TOLL HOUSE
Tried and True Recipes

TOLL HOUSE
Tried and True Recipes

by
Ruth Graves Wakefield

❧

DOVER PUBLICATIONS, INC.
NEW YORK

Published in Canada by General Publishing Company, Ltd., 30 Lesmill Road, Don Mills, Toronto, Ontario.

Published in the United Kingdom by Constable and Company, Ltd., 10 Orange Street, London WC2H 7EG.

This Dover edition, first published in 1977, is an unabridged and unaltered republication of the sixth (1948) edition, as published by M. Barrows & Company, Inc., New York, in 1949.

International Standard Book Number: 0-486-23560-2
Library of Congress Catalog Card Number: 77-86264

Manufactured in the United States of America
Dover Publications, Inc.
180 Varick Street
New York, N.Y. 10014

Affectionately dedicated
to my
MOTHER
whose encouragement and confidence
have been unfailing

CONTENTS

ᴇᵍ CONTENTS ᵍᵇ

FOREWORD

In August of 1930 my husband and I bought a lovely old Cape Cod house, built in 1709 on the outskirts of Whitman, Massachusetts. Many years ago it was used as a toll house where passengers ate while the horses were changed on the way from Boston to New Bedford. At this time the whaling industry in New Bedford was at its height and there was much travel. Our house was the half-way point where toll was collected for this particular section of the road. During the Revolution the house was also the center of much activity, so we started our business here in the midst of many traditions and called the place Toll House.

In my childhood my mother and I lived with her parents so that my first experience in cooking was under Grandmother's watchful eyes. She loved to teach me but did deplore the number of pans left to wash after my efforts were over.

After I was graduated from Massachusetts State Teachers College, I spent two years teaching home economics in Brockton High School and the summers in dietetic work at the Brockton Hospital. Then I married and my interest in cooking was part of my own homemaking. For four years my husband, who was also in the food business, and I dreamed of the kind of eating place we would like to have. Finally we invested all our savings in Toll House, taking over the mortgage as well, and started out with more courage than capital.

The original little house was left with its front hall and parlor to welcome guests. The other rooms were made into dining rooms with seven tables seating about thirty-five guests. In three years' time the business expanded to sixty-four tables. Now we serve from one to more than two thousand guests a day, at ninety or

9

so tables, depending on the season. Although we have enlarged the buildings considerably, we have for many years kept the seating capacity the same for we do not wish to lose our homey atmosphere in commercialism. Our aim has always been to offer a restful atmosphere and, in expanding, never to sacrifice fine quality or the kind of service we all want in our own homes. We set each table with different patterns of china, glass, and linens from its neighbor and place on it, too, a flower arrangement that has no counterpart elsewhere in the room.

Our original male assistant is still with us as our chef and his assistant is his original second cook. Our pastry cook and the other key people in the kitchens have been with us almost since the beginning. Our hostess, Helen Morton, now our manager and a member of the firm, came to us directly from college in 1934 and it is her devotion to Toll House and her attention to detail which now enables me to have more home life with our children than would otherwise be possible. Our staff has always called itself the Toll House Family and today numbers about one hundred and twenty-five.

During the first year of our business—there have now been eighteen—I published my collection of recipes in book form at the request of Toll House guests and friends. And in subsequent printings have added recipes which we devised at Toll House or which came to us from friends and cooks whom my husband and I met in our travels. Before our children came to us, we used to travel during the quiet winter months and there are few spots famous for food in the world which we have not visited in our quest of ideas.

I still believe in small-quantity cookery. I feel it is the only means to flavor, consistency, and general high quality, especially in baking, and I know there are no substitutes for butter, cream, whole milk, fresh eggs, fruits, and vegetables in preparing a fine meal.

RUTH GRAVES WAKEFIELD

September 1, 1948
Toll House
Whitman, Massachusetts

TOLL HOUSE
Tried and True Recipes

CONVERSION TABLES FOR FOREIGN EQUIVALENTS

DRY INGREDIENTS

Ounces	Grams	Grams	Ounces	Pounds	Kilograms	Kilograms	Pounds
1 =	28.35	1 =	0.035	1 =	0.454	1 =	2.205
2	56.70	2	0.07	2	0.91	2	4.41
3	85.05	3	0.11	3	1.36	3	6.61
4	113.40	4	0.14	4	1.81	4	8.82
5	141.75	5	0.18	5	2.27	5	11.02
6	170.10	6	0.21	6	2.72	6	13.23
7	198.45	7	0.25	7	3.18	7	15.43
8	226.80	8	0.28	8	3.63	8	17.64
9	255.15	9	0.32	9	4.08	9	19.84
10	283.50	10	0.35	10	4.54	10	22.05
11	311.85	11	0.39	11	4.99	11	24.26
12	340.20	12	0.42	12	5.44	12	26.46
13	368.55	13	0.46	13	5.90	13	28.67
14	396.90	14	0.49	14	6.35	14	30.87
15	425.25	15	0.53	15	6.81	15	33.08
16	453.60	16	0.57				

LIQUID INGREDIENTS

Liquid Ounces	Milliliters	Milliliters	Liquid Ounces	Quarts	Liters	Liters	Quarts
1 =	29.573	1 =	0.034	1 =	0.946	1 =	1.057
2	59.15	2	0.07	2	1.89	2	2.11
3	88.72	3	0.10	3	2.84	3	3.17
4	118.30	4	0.14	4	3.79	4	4.23
5	147.87	5	0.17	5	4.73	5	5.28
6	177.44	6	0.20	6	5.68	6	6.34
7	207.02	7	0.24	7	6.62	7	7.40
8	236.59	8	0.27	8	7.57	8	8.45
9	266.16	9	0.30	9	8.52	9	9.51
10	295.73	10	0.33	10	9.47	10	10.57

Gallons (American)	Liters	Liters	Gallons (American)
1 =	3.785	1 =	0.264
2	7.57	2	0.53
3	11.36	3	0.79
4	15.14	4	1.06
5	18.93	5	1.32
6	22.71	6	1.59
7	26.50	7	1.85
8	30.28	8	2.11
9	34.07	9	2.38
10	37.86	10	2.74

PREFACE

POINTS TO REMEMBER

All measurements in this book are level unless otherwise stated.

All measurements for flour are given for flour sifted once before measuring.

All recipes call for pastry or all-purpose flour unless the recipe specifically states bread flour.

"Bad Luck" is blamed for much waste. You can eliminate most failures by letting rules replace guesswork.

Measure ingredients accurately and combine carefully. Results will be more uniform if you know at what temperature the oven should be held and keep it there. The time consumed in hovering near the stove to "see how it is coming along" is then saved for something more profitable.

The New England term, spider, refers to a frying pan or skillet.

Recipes in this book are always capitalized each time they are mentioned. If you see Roast Chicken, it is here and you can find it in the Index, but roast pig, without capitals, is not.

Recipes given me by friends have been printed in the friend's own words. In such cases you will notice "butter, size of an egg," for ¼ cup butter, as standard recipes are given. I hesitated to change wording and so lose the donor's personality.

HELPFUL HINTS

Dip peeled bananas in lemon juice to prevent discoloration. Drop peeled peaches into a bowl of milk to prevent darkening.

To peel a tomato easily, insert a two-tined fork into stem end, hold over a lighted gas burner, and turn constantly. When skin bursts, remove from fire and peel off skin.

To peel oranges or grapefruit and free fruit entirely of the membranous white pulp underneath skin, first place fruit in hot water for 5 minutes. You will then be able to peel every particle of outside from the fruit pulp.

A rubber plate scraper from the ten-cent store efficiently removes every speck of batter from a bowl when you are transferring a mixture to a baking or serving dish.

To save time and dishwashing when baking, place paper baking cups inside muffin tins, which are so tedious to wash.

If a vegetable or cereal burns, plunge vessel containing the burned mass into cold water and allow it to remain for a few minutes before pouring contents into another pan. This will do away almost entirely with the burned taste.

If cream seems too thin to whip, place the dish containing it in another dish of cold water. Leave it there until it is well chilled. Then put it into a pan of hot water. It will usually whip without difficulty.

When measuring solid fat, use the measuring-cup-and-cold-water method. For instance, if ½ cup fat is called for, fill cup half full of water, drop enough fat into water until water reaches the 1-cup mark. Pour off water and correct amount of fat will remain.

Wherever possible, scrub or scrape vegetables instead of peeling them. For instance, new carrots and mushrooms need only scrubbing.

Follow the chef's way of dicing vegetables and meats. Using a large knife, place the point down on a board. Push the food under blade and chop with an up and down motion, swinging large end of knife in a semicircle.

Make use of the prepared foods now on the market. Strained or chopped baby foods are excellent when a recipe calls for fruit or vegetable purée. Use these in combination with canned soups for last minute meals which will appeal to everyone. Try mixing cream of tomato with cream of green pea soup for Purée Mongole or cream of mushroom with cream of spinach. If you keep on the emergency shelf tomato and cream of mushroom soups, chicken and beef consommé you will always have a feeling of security. The consommés are especially valuable when meat stock is called for.

To improve the flavor and color of corn, cauliflower, and cabbage, use half milk and half water in cooking.

Do not use cooked bones or starchy vegetables for soup if you wish a clear stock. The French use two soup kettles, one for clear stock made with new bones and a secondary kettle for scraps.

Avoid using too much shortening in a soufflé or it will not rise.

Do not be afraid of mixing varieties of cheese when making a cheese soufflé. Parmesan, sharp Cheddar, and Camembert make a delightful combination.

To clear fat you have saved for deep frying, bring it to a boil with 1 slice apple, 1 slice potato, and ¼ cup water. Remove apple and potato after cooking and strain fat.

When a flour and fat roux is used to thicken a sauce, add flour to melted fat *away from heat*. This allows flour to absorb fat slowly and expand gradually. (When flour is cooked too quickly, the outside coating of each grain hardens and a coarse texture results.) Liquid is then added and the sauce brought to a boil over low heat. Constant stirring and slow cooking are important in achieving a velvety smooth sauce without a raw pasty taste.

For gravies, many cooks prefer a potato flour as it cooks more quickly and less of it is required than of ordinary flour. One teaspoon potato flour may be substituted for 1 tablespoon wheat flour.

Many people find it difficult to select a ripe melon. Choose cantaloupes and honeydews by fragrance. A ripe one has a faint but noticeable aroma; a sharp nose can detect an overripe odor too. The blossom end is rather soft and yields when pressed. If very soft, the melon is overripe. Some people shake a honeydew and if the seeds rattle inside, they consider the melon ready to eat. With watermelons, rapping on the sides is the test. A dull, hollow sound means a ripe melon; a ringing sound, a green melon. A dead ripe melon gives a hollow "clunk" also, but rapping still seems to be the only test.

Here are two recommended methods for cleaning pewter: Mix juice of 1 lemon with 2 tablespoons soda and dissolve. Use the lemon rind as a sponge to apply the liquid to pewter. Then rinse, dry, and polish with soft flannel. Or prepare a paste of denatured alcohol or ammonia and a mild abrasive that will not scratch. Apply with a clean cloth, rub dry, then polish.

Old gilt frames or old brass cornices and curtain tiebacks may be cleaned with the water in which onions were boiled. The accumulation of smoke and dust is removed with a little polishing which does not destroy the soft antique look.

EQUIVALENTS

3 teaspoons = 1 tablespoon
4 tablespoons = ¼ cup
8 tablespoons = ½ cup
16 tablespoons = 1 cup
1 heaping cup = 1 cup and 3 to 4 tablespoons
2 cups = 1 pint
4 cups = 1 quart

Dash, pinch, or speck = ⅟₁₆ teaspoon
Size of nut = 1 tablespoon
Size of egg = ¼ cup
2 tablespoons = 1 fluid ounce
480 drops = 1 ounce
8 drams = 1 ounce

PROPORTIONS

Baking Powder
2 teaspoons to 1 cup flour
Reduce to ½ teaspoon to 1 cup flour for each egg added *after the first*

Gelatin
1 tablespoon to 2 cups liquid

Soda
½ teaspoon to 1 cup sour milk
½ teaspoon to 1 cup molasses
If acidity of milk or molasses is considerable, use a little baking powder also. If soda is not available, use 2 teaspoons baking powder for every ½ teaspoon called for.

Salt
1 teaspoon salt to 1 quart of soup or sauce
1 teaspoon salt to 3 to 4 cups flour in dough
1 teaspoon salt to 2 cups water for cereals

Sugar
1 cup to 1 quart of mixture to be chilled

Flavoring
1 teaspoon to 1 quart to be chilled
1 tablespoon to 1 quart to be frozen

THIS FOR THAT

Baking Powder
1 teaspoon = ⅓ teaspoon soda and ½ teaspoon cream tartar

Chocolate and Cocoa
⅓ cup cocoa = 1 square (1 ounce) chocolate plus ½ tablespoon shortening

Cornstarch
1 tablespoon = 1¾ tablespoons flour

Molasses
¾ to 1 cup = 1 cup sugar

Tapioca
1½ tablespoons cooking tapioca = ¼ cup pearl tapioca (soaked at least 1 hour)

Shortening Substitutes
For 1 cup butter use:
⅘ cup bacon fat, clarified
⅔ cup chicken fat, clarified
⅞ cup vegetable oil
⅞ cup lard
½ cup suet

Crumbs
¾ cup cracker crumbs = 1 cup bread crumbs

FAMILY PURCHASING GUIDE

Almonds	1 lb. in shell	= 1–1¾ cups shelled
Apples	3 medium-sized (1 lb.)	= 3 cups, pared, sliced or diced
Asparagus	1 bunch, fresh	= 4 servings
	1 pkg., frozen	= 4 servings

Bacon	1 lb.	= 18–20 slices
Bananas	1 lb.	= 3 medium-sized
Beans, dry	1 lb.	= 2 cups
green	1 lb., fresh or frozen	= 5 servings
Brown Sugar	1 lb.	= 2⅓–3 cups, well-packed
Bread	1 loaf	= 16–20 slices
	3 slices	= 2 cups soft crumbs
Butter	1 lb.	= 2 cups
Celery	1¼-lb. bunch	= 3 cups, cut up
Cheese, American	½ lb.	= 2 cups, grated
Cottage	½ lb.	=: 1 cup
Cream	3-oz. pkg.	=: 6 tbsp.
Chicken, cut up	4 lbs.	=: 3½–4 cups, cooked
Broiler	2½ lbs.	=: 2–4 servings
Fryer	2½–3½ lbs.	= 3–4 servings
Roaster	4 lbs.	= 6–8 servings
Coffee	1 lb., ground	= 5 cups, dry
Corn	1 No. 2 can	= 5 servings
Corn Meal	1 lb.	= 2⅔ cups
Cranberries	1 lb.	= 4 cups sauce
Cream, heavy	½ pt. (1 cup)	= 2 cups, whipped
light	½ pt. (1 cup)	= 8 servings, 2 tbsp. each
Dates	7¼-oz. pkg., pitted	=: 1¼ cups
Duck	4 lbs.	= 3–4 servings
Eggs	8 average-sized	= 1 cup
whites	8–11	= 1 cup
yolks	12–14	= 1 cup
Fish, broiled or baked	1 lb.	= 2 servings
Flour, white	1 lb.	= 4 cups
cake	1 lb.	= 5 cups
rye	1 lb.	= 3⅞ cups
graham	1 lb.	= 3½–3¾ cups
rice	1 lb.	= 2 cups
Frankfurters	1 lb.	= 9 frankfurters

Fresh Pork Sausage	1 lb.	= 15 small link sausages
Graham Crackers	11	= 1 cup crumbs
Ice Cream	1 qt.	= 6–7 servings
Lemon	Juice of 1	= 3–4 tbsp.
Lobster	2½ lbs.	= 2 cups cooked and cut up
Macaroni	½ lb.	= 2¼ cups raw, broken up
		= 5⅓ cups, cooked
Marshmallows	¼ lb.	= 16
Meat, ground or boned	1 lb.	= 4 servings
with bone, steaks or roasts	1 lb.	= 2 servings
Nuts in shell	1 lb.	= ½ lb. shelled
Onion	1 medium-sized	= ¾ cup, minced
Orange	1 medium-sized	= ⅓ cup juice
Peas, split	1 lb.	= 2 cups
frozen	12-oz. pkg.	= 4–5 servings
fresh, in pod	2 lbs.	= 4 servings
Peaches or Pears	1 lb.	= 4 medium-sized
Pecans in shell	1 lb.	= 1⅔ cups, cut fine
Potatoes, white or sweet	1 lb. or 3 medium-sized	= 3 cups, pared, diced or sliced
Rice, white	1 cup raw	= 2¼ cups, cooked
wild	1 cup raw	= 4 cups, cooked
Salmon	7¾-oz. can	= 1 cup, flaked
	1-lb. can	= 2 cups, flaked
Sugar, granulated	½ lb.	= 1 cup
brown	½ lb.	= 1⅜ cups
Confectioners	½ lb.	= 2 cups
Shrimp, canned	7-oz. can	= 1–1¼ cups
fresh	1 lb.	= 20–24 shrimp, shelled
Squash	1 can or 1 lb.	= 2¼ cups
Tomatoes	1 can	= 2–3 cups
	1 lb.	= 4 small
Tuna	6½–7-oz. can	= 1 cup, flaked

TIMETABLE FOR BAKING

Food	Oven Temperature in Degrees F.	Minutes (except as indicated)
Baked Apples	375	30–40
Baked Beans	275	6 hours
Breads	Preheat to 400	
Yeast Loaf	Reduce to 350	60
Rolls, Solid pan	400–425	20–25
Rolls, in muffin pan	450–475	15–20
Biscuits	450–500	10–15
Muffins		
Plain	400–425	20–25
Corn Bread	425–450	15–30
Bran	375–400	20–30
Popovers	425–450	35–45
Cookies	350–375–400	8–15
Angel Cake (start in cold oven)	300–325	60–75
Large Spongecake	325–350	45–60
Layer Cake	375–400	20–30
Loaf or Sheet Cake	350–360	45–60
Fruit Pie	Preheat to 425	15 then
	Reduce to 350	20–35
Custard Pie	Preheat to 450	10 then
	Reduce to 325	30–40
Pie Shells	450–475	10–15
Turnovers	450	20–25
Meringue	350	12–15
Cream Puffs	425	35–45
Potatoes	400	60
Casserole Dishes	350–400	30–45–60
Puddings	350–400	30–45–60
Baked Custard	325–350	45–60

TIMETABLE FOR ROASTING

For best results with meat and poultry roasting, use an open shallow pan with rack. Select a pan that fits the meat. No water is necessary with the lower temperatures now recommended, and no basting at all. Start with a cold oven and roast will be more juicy and shrink less.

Remove roast from refrigerator well ahead of time to lose extreme chill. Wipe the meat with damp cloth or scrape outside clean. Rub surface with flour and sprinkle with salt and pepper for a well-seasoned outside crust. Place in pan with fat side up.

Follow roasting directions. When meat is cooked to family's taste, remove to serving platter and keep warm while gravy is being made.

Beef	Oven Temperature in Degrees F.	Minutes Per Pound
Rib Roast, 4–6 pounds	rare, 325	15–20
	medium, 325	24–28
	well done, 325	28–34
Rolled Roast, 4–6 pounds	same as above	add 8–10 minutes per pound to above timing
Chuck or Rump Roast, 4–6 pounds	medium, 325	35–45
Lamb		
Leg, 6–8 pounds	well done, 325	30–35
Shoulder rolled, 3–5 pounds	well done, 325	35–40
Veal		
Leg, 6–8 pounds	well done, 325	25–30
Shoulder rolled, 5–6 pounds	well done, 325	35–40
Loin, 4–5 pounds	well done, 325	30–35

	Oven Temperature in Degrees F.	Minutes Per Pound
Duck, 5–7 pounds	350	25–35
Pork		
Fresh ham, 10–12 pounds	well done, 350	35–40
Fresh loin, 3–5 pounds	well done, 350	40–50
Smoked ham, tenderized, 18–20 pounds	well done, 300	18–20
Chicken, 3–6 pounds	350	20–30
Turkey		
Small, 6–12 pounds	325	18–25
Medium, 12–18 pounds	300	18–20
Large, 18–25 pounds	300	15–18

TIMETABLE FOR BROILING

Use a broiler pan with rack made with wide grids and one which fits the food; if using a small food, use a small pan to reduce spattering and smoke. In many cases a shallow pan or pie plate is best, especially when broiling foods like mushrooms, where it is important to retain moisture in which food is broiled, and especially in cases where food does not need to be turned. This applies to fish.

No preheating is necessary with electric broiler but 5 minute period of preheating at 550° F. or "Broil" is recommended for gas stoves.

Most foods are broiled best when placed 3 inches below heat unit, particularly steaks, chops, patties, fish, sandwiches. Place chicken and lobster, which should not be as brown, 4 to 5 inches below to insure thorough cooking.

Keep broiler door of gas range *closed.* Leave door of electric broiler open a few inches.

		Time in Minutes
Beef—3 inches below heat		
Sirloin or Porterhouse		
1 inch thick	medium	10–15
1½ inches thick	rare	13–18
2 inches thick	rare	20–22
Ground beef patties		
1 inch thick	rare	12–15
	medium	15–20
Liver (oiled)		
½ inch thick		10–15
Lamb—3 inches below heat		
Chops		
¾ inch thick		10–12
1½ inches thick		15–20
Ground lamb patties		
1 inch thick		15–20
Pork—4–5 inches below heat		
Bacon		4–5
Slice of ham (smoked, tenderized)		
½ inch thick		10–15
1 inch thick		15–20

(National Meat Institute does not advise broiling pork chops. Always pan fry or bake slowly and thoroughly for tenderness, flavor, and health.)

Chicken—4–5 inches below heat		
Half broiler-size		20–40
Fish—2 inches below heat		
Cut thick, buttered		15–18
Cut thin, heavily buttered		8–10
Lobster		
Split		20–40

23

TIMETABLE FOR BOILING

In vegetable cookery use as small amount of hot water as possible; never cover vegetables with water. Always cover utensil and keep covered until cooking period is over. Several vegetables may be cooked together without mingling of flavors if cover is removed while there is still live steam in utensil or before steam condenses while cooling. The time periods given are approximate since they will vary with such conditions as age and size of vegetables.

Fresh Vegetable	*Preparation*	*Minutes in Tightly Covered Saucepan*
Asparagus	Tied in bunches	20–25
Beans, Lima	Shelled	20–30
Beans, snap	1 to 1½-inch pieces	20–30
Beets, young	Whole	35–45
Broccoli	Stalks split	15–30
Cabbage	Shredded or quartered	10–15
Carrots, young	Pared, sliced, or whole	20–30
Cauliflower	Medium-sized head	25–30
Corn	On cob (water to cover)	10–15
Greens	Tough stems removed	15–30
Okra	Whole or in ½-inch slices	15–25
Onions	Medium-sized, peeled, whole	30–35
Parsnips	Pared, quartered, or in ½-inch pieces	30–40
Peas	Shelled	15–25
Potatoes, white	Medium-sized, whole	25–40
Potatoes, sweet	Medium-sized, whole	20–35
Squash, Hubbard	Pared, cut in 2-inch pieces	30–45
Squash, summer	Pared, cut in 1-inch pieces	15–20
Tomatoes	Quartered	10–20
Turnips	Pared, cut in 1-inch pieces	15–40

OVEN STEAMING

Vegetables may be steamed in oven in any utensil with tight-fitting cover. Use temperatures of 325° F., 350°, 375°. Approximately double usual surface cooking time should be allowed for oven steaming. In this way you may cook a whole meal at one time. Select meats or fish and other dishes which take 1 to 1½ hours for satisfactory results as, for example, Spanish Steak, Meat Loaf, Hawaiian Ham, Smothered Chicken.

PROBLEMS OF HIGH HUMIDITY AND HIGH ALTITUDE

Many inquiries have come to me from southern cooks who have trouble with sugar cookery as in cooked icings and candies. Their difficulties are due to the high humidity of certain sections. If this is your problem, reduce the amount of liquid ordinarily required in a recipe about one quarter and take care to under- rather than over-cook candy or frosting since normal evaporation does not take place under conditions of high humidity.

In mountainous sections the high altitude has an effect on cooking and temperatures must be regulated accordingly. Remember that in boiling foods there is a 1 degree drop for every 500 feet above sea level. At sea level, water boils at 212° F., but in Denver, Colorado, which is 12,000 feet water boils at 202° F.

If you are baking, or using a pressure cooker for meats and vegetables, you can regulate heat without special consideration of altitude unless you are more than 7,000 feet above sea level. At greater heights, allow a little more time, than recipe indicates.

With the pressure cooker, there is no change in amount of pressure unless the altitude is more than 2,000 feet above sea level. In that case allow 1 pound pressure for each additional 1,000 feet or part thereof.

Sugar cookery is also affected so that you must test by finger for consistency rather than thermometer for heat. The soft ball stage, for instance, at sea level and up to 1,000 feet is reached at 236° F., but at 7,000 feet it will be reached sooner, at 200° F.

Baked foods containing sugar, baking powder, and shortening are the most difficult so careful study must be made of each recipe. Less sugar, baking powder, and shortening are required at high altitudes but you will get the most accurate results if you will write to the Colorado State College for a resume of the experiments they have made in cooking.

YOUR RANGE, CARE AND POSSIBILITIES

The days of taking ranges apart and boiling in soda or ammonia water are past. Ranges of today are cared for in the same way you clean a china dish or porcelain utensil.

The best method is to make a habit of wiping off all parts of the stove you have used for the meal at each dishwashing time. A thorough wiping with clean soapy water is usually all that is needed. If not wiped off at once, acids from such foods as tomatoes, vinegar, or milk may take away glaze from some enamels, leaving a dull spot.

When spill-overs occur, try to wipe off food quickly before it has a chance to "cook on" to burner or heating element. When a thorough cleaning is necessary, remove grates or pan under electric heating element and wash in hot soapy water. A mild cleaning powder may be used for stubborn spots. Dry parts thoroughly.

Occasionally food boils into the oven and burns on the bottom, or the sides are splattered with grease. When it is not possible to clean the oven immediately afterward, do it at the earliest moment so that food does not become cooked on permanently. Oven racks and the bottom of the oven too can be easily removed for cleaning.

When not in use, keep broiler pan out of its cooking place. Most stoves now have a compartment separate from heating space in which the broiler is kept to avoid overheating it and "crazing" or "cracking" of enamel when baking oven is in use for long periods.

Leave oven door open slightly after each use so oven will cool without sweating.

HOW TO SAVE FUEL

1. Water will not heat above 212° F., so use simmer position to keep water just at boiling point.
2. When water is gently boiling, several times as much gas is required for utensil with lid off as with lid on.
3. Remove lids only when evaporating water from a product, for example, in jelly- or candy-making.
4. Use simmer-set position for stewing and other slow cooking processes.
5. Use double boiler and triple pans over burner wherever possible; for example, cook frankfurters in lower part, place rolls in upper part to heat at same time.
6. Place utensil on burner before turning on heat.
7. Turn off heat before, not after, removing utensil from range.
8. Never leave burner turned on when not in use.
9. When a quart of water is enough, do not heat a gallon.
10. Do not heat oven too long before you are ready to put in food.

OVEN MEALS

When a busy day of cleaning comes along or when you want to go out for the afternoon, you will find oven meals of great assistance. On the heat-controlled gas stove the pilot burns constantly when the oven is lighted and the heat control automatically regulates the temperature so that there is no danger whatever.

Meats, vegetables, fruits, and puddings may be cooked together. I do not advise baking pastries, cakes, muffins with other foods except for short-time (1 hour) meals. Use tightly covered baking dishes.

Suggestions for foods efficiently cooked at one time are roasts, baked fish, soups, cereals, stews, applesauce, prunes, vegetables, scalloped dishes, casserole dishes and those puddings which will stand long cooking such as bread puddings, Indian pudding, etc.

Vegetables like potatoes and carrots, which do not require long cooking, are best started with 1½ cups cold water and a pinch of salt in the covered kettle. With other vegetables, such as onions, string beans, etc., it is best to use hot water in the same quantity.

The following combinations are successfully cooked at one time:

One-Hour Meal at 350° F.	*One and One-Half Hour Meal at 350° F.*
Neapolitan Meat Loaf	Spanish Steak
Baked Potatoes en Casserole	Franconia Potatoes
Carrots	Harvard Beets
Baked Cup Custards	Scotch Betty

YOUR REFRIGERATOR, CARE AND POSSIBILITIES

Temperature Regulation. Read carefully the directions which come with your refrigerator and set controls accordingly. Gas and electric refrigeration differ in their control markings. For normal everyday use, set at position advised and your refrigerator will adjust itself to changes in kitchen temperature. For fast freezing of cubes, ice cream, and salads set controls to fastest freezing and turn back to normal position as soon as freezing is completed.

Vacation Setting. For vacations of a few days, it is more economical not to turn refrigerator off, but to allow it to operate at a point a little below usual "set" since the cabinet door is to remain closed and this setting will maintain safe refrigeration for most types of food. During extended holidays it is best to disconnect plug from wall or turn off gas completely, remove all food, and clean interior of cabinet. While you are away, leave door partially open to air out and avoid stale odor.

Defrosting. Most refrigerators automatically defrost, but many of us still prefer to have periodic defrostings and cleanings. When excessive frost collects on freezing unit, it acts as an insulator, reduces freezing efficiency, raises operating costs, and also harbors food odors that may be present within the food storage compartment. It is most convenient to defrost at night. If temperature control is set at defrosting position before you retire, the freezing unit will be completely defrosted by morning and the inconveniences of daytime defrosting will be eliminated. During the night there is no occasion for frequent opening of the door and inside temperatures will not rise enough to endanger food preservation.

To defrost set control at "Defrost." Remove meats or fish from pan under unit and wrap in newspaper to keep well chilled. Also wrap any packages of frozen foods in newspaper, to hold the frost. Remove all trays of ice cubes. In the morning set refrigerator to normal position, empty water in defrosting pan, wash in warm soapy water, rinse, dry, and place meat and fish back in tray under freezing compartment. Place frozen foods in receptacle. Remove other dishes and foods so that interior can be quickly wiped out. Use a solution of 2 tablespoons of baking soda to 1 quart warm water and rinse with clear water. Wipe dry and replace all foods and ice trays, refilled with fresh water. The defrosting period during the day may be shortened if ice cube trays, meat storage trays, and vegetable fresheners are filled with warm water and set back in place. The ice will be easier to remove. *Never* use a sharp knife to remove frost.

FOOD STORAGE

Put milk in refrigerator as soon after delivery as possible.

Although a number of refrigerator firms do not advise covering food, many of us prefer covered dishes to prevent transfer of odors, especially from strong to mild-flavored foods.

Cheese should be wrapped in wax paper for overnight storage. For longer periods use moisture-proof cellophane-type materials or wrap in cloth moistened with vinegar and wrap again in wax paper.

Wrap meats lightly in wax paper to retain color, never use brown paper as it acts as an insulator and keeps out the cold.

Fish should be kept as near freezing point as possible and used quickly.

Lettuce and other vegetables are best kept covered. Most refrigerators have Hydrators or Crispers to hold vegetables and fruits. Lettuce, celery, and similar vegetables keep best if they are washed first but not trimmed or cut up. Most vegetables are best washed and dried before placing in receptacle but asparagus and Brussels sprouts should not be washed until time for use. Use leafy vegetables as soon as possible, the longer they are kept the fewer the vitamins they contain.

Fruit may be kept in perfect condition for a week or more, depending upon ripeness. Berries and cherries should not be washed before being placed in refrigerator. Keep them until ready for use in well ventilated containers such as a wire sieve. Use as quickly as possible.

Bread dough, coated with fat and then covered, will remain sweet for one week. Cut off a piece for a pan of rolls each day, if you wish, but allow two hours or more for dough to rise after the extreme cold of the refrigerator.

Pastry dough may be kept longer than bread dough, even for 2 weeks, by wrapping it securely in wax paper.

Baked bread keeps perfectly without mildewing in refrigerator. This is especially helpful in warm weather.

Eggs should not be washed before refrigerating as it removes protective coating.

Parsley and mint keep a week or more when washed, trimmed, stems bunched, and placed in covered jar or cellophane bag, tightly covered.

Nuts are best refrigerated to prevent rancid flavors from developing. Keep in cellophane bag.

Cut flowers will keep fresh much longer if put into refrigerator each night.

Cover all moist foods after cooking. Never put hot food into refrigerator. Cool first. Store tiny amounts of leftovers in low jelly glasses or small mayonnaise jars which have tight covers.

PLACEMENT

We still speak of mechanical refrigerators as iceboxes but the placement of food in a modern refrigerator is quite different from what it had to be in an ice chest. The opportunities which new boxes offer are unlimited. Remember when we never thought we could serve fresh pork in the warm months without illness resulting? Now extremely low temperatures keep food as fresh in summer as in the middle of winter.

Avoid overcrowding refrigerator so that cold air can circulate around food. Meat should be stored, uncooked if possible, in tray under freezing compartment. Wrap fish securely in wax paper and store in freezing compartment, if it has to be kept long.

Most refrigerators provide room for tall beverage bottles and milk and cream on shelves next the freezing unit. Eggs should be placed directly under the unit as they are highly perishable. Place butter in a covered container to prevent its absorbing other food flavors.

Modern refrigerators have deep covered trays at the bottom for vegetable and fruit freshening.

Be sure to cover leftover cooked foods before storing to prevent transfer of odors and flavors.

Place packaged frozen foods on the bottom of freezing storage compartment in direct contact with metal floor of compartment.

When you buy packaged ice cream, remove it from wax package (which acts as an insulator) and place in freezing trays. When ice cream or packaged frozen foods have thawed, do not refreeze.

Do not attempt to freeze fresh fruits and vegetables unless refrigerator has a separate compartment for quick freezing. Use only a deep-freeze box for the purpose of large-scale quick freezing. The regular home refrigerator is a safe place for "storage" of frozen foods but does not freeze fresh foods quickly enough. In fact, the extremely low temperature needed for the process of quick freezing is not desirable in a home refrigerator.

SUCCESS WITH FROZEN DESSERTS

Fast freezing is the key to success in making refrigerator ice creams that are soft and smooth. The following guides will help you:

1. Keep refrigerator free from excessive frost.
2. Set control dial to lowest temperature.

3. Do not freeze ice cubes or chill warm foods when freezing mixtures.

4. Chill all ingredients before mixing and all utensils, including bowls and beater.

5. Use two trays rather than one large tray; fill half full of mixture.

6. Moisten underside of tray with warm water for good contact.

7. Place trays on lowest shelf of freezing compartment as that is coldest.

8. Keep refrigerator door closed.

9. When mixture is mushy, beat until light and fluffy. Work fast, stop beating before mixture starts to melt. This step is not necessary in sherbets with beaten egg white.

10. Scoop mixture into one big tray and place in freezing compartment again.

11. Turn control back to a little colder than normal so as to continue freezing but to keep mixture from freezing solid.

12. A very sweet mixture takes longer to freeze than one with little sugar.

13. If frozen dessert refuses to freeze, it may be because you have used too much heavy cream, (light cream is rich enough), too much sugar, or too much acid fruit in mixture. Soft mixtures may sometimes be stiffened by adding stiffly beaten egg whites when mixture is at point of mushy consistency.

ICE CUBES

While using trays for freezing desserts, place frozen ice cubes in defrosting pan under freezing compartment to "hold" them.

Most automatic refrigerators now have trays with devices for easy removal of ice cubes. If they are stubborn, turn tray upside down and run cold water over bottom of tray.

If ice cubes are to be used in iced tea or punch, substitute fruit juice for water. Other colorings and flavorings are also attractive changes. Grape juice or cranberry juice adds much color. For iced coffee try freezing leftover breakfast coffee into cubes and the iced coffee will not be diluted.

TABLE SETTING AND SERVICE

Place mats are attractive for breakfast, luncheon, or supper, but the formal dinner table should have its silence cloth and tablecloth.

Centerpieces should be low enough to see over or high enough to see under.

Silver, napkin and plate should be placed one inch from edge of table; with the butterplate and glass they constitute a "cover."

Silver is placed in order of serving: the first piece used being farthest from the plate. The dinner knife and fork come next to plate (on opposite sides) unless salad is placed on table with main course. Then the salad fork will be next to plate.

Knives and spoons are placed at the right, cutting edge of knives toward plate. Forks, as a rule, are placed at left, tines up. However, oyster forks are placed at right of spoons; salad forks, when used with salad course alone, are placed at right.

Service plates, also called place plates, are not generally used unless you have a servant. The service plate remains on the table through the appetizer and soup service with the food dish placed upon it. The service plate is not removed until the main course (fish or meat entree) is served, when the maid removes it with her right hand and immediately replaces it with the hot dinner plate. She then passes the food for the main course. If the salad is served as a separate course, the service plate is again used when removing the dinner plate, with the salad plate directly set upon the place plate. Only when it is time for dessert is the individual place allowed to be uncovered.

The water glass is placed at the right, just above the point of the knife. The salad plate may be placed beside the forks or directly above the plate.

The bread and butter plate is placed at the left above the fork. The butter knife is laid across this plate at right angles to the other silver. For formal dinners the bread and butter plate is omitted.

The napkin is at the left of the forks or on the service plate, with open edges toward the plate.

Don't be sparing with salt and pepper. There should be a set within easy reach of every two guests.

At luncheon, the soup is served in cups, cream soup dishes, or in rimless soup plates. At a formal dinner a more shallow rimmed soup plate is used. Bouillon, cream soup, or dessert spoons are used at luncheon; tablespoons are for dinner-soup service. Celery, olives, crackers or any other accompaniments are served during the soup course.

Luncheon beverages are served at the table. For formal dinners the custom is to serve coffee in small cups after dinner in the living room. Coffee may be poured at the table for informal dinners.

A waitress stands at the left of each person whether she is passing a dish from which you help yourself or placing or removing a plate. In filling the beverage glass or cup, the waitress refills or sets the glass down from the right-hand side.

Plates should be placed and removed one at a time. When the table is cleared, all food is removed first, then the plates, and next the bread and butter dishes, all without stacking. When two or more guests have finished eating, the waitress may start to clear the table. At a *family meal* she waits until everyone has finished eating.

In arranging the seating of guests, place the most distinguished woman guest at the host's right, the most distinguished gentleman guest at the hostess' right.

If finger bowl service is included in the meal, the bowl is brought in resting on a doily placed on the dessert plate along with the dessert fork, on the left, and the dessert spoon, on the right, of the bowl. The guest removes the silver and places it on the table at either side of the plate, then slips the doily and finger bowl off the dessert plate, setting it on the table directly above the plate. Dessert is then passed by the maid.

In recent years it has become unpopular to serve the hostess first. Many of us prefer this service, however, for if any unfamiliar dish is present, she can give the cue as to how it is to be handled. It is now considered more gracious to serve the guest at the hostess' right first, with the maid continuing in order around the table, serving the hostess last.

MENUS—CHALLENGE OR CHORE

Menu-making may be lots of fun or a hard task. Actually it is just as easy to prepare interesting food as to serve the same dreary dishes week after week. Imagination enters into menu-planning as much as in arranging an attractive table centerpiece. Do give your family a lift now and then by offering them a variety of food-flavor surprises, one at a time.

The following menus include only the recipes in this book. Perhaps you will wish to use vegetables requiring less preparation or fewer cooked desserts, substituting fruits, for instance.

Please remember these are only suggestions for the use of my own recipes. These menus offer combinations which I have found pleasing, considering individual tastes and the circumstances under which they are served. Some luncheons are planned to be heartier than others—a salad can often be substituted for one of the vegetables or even for the dessert course to please those who like salads. In many cases the menu is planned so that everything may be baked in the oven at the same time.

Several menus include breads; in others they have been omitted. Relishes or jellies are sometimes suggested but not always.

In planning menus, of course, your first consideration must be the individual favorites and dislikes of your family or guests. If there are children who don't like to drink milk, try to plan meals with a good deal of milk in the cooking. Plenty of vegetables and fruits too should appear on the menus for adults as well as children.

Try to visualize colorful meals, for we feast *first* with our eyes.

Consider the consistency of food, too. A number of soft foods served at the same meal are not appealing as, for instance, creamed chicken, mashed potato, and mashed white turnip. These are a most uninteresting combination from every point of view. Creamed chicken is pale, somewhat soft; mashed potato is also soft and white; the turnip is both light and soft, besides being of too strong a flavor to harmonize with the delicacy of creamed chicken. A much more appealing plate results if sweet potatoes, glazed or fried, even white potatoes French fried, perhaps, are substituted to give color and texture contrast. Then mildly flavored vegetables such as string beans, peas, carrots, or tomatoes are a more appealing color and consistency than turnips with the chicken.

So much depends upon the part of the country you live in as to your tastes and the heartiness of your meals that I do not expect to be able to suggest menus which will please everyone. My only hope is that you will find here a few suggestions to help you over the hurdle of menu-making.

Every dish listed has its recipe in this book under the name given in the menu.

INEXPENSIVE EVERYDAY MEALS

LUNCHEONS OR SUPPERS

Syrian Stew
Souffléed Crackers
Cole Slaw
Apricot and Pineapple Tapioca

•§ ₹•

Fish Balls
Baked Beans
Double Boiler Brown Bread
Piccalilli
Puffed Tomato Salad
Harlequin Jelly
Ginger Snaps

•§ ₹•

Fish or Clam Chowder
Water Crackers
Delicious Pickles
Mary Jane Gingerbread with
Sliced Bananas and Pudding Sauce

❧ ☙

Potatoes à la Suisse
Red Crest Salad
Winchester Nut Bread
Amber Pudding

❧ ☙

Cornucopia Salad
Graham Prune Bread
Pineapple Pie, Chinese Style

❧ ☙

Irish Stew with Dumplings
Tropical Salad   Orange Nut Bread Sandwiches

❧ ☙

Codfish Soufflé
Beet, Cabbage, and Pineapple Salad
Chocolate Spanish Cream
Nut Tea Wafers

❧ ☙

California Chicken Pie
Vegetable Salad
Bran Muffins
Never-Fail Chocolate Cake, Richmond Chocolate Frosting

❧ ☙

Corn and Cheese Fondue
Pickled Beets
Lettuce with Chiffonade Dressing
Coffee Whip
Chocolate Cookies

~§ §~

Escalloped Macaroni and Ham
Baked Carrots
Spiced Peach Salad with Heavenly Dressing

~§ §~

Vegetable Chowder
Popovers
Dutch Apple Cake with Lemon Sauce

~§ §~

Haddock à la King in Croustades
Harvard Beets
Pumpkin Chiffon Pie

~§ §~

Tomato Juice Cocktail
Stuffed Peppers
Carrot and Pineapple Honey
Coconut-Date Surprise

~§ §~

Southern Bisque
Bacon Salad
Popovers
Steamed Chocolate Pudding with Mock Maple Sauce

~§ §~

Epicurean Finnan Haddie in
Potato Nests
Stewed Tomatoes with Corn
Scotch Pudding

⋆§ §⋆

Neapolitan Meat Loaf
Oriental Relish
Harvest Salad
Peach Cobbler

⋆§ §⋆

Cold Sliced Meat
Sweet Pickled Prunes
Potato Cheese Puff
Rosy Apples
Toll House Ting-a-lings

⋆§ §⋆

SIMPLE DINNERS

Planked Hamburg with Border of Duchess Potato
Glazed Onions
Grilled Tomato Halves
Twopenny Salad
Coconut Custard Pudding

⋆§ §⋆

Vermont Special Chops
Apples stuffed with Sweet Potatoes
Cabbage au Gratin
Lime Sherbet
Soft Ginger Cookies

⋆§ §⋆

Baked Stuffed Haddock with Tomato Rice
Orange Beets
Jellied Waldorf Salad
Indian Tapioca Pudding

⊷§ ౿↩

Shepherd's Pie with Potato Top
Lyonnaise Carrots
Cabbage Salad
Slop-Over Cake with Apricot Filling

⊷§ ౿↩

Fish Spencer with Egg Sauce
Pan Fried Potatoes
Hot Red Cabbage
Applesauce Cake
Frappéed Fruit Juices

⊷§ ౿↩

Rolled Flank Steak
Pimento and Cheese Potato
Ten-Minute Cabbage
Butterscotch Pudding
Curried Salmon   Ripe Cucumber Pickles
Buttered Green Beans
Lemon Pie

⊷§ ౿↩

Braised Short Ribs
Baked Potatoes in Casserole
Fresh Spinach   Pepper Relish
Grapenut Pudding

⊷§ ౿↩

Broiled Steak
Mashed Potato and Carrot
Spanish Eggplant
Reed Family Tomato Relish
Peach Melba Salad
Honolulu Date Squares

⊷§ ᠍§ᡒ

Ham and Veal Loaf
Parsley Butter Potatoes
Cheese Spinach
Cardinal Pear Salad
Shredded Wheat Pudding

⊷§ ᠍§ᡒ

Sole Fouquet
Potato Cheese Balls
Gingered Carrots
Lemon Rice Pudding

⊷§ ᠍§ᡒ

Lamb Chops with Fruit Dressing
Sweet Potato Balls
Cheese Beans
Orange Layer Cake

⊷§ ᠍§ᡒ

FOR SPECIAL OCCASIONS

LUNCHEONS WITH THREE COURSES

Orange Baskets with Lime Sherbet
Chicken Soufflé Ring with Creamed Mushroons
Sweet Potato Balls with Pineapple Centers
Jellied Beet and Celery Salad   Orange Biscuits
Fudge Pecan Cake Ball

⊷§ §⊷

Fresh Pineapple Ring
Sweet Breads Chantilly with Wild Rice
Asparagus, Hollandaise Sauce   Gingered Carrots
Melba Toast
Pear Macaroon Salad   Cheese Sticks
Individual Chocolate Chiffon Pies

⊷§ §⊷

Seafood Spread Canapé
Curried Chicken with Fluffy Rice
Tray of Chutney and Accompaniments
Gingered Carrots
Toll House Frozen Fruit Salad
with Tiny Cream Puffs

⊷§ §⊷

Fruit Shrub
Ham Baked with Cheese
Potato Nests with Carrots and Peas
Persian Salad
Pineapple Icebox Cake

⊷§ §⊷

Vichyssoise Crème
Sausage and Oyster Loaf with Horseradish Sauce
Baking Powder Parker House Rolls
Harvard Beets   Cabbage Salad
Stephanie Pudding

⋟ ⥊

Tomato Juice Cocktail
Shrimp and Mushrooms
Potatoes in Half Shell with Cheese
Sautéed Corn with Peppers
Pineapple Supreme Salad   Graham Prune Bread
Orange Fairy Fluff

⋟ ⥊

Southern Bisque
Shirred Clams
Potato Cheese Puff   Escalloped Celery and **Carrots**
Frozen Tomato Salad   Squash Biscuits
Soufflé Parisienne

⋟ ⥊

Cream of Mushroom Soup
Bouquet of Salads
Fresh Crab with Russian Dressing
Molded Jelly Salad with Boiled Dressing
Puffed Tomato
Roquefort Dressing
Hot Butterscotch Pecan Rolls
Chocolate Peppermint Layer Cake
Peppermint Stick Ice Cream

⋟ ⥊

Frappéed Fruit Juices
Hawaiian Chicken
Glazed Sweet Potatoes   Cheese Beans
Cranberry Salad in Ring Mold   Golden Corn Cake
Mary Janes

ॐ ॐ

Clam Bisque
Noodle Ring with Creamed Lobster
Cheese Spinach
Molded Mexican Salad   Rum Biscuits
Orange Blossoms

ॐ ॐ

LUNCHEONS WITH TWO COURSES

Molded Salmon Ring with Cucumber Dressing
Corn and Cheese Fondue   Hot Popovers
Macaroon Pear Salad with Cheese Straws

ॐ ॐ

Avocado and Fresh Crab Salad
Cheese Soufflé   Broccoli with Buttered Crumbs
Caramel Cornflake Ring with Ice Cream Center
Butterscotch Sauce

ॐ ॐ

Ramekin of Delmonico Chicken and Noodles
Black Raspberry and Golden Glow Layer Salad
Hot Cheese Biscuits
Concord Grape Delight

ॐ ॐ

44

Escalloped Lobster
Baby Green Lima Beans   **Baking Powder Biscuits**
Savory Grapefruit Salad
Apricot Upside-Down Cake

⊷§ §⊷

Chicken and White Grape Salad
Sweet Potato Balls with Pineapple
Cheese Beans   **Cream Scones**
Baba au Rhum

⊷§ §⊷

Lobster Salad
Potato Chips   **Casserole of Corn and Tomato**
Hot Apricot Sponge Cake

⊷§ §⊷

DINNERS

Grapefruit Stuffed with **Crab**
Chicken Supreme
Apples Stuffed with Sweet Potatoes   **Green Peas**
Orange Beets
Green Salad
Raspberry Ice with Italian Meringue

⊷§ §⊷

Honeydew Melon
Vichyssoise Crème
Lobster Thermidor
French Fried Potato Balls   **Cheese Beans**
Stuffed Celery
Puffed Tomato Salad
Orange Layer Cake   **Orange Ice**

⊷§ §⊷

Cantaloupe Ring
Oyster Bisque
Smothered Chicken
Stuffed Sweet Potato   Buttered Cauliflower
Baked Peas
Toll House Frozen Fruit Salad
Daffodil Pudding

◄§ §►

Avocado and Crab Cocktail
Clam Bisque
Broiled Live Lobster
Potatoes à la Maître d'Hôtel   Green Peas
Baked Tomato Ring with Summer Squash
Cole Slaw
Lemon Meringue Pie

◄§ §►

Fresh Pineapple Ring
Mixed Grill Dinner
Sweet Potato Slices   Grilled Tomatoes
Grilled Pineapple
Vegetable Salad
Daffodil Cake   Coupe Espérance

◄§ §►

Oyster Casino
Lobster Toll House
Potato Nests with Lima Beans and Kernel Corn
Orange Beets
Peach Melba Salad
Angel Pie

◄§ §►

Grapefruit Supreme
Southern Bisque
Parisian Baked Chicken
Franconia Potatoes　　　Brussels Sprouts
Harvard Salad
Lemon Rice Pudding　　　Nut Tea Wafers

ઙ&

Fruit Cup
Crown Roast of Pork
Mashed Potato and Carrots　　　Apple Circlets
Glazed Onions
Hearts of Lettuce with Chiffonade Dressing
Baked Indian Pudding

ઙ&

Marinated Herring
Roast Beef
Mashed Potato　　　Stuffed Onions
Broccoli, Hollandaise Sauce
Green Salad with Roquefort Dressing
Individual Pumpkin Chiffon Pies

ઙ&

Cream of Mushroom and Spinach Soup
Spanish Steak
Pimento Cheese Potato　　　Escalloped Celery and Carrots
Cabbage au Gratin
Pineapple Waldorf Salad
Manhattan Pudding　　　Butterscotch Chews

ઙ&

Jellied Clam Bouillon
Hawaiian Ham
Candied Sweet Potatoes   Cheese Spinach
Hubbard Squash
Pineapple-Mint Ice Cream   Brownies

⊷ ⊷

Prune Cocktail
Toll House Onion Soup
Broiled Steak
Baked Potatoes   Lyonnaise Carrots
Spanish Eggplant
Crème Brulée   Toll House Chocolate Crunch Cookies

⊷ ⊷

SUNDAY NIGHT SNACKS

Framingham Sandwich Loaf
South American Chocolate
Peach Mousse   Date Nut Meringues

⊷ ⊷

Ring-Tum-Diddy
Toasted Crackers
Pineapple Waldorf Salad   Brownies

⊷ ⊷

Cold Sliced Neapolitan Meat Loaf
Macaroon Pear Salad
Hot Milk Sponge Cake with Strawberry Meringue Frosting

⊷ ⊷

Goldenrod Eggs
Cardinal Pear Salad with Heavenly Dressing
Maple Almond Layer Cake

⋅⋅§ ₷⋅

Toll House Onion Soup
Melba Toast
Cottage Cheese and Chives Spread   Lemon Chiffon Pie

⋅⋅§ ₷⋅

Chicken and Pineapple Salad
Potato Chips
Chocolate Peppermint Stick Layer Cake

⋅⋅§ ₷⋅

Baked Beans and Brown Bread
Cabbage Salad
Coconut Strips

⋅⋅§ ₷⋅

Open Cheese and Bacon Sandwich
Spiced Orange Peel
Pineapple Trifle

⋅⋅§ ₷⋅

Merrymount Lobster
Hot Cheese Biscuits
Frozen Orange-Prune Whip

⋅⋅§ ₷⋅

Cheese Soufflé   Orange Nut Bread
Green Salad with French Dressing
Toll House Chocolate Crunch Cookies

⋅⋅§ ₷⋅

Rice Waffles   Maple Syrup
Crisp Bacon
Stephanie Pudding

Little Pigs in Blankets
Tomato Jelly Ring Salad
Orange Layer Cake

French Toasted Ham Sandwich
Venison Jelly
Pineapple Mint Ice Cream   Butterscotch Chews

Crab Meat Soufflé
Frozen Tomato Salad
Cheese Puff Straws

Savory Milk Toast
Reed Family Tomato Relish
Cream Puffs with Chocolate Sauce

Cornucopia Salad
Hot Squash Biscuits
Fruit Shrub

Peach Melba Salad
Hot Cream Scones
Mocha Chiffon Pie

Assorted Sandwiches
Cardinal Punch
Maple Fango

☙ ❧

Molded Salmon Rings with Cucumber Dressing
Winchester Nut Bread
Caramel Custard   Peanut Butter Cookies

☙ ❧

GLOSSARY OF COOKING TERMS

Bake. To cook in oven or by dry heat; referred to as roasting for meat cookery.

Baste. To keep food moist while cooking. Usually applied to meat when pan juices or other sauce is spooned over roast.

Beat. A rapid lifting motion to incorporate air or to smooth mixture by an up-and-over motion with spoon, or from bottom of bowl to top, or a round-and-round motion with rotary beater.

Blanch. To immerse in boiling water from 1 to 5 minutes for easy removal of outer skin, often followed by a second immersion in cold water to prevent overheating of food.

Blend. To mix ingredients until they are a smooth mass.

Boil. To cook in liquid over sufficient heat to keep mixture at 212° F. or boiling.

Braise. To sear or fry outside of meat or vegetables in just enough fat to brown; then to cook slowly in covered pan on stove top or in oven with additional liquid.

Broil. To place food directly under heat, usually on flat rack or pan.

Brush. To spread thinly with melted fat, egg, or cream, usually before placing in oven to hasten browning.

Caramelize. To slowly melt sugar until it turns brown.

Chop. To cut in tiny pieces, either by hand with knife or through blades of food chopper.

Combine. To mix assorted ingredients thoroughly.

Cream. To soften shortening to consistency of heavy cream by using wooden spoon or mechanical beater.

Cube. To cut into small squares.

Cut. To work fat into flour for pastry by cutting fat with two knives or pastry cutter until all small pieces are coated with flour.

Dice. To cut into tiny squares.

Dot. To arrange small sections of food, such as butter, over top of food.

Dredge. To cover outer surface of food with light coating of flour or sugar.

Dust. To sprinkle outside of food with a powder such as confectioners sugar or flour.

Fold. To cut down through mixture with spoon, then turn across bottom of utensil, bringing spoon up to surface and turning only handle of spoon so that no air escapes from mixture.

French Fry. To cook in spider with hot fat deep enough to immerse food.

Fry. To cook in spider with 1 to 2 inches of fat. See also French Fry, Pan Fry, Sauté.

Garnish. To decorate one food with another for affinity of taste or attractiveness of color, as parsley on steak.

Glacé. To cover with thin sweet coating such as jelly or sugar.

Grate. To rub on rough open surface or grater to reduce food to desired size of small particles.

Grill. To broil with food in direct contact with heat.

Julienne. To cut food in long, very slim strips.

Knead. To press dough with palms, pushing, then turning small amount over on itself with knuckles.

Lard. To incorporate fat into lean meat by covering with strips of fat or inserting pieces of fat into gashes made in meat, or draw fat through meat with larding needle. Also a type of shortening.

Marinate. To incorporate salad dressing, usually French dressing, in dry ingredients by letting them stand in liquid until it is absorbed.

Mince. To cut into very fine pieces.

Mix. To stir ingredients.

Pan Broil. To cook in hot spider with little or no fat, pouring off repeatedly any fat which accumulates.

Pan Fry. To cook in spider with very small amount of fat.

Parboil. To boil food so as to partially cook before continuing with another type of cooking, such as baking or frying.

Pare. To remove skin with knife, as for potatoes, apples.

Peel. To remove skin by pulling as for oranges, tomatoes, avocados.

Pit. To remove stones or pits from fruits, such as cherries or dates.

Poach. To cover food with liquid and cook gently with heat below boiling point.

Purée. To force food through coarse sieve or ricer.

Render. To free fat from tissue in suet or salt pork, for example, by cutting fat into small pieces and heating it slowly until liquid fat can be drained off.

Roast. To cook by dry heat in oven, usually applied to meats.

Roll. To place on board and smooth thin and flat with rolling pin.

Sauté. To cook in spider which is barely greased.

Scald. To heat until very hot but not quite boiling or to dip food into boiling water. To scald milk, heat until bubbles form around side of pan.

Scallop. To bake food with added liquid, such as milk or stewed tomatoes in heat proof dish in oven, often with covering of bread crumbs or cereal flakes.

Score. To cut narrow gashes in even line on surface or along edge and part way through food.

Sear. To seal and brown outside of meat by contact with heat: hot fat in spider, or under heating unit of broiler or in oven.

Shortening. The term applied to fats used in batters or doughs; so-called because it rendered the mixture tender or "short." Fats differ in shortening power. Lard has more shortening power than other fats. Oils lack plasticity, being liquid, and, for good results, must be combined differently in a mixture. Butter, lard, vegetable oils, hydrogenated fats, oleomargarine, bacon, salt-pork fat, and suet are types of shortening.

Sift. To put dry ingredients through a fine sieve so as to incorporate air or remove larger particles as from flour or lumps from sugar.

Simmer. To cook slowly in liquid kept just below boiling point.

Skewer. To pierce with sharp piece of wood or metal and fasten to hold together as for pot roast, or to support small cubes of meat, vegetables, or fruit when broiling so as to serve *en brochette*.

Soak. To steep in liquid for a short time.

Spider. The New England term for a frying pan.

Steam. To cook over boiling water or to cook surrounded by steam in a double boiler or in a perforated dish through which steam can pass from water boiling below.

Steep. To cover with boiling liquid and allow to stand until flavor has been extracted.

Sterilize. To subject to boiling (212° F.) water, steam, or great heat for period of time to destroy all bacteria.

Stew. To cook slowly in liquid for a long period.

Stir. To mix ingredients until well blended using a round-and-round motion.

Toast. To brown lightly by heat in oven or under broiler as for bread, marshmallows.

Truss. To skewer or tie meat so that it will not separate during cooking; term usually applied to poultry after stuffing when it is tied to hold wings and legs of fowl close to body.

Try Out. To cook in spider solid fat or meat containing considerable fat until fat is liquefied and separated from membrane.

Whip. To incorporate air by rapid beating and so double volume of such foods as cream, gelatin, egg whites.

Ruth Wakefield's

PRIMER FOR BRIDES

Portfolio
of
Thirty-Six Essential Dishes
for the
New Homemaker

PRIMER FOR BRIDES

In this book there are hundreds of recipes for wonderful, wonderful dishes—dishes that have pleased our visiting families for many years. Perhaps as a child you were brought to Toll House to enjoy them too. Perhaps you were one of the youngsters I once put into a highchair.

Now for the first time you become a homemaker in your own new and shining kitchen. You will want to try a lot of these recipes, especially those which are your husband's favorites. But before you branch out too far there is an essential group of dishes you should be able to prepare *with assurance*. I have set these down here at the beginning so you can find them easily and if possible, before you are married, learn to prepare them one by one in your mother's kitchen. Check each one as you are successful with it. Once your thirty-six check marks are in place, I, for one, consider you well-launched toward your goal of being a proficient wife and hostess. And if I were still teaching young brides, as I used to, I would give every one of you at this point a well-ribboned diploma!

So let's start with coffee, a *good* cup of coffee.

HOT COFFEE OR ICED

For each person to be served allow
1 tablespoon coffee, ground according to method, to

1 cup water. Add
1 extra tablespoon coffee "for the pot"

Percolated. Use boiling or fresh cold water. Let "perk" until color of coffee indicates desired strength reached, usually about 5 to 10 minutes, unless a large quantity is being made.

Drip. Place coffee in container and pour boiling water over it.

Vacuum. Use hot water. When it boils, fasten securely upper bowl, containing coffee. Control heat to keep coffee and water in contact for 5 minutes.

Boiled. Use cold water. Let coffee and water come to a boil. Then strain and serve immediately. This method is largely used for large-quantity coffee-making or on camping trips.

Variation: I C E D C O F F E E. Double the amount of coffee. Fill tall glasses with ice cubes and pour hot coffee over them. Serve with plain or whipped cream, and sugar.

Coffee Pointers: Be certain you are buying fresh coffee and the "grind" suited to your coffee maker. Vacuum-packed coffee can be kept a long while unopened, but keep lid on tight after you start using it. A tightly covered jar in the refrigerator is the best place for all coffee. Keep coffee-maker absolutely clean, dry well before fitting parts together after washing, and sun and air inside parts frequently. It is difficult to make well less than 3 cups of coffee.

HOT TEA OR ICED

| For each person to be served allow | ½ teaspoon tea to 1 cup boiling water |

Scald teapot and place the tea in holder or directly in pot. Add desired number of cups of boiling water. Let stand 5 minutes and serve. After adding water to tea leaves, do not place pot over heat again. My English grandmother used to warn me, "Carry the teapot to the tea kettle of boiling water not vice-versa."

Variation: I C E D T E A. Double the amount of tea. Fill tall glasses with ice cubes and pour hot tea over them. Squeeze ¼ lemon into each glass and fasten a slice of lemon on the rim of each glass. Serve with cream and powdered sugar.

TOMATO BISQUE *(A Typical Cream Soup)*

Simmer together until soft:
3 tomatoes (2 cups, canned,)
½ small stalk celery. Add
Speck of soda, and strain.
(There should be 2 cups.)
Blend:
2 tablespoons butter, melted,

2 tablespoons flour. Add
slowly
2 cups milk. Cook until thickened. Add:
⅛ teaspoon white pepper
1 teaspoon salt

Combine and beat two mixtures. A few pieces of popcorn make a nice garnish for each service and your favorite herbs may be added sparingly to give a subtle and different flavor. Serves 4. (Nice for a party, or once as main-dish and once as first course for two.)

Variations: Add 1 cup canned or 1 cup leftover vegetables. This Tomato Bisque is excellent as a casserole dish with rice, macaroni, or spaghetti and leftover meat.

VEGETABLE SOUP

Bones remaining from a cooked rib roast of beef or the short ribs you saved from your roast are fine for soup. Or you can buy 4 pounds of shin bones. Place in deep kettle and cover with cold water. Add 1 teaspoon salt, 1 sliced onion, 1 sliced carrot and the outside stalks of celery, leaves included. Bring to a boil. Skim and reduce heat. Simmer slowly for 2 to 3 hours, depending upon amount of bones you are cooking. When meat clinging to them is tender and bones are whitened, strain liquid through a fine sieve and cool, uncovered. Chill in refrigerator. When fat hardens on surface, skim it off. For every 4 cups of soup stock prepare the following:

1 onion, cut fine,
1 cup diced celery
1 cup diced carrots

1 cup peas
1 cup Lima beans
1 cup canned tomatoes

Add 2 cups hot salted water. Cover and cook until vegetables are tender, about 20 minutes. Then season to taste with salt and pepper and simmer a few minutes more. Make soup well ahead and, if possible, allow to stand before reheating to serve.

Variations: **HURRY-UP SOUP.** Substitute for stock, beef bouillon cubes dissolved in hot water, according to directions.

MAIN-DISH SOUP. Add along with vegetables ¼ cup rice, macaroni, or cubed potatoes. At Toll House we pass grated Parmesan cheese to sprinkle over this soup. It makes good soup just that much better.

IRISH STEW

Heat in spider
2 tablespoons fat. Add
1 pound beef, lamb, or mutton, cubed and rolled in flour. When browned, place in kettle with:
½ small onion, sliced,
1 teaspoon salt
Few grains pepper

1 quart cold water. Simmer until meat is tender. Add:
1 carrot, diced,
2 potatoes, diced. Cook until vegetables are done, about 10 minutes. Thicken with
2 teaspoons flour, mixed with water

Bring all to boiling point and serve. Serves 2.

NEW ENGLAND CLAM CHOWDER *(Basic Recipe for New England Brides)*

Try out a
1½ inch-cube salt pork, cut fine. Fry in it
1 onion, sliced. Add:
4 cups diced raw potatoes
2 cups boiling water. Cook 5 minutes. Add liquor of

1 peck clams, steamed and shucked. Remove black necks. Add clams. Simmer until potatoes are done. Add:
4 cups milk, scalded. Season with
Salt and pepper

Prepare 1 hour ahead of serving to allow chowder to develop best flavor. Dot with butter and serve with Boston common crackers or water crackers. Serves 8. (This is splendid for a hot easy-toprepare company supper in winter or to reheat for the second even better meal.)

Variation: **NEW YORK CLAM CHOWDER.** Omit milk and add 3 cups water and 1 cup stewed tomatoes.

CRUSTY BISCUITS *(A Typical Drop Biscuit)*

Sift together:
1 cup flour
2 teaspoons baking powder
½ teaspoon salt. Cut in
1 tablespoon shortening until consistency of corn meal. Add
⅓ to ½ cup milk and water combined

Mix with enough milk for dough to drop from spoon. Drop by tablespoonfuls onto a greased baking sheet. Bake in hot oven, 500°F., for 12 to 15 minutes. Makes 6 large biscuits. (This is worth doubling. You can split the extras and toast for breakfast or serve as a shortcake for dessert.)

Variations: **CHEESE BISCUITS.** Add ½ cup grated cheese.

ORANGE BISCUITS. Substitute orange juice for milk.

BREAKFAST MUFFINS

Sift together:
1 cup flour
2 teaspoons baking powder
1 tablespoon sugar
¼ teaspoon salt. Add gradually
⅓ cup milk
1 egg, well beaten,
1 tablespoon melted butter

Do not beat. Just stir enough to blend well. Pour into buttered muffin pans and bake in hot oven, 400°F., for 25 minutes. Makes 6 large muffins. (This is well worth doubling. Split, butter, and sprinkle the extras with cinnamon and sugar for a delightful second-breakfast bread.)

Variations: It is also nice to use ½ cup white flour and ½ cup graham or rye flour, or corn meal. Then add ¼ cup chopped dates or whole cranberries or place 1 whole pitted prune in the center of batter for each muffin.

SOFT- AND HARD-COOKED EGGS

Always cook eggs at the lowest practical temperature. First bring water just to boiling point, add eggs, turn heat off, cover pan and let eggs stand about 5 minutes. The result is a very soft or "coddled" egg, the kind served to invalids.

For average or family use, fill an enamel or stainless steel pan—aluminum pans turn black when eggs are boiled in them—three-quarters full of water. Bring water to boil and slide eggs carefully into water to prevent cracking of shells. Time cooking from this period. Allow about 4 minutes for soft-cooked eggs. If eggs are taken directly from the refrigerator, allow about 5 minutes. When water resumes boiling turn heat low to simmer.

For hard-cooked eggs allow 10 to 15 minutes. After removing from heat, run cold water over eggs immediately to prevent outside of yolk from turning black.

FRIED BACON AND EGGS

Place bacon strips in heavy spider, turn on heat, and cook bacon very *slowly* until light brown, turning it once. (Remember bacon will darken when removed from pan.) Place on absorbent paper after cooking to remove excess fat. If a great deal of fat accumulates in spider, pour it off during frying and save it for other cooking. Never allow heat to become so great that fat smokes and turns brown.

After bacon is cooked, reserve about 2 tablespoons of fat in spider. Break eggs, one at a time, into a saucer and slide into heated spider. Cover pan for a minute to cook viscous part of egg not in direct contact with pan. (Or you can spoon fat over top of egg to accomplish this.) Season with salt and pepper. When white is firm, eggs are done. Remove to warm platter, garnish with the bacon strips, and serve at once. These are eggs "sunny side up." If you prefer, break the egg yolk and turn the egg once during the frying. The result is a firm yolk and generally a harder egg.

SCRAMBLED EGGS

Combine in bowl:
3 eggs
3 tablespoons milk
½ teaspoon salt
Few grains pepper. Stir to
break yolks and mix all thoroughly. Melt
2 tablespoons butter in frying pan

Pour in egg mixture. Cook until creamy, stirring constantly and scraping from bottom of pan. (The top of a double boiler may be used instead of frying pan.) Serves 2 to 3.

Variations: With this recipe, you can add ¼ cup stewed tomatoes, 2 tablespoons fine cut cheese, or ½ teaspoon fine herbs.

ESCALLOPED MACARONI AND CHEESE

Cook for 12 minutes
½ cup macaroni in
1 quart boiling salted water.
Drain. Combine:
½ cup sharp cheese, cut fine,
½ cup cold milk. Heat slowly.
Season with
Salt and Pepper

Combine macaroni with cheese mixture in buttered casserole. Cover with cornflakes or crushed shredded wheat or bread crumbs. Dot with butter. Bake in moderate oven, 375°F., for about 30 minutes. (Starch of macaroni thickens milk.) Serves 2 to 3.

Variations: You can double this recipe also to advantage. Add leftover scraps of roast pork, ham, slices or flakes of fish to mixture and stir in well before baking, or if you have macaroni left over, add meat to it as a change for another meal. In reheating, add about ½ cup milk.

BAKED HALIBUT STEAK *(A Typical Baked Fish)*

Wipe dry 1 large ¾-pound halibut steak. Place in greased baking dish.

Blend:
2 tablespoons butter
2 tablespoons flour. Add:
½ teaspoon salt
⅛ teaspoon pepper

2 tablespoons pimento, chopped fine,
1 tablespoon onion, chopped fine

Spread mixture over fish. Bake in hot oven, 450°F., for about 30 minutes. Serve at once. Steak serves 2 to 3.

Variations: Haddock, cod, lake trout, or any thick white fish may be cooked the same way.

BROILED STEAK
(See Timetable for Broiling, page 22)

Purchase a sirloin, porterhouse, or tenderloin steak cut 2 to 3 inches thick. Have the "end" ground. (Weight depends on size of loin.) Wipe steak, slash fat in 4 or 5 places and place meat on wire rack of broiling pan. Preheat broiler to 550°F., or as hot as possible, for 15 minutes. Place steak 3 inches below heat. Sear steak on one side. Turn and sear on other side, inserting fork in fat so as not to pierce meat. Reduce heat to 350°, when steak is well browned, and cook until meat is done to individual taste: about 20 minutes for rare; 25 minutes for medium; and 35 minutes for well done. Place on platter and rub butter over steak. Season with salt and pepper. Serve at once. Serves 4. (Broil the ground end or flank as meat cakes for a second meal.)

BROILED LAMB CHOPS
(See Timetable for Broiling, page 22)

Purchase rib or loin lamb chops about ½ pound each. Allow 1 or 2 per person. Preheat broiler to 550°F. Slash rim of fat in 3 places to avoid curling. Place chops on rack about 3 inches below heat. Brown, season with salt and pepper. Turn, brown, and season other side. Reduce heat to 350° and cook about 15 minutes (medium) or 20 minutes (well done). Place on hot platter and serve.

ROAST BEEF WITH ROAST POTATOES AND GRAVY
(See Timetable for Roasting, page 21)

For best flavor buy a 2- or 3-rib standing roast of beef. Allow ½ pound per person but plan roast for 2 or more meals. Your butcher will trim off what are known as the short ribs. Be sure to have him include these with your roast to bring home as they are excellent for braised beef, stew, or soup stock.

Remove roast from refrigerator about 30 minutes ahead of roasting. Wipe meat with damp cloth. Dredge bottom of roasting pan with flour which will brown for a rich brown gravy while roast is cooking. A rack may or may not be used in the roasting pan. Place roast on rack or directly on bottom of pan with fat side up. Dredge lightly with flour and season the fat with salt and pepper. Place in oven preheated to low heat of 325°F. Add no water, nor will basting or turning be necessary. Allow 15 to 20 minutes per pound for rare meat, 24 to 28 minutes for medium, and 28 to 34 minutes per pound for a well-done roast. The larger the roast, the less time per pound is required. A rare 5-pound roast requires 20 minutes per pound but a 10-pound roast will require only 15 minutes per pound. Place roast on a hot platter and cover while you prepare gravy.

In our family we enjoy a rare roast for two dinners. We allow a little less time per pound for the first roasting and cut slices from each side of roast, leaving center of the roast almost raw. We re-roast it again another day and enjoy hot rare roast beef. The remaining meat is then sliced to serve cold for a third meal.

Roast Potatoes
Pare medium-sized white or sweet potatoes, parboil about 5 minutes, and place around roast during last 45 minutes of cooking. Turn twice to produce even browning.

Gravy
Pour off all but 2 tablespoons fat from drippings in roaster. Blend in 2 tablespoons flour. Add very slowly 1 cup hot water or vegetable juices and blend carefully. Cook slowly, scraping from bottom of pan the browned pieces which will usually be sufficient

to give the gravy a nice brown color. Strain before serving, if there are any large particles. Be sure to cook long enough to eliminate "raw" taste of flour.

ROASTED HAMBURG STEAK

Soak
2 slices bread, broken fine, in
1½ cups milk. Combine with:
1 pound hamburg and
½ pound lean pork, put

through food chopper. Season with:
1 teaspoon salt
1 teaspoon poultry seasoning
1 onion, cut fine. Stir in
1 egg

Shape into loaf. Place in loaf pan and pour 1 can (2½ cups) tomatoes over all. Place strips of bacon across top. Bake in moderate oven, 350°F., for 1 hour. Baste meat frequently with tomatoes. Serves 4. (If desired, add 1 tablespoon pimento and 1 tablespoon chopped green pepper for flavoring.)

BAKED PICNIC OR COTTAGE HAM

In using packers' hams follow directions given by them. Most of the hams we purchase today have been "processed" or "tenderized." They will not need the preliminary soaking or boiling which used to be required. Ham can be immediately baked and some types will not even need as much baking time as I have indicated below. A thorough heating will suffice.

Place well scrubbed 3½- to 4-pound picnic ham, rind side up, in roaster or large pan and bake, uncovered, in slow oven, 275°F., to 300°, allowing 15 to 20 minutes per pound. If ham weighs over 12 pounds, reduce baking to 10 minutes per pound.

About ½ hour before meat is done, remove from oven, strip off rind and any extra-thick sections of fat. Leave about ½ inch coating of fat over all. Score fat by running sharp knife evenly across surface of fat to make a pattern of 1-inch squares or diamonds. Rub with brown sugar. Insert a clove in center of each scored square or diamond, and pour ¼ cup cider, ginger ale, cranberry, or pineapple juice over all. Return to oven and continue baking. Baste twice with drippings. When done, garnish with maraschino cherries, inserted into fat and held there with toothpicks.

Variations: Arrange over scored fat and fasten with toothpicks pineapple slices or peach halves with a cherry in center of each. Then sprinkle with brown sugar. Pour ¼ cup fruit juice over all and baste. Serves 6 to 8. (This is an excellent party meat served hot at the table or cold at a buffet. Of course it can be prepared the day before.)

ROAST STUFFED CHICKEN WITH GIBLET GRAVY
(See Timetable for Roasting, page 21)

Select a 4- to 5-pound chicken. Have butcher draw (clean) it, but go over it at home before cooking. Remove pin feathers with tweezers, singe to remove any hairs. To do this hold chicken over low heat, moving to expose all areas for a moment to the flame or heat. Wash by allowing water to run through carcass; do not let it soak in water. Wipe dry inside and out; stuff, tie or "truss." This means tying legs and wings close to body. Rub entire surface with blended mixture of ½ teaspoon salt, 1½ tablespoons soft butter, and 1 tablespoon flour. Place on rack in dripping pan with breast down.

Dredge bottom of pan with flour. Place chicken in preheated oven, 350°F. Allow 20 to 30 minutes per pound (weight before cleaning) for roasting. A 4-pound chicken will serve 4 to 6 and take about 2 hours.

Poultry Stuffing

Pour
¾ cup boiling water over:
3½ cups stale bread crumbs
1 tablespoon butter. Let stand a few minutes. Add:
1 tablespoon poultry seasoning

1½ teaspoons salt
¼ teaspoon pepper
¾ cup finely chopped celery
1 onion, chopped (optional)

If mixture seems too moist, add more bread crumbs. This is ample stuffing for a 4- to 5-pound fowl. Allow about 1 cup stuff-

69

ing for each pound poultry. (Double or triple recipe for a turkey.) Pack stuffing lightly into cavity of fowl as stuffing swells in baking.

Variation: Add either ¾ cup chopped chestnuts, or ¾ cup chopped cooked giblets, or 1 cup chopped oysters to recipe.

Giblet Gravy

While fowl is roasting, cook in saucepan of water to cover the cleaned and washed giblets—heart, liver, and gizzard. Simmer until liver is tender. Remove liver and continue cooking heart and gizzard until tender. Remove them from stock and chop into small pieces. Strain stock to use in gravy.

When fowl is tender, remove to serving platter and keep hot. Pour off all but 2 tablespoons of fat from drippings in pan. Blend into them 2 tablespoons flour. Add very slowly 1 cup giblet stock and hot water or add any available vegetable juices to make 1 cupful. Blend carefully. Simmer while scraping the browned pieces from bottom of pan. These browned pieces will be sufficient to give the gravy a rich brown color. Season with salt and pepper. Add chopped giblets and serve at once. (Double this recipe for roast turkey gravy.)

FRIED CHICKEN WITH CREAM GRAVY *(Typical Breaded and Fried Food)*

Allow half of a 2½-pound broiler per person. Prepare for cooking (see Roast Stuffed Chicken), wash, wipe dry, and split chicken down through backbone. Separate breast and thigh sections so that there are 4 pieces.

In paper bag place small amount of flour with ample seasoning of salt and pepper. Dip chicken in cold milk, then drop into bag of flour, and shake to coat well. Fry in drippings, made up of about 4 tablespoons salt pork (or other shortening) and 4 tablespoons butter, having fat deep enough to reach well up on sides of chicken while it is browning in pan. Keep pan covered and when chicken is well browned on one side, turn and brown on other side. Cook until fat has reduced in amount and at end of frying there is just enough to use in the making of gravy, about

2 tablespoons. Do not crowd chicken into spider while frying. Use two pans if necessary to keep chicken in contact with hot fat on all sides. When fried to perfection, remove chicken to hot serving platter and make gravy.

Cream Gravy

Remove spider from heat and measure approximate number of tablespoons of fat left in pan. Use same number of tablespoons of flour and blend well with water to make thin paste. Then add milk. Cook slowly over low heat and stir constantly until gravy is smooth, creamy, and with all starchy taste gone. There will be bits of chicken crust, etc. Keep these to enhance the flavor of the gravy. Season with salt and pepper before serving. For 1 cup gravy, allow 2 tablespoons fat, 2 tablespoons flour, and 1 cup milk.

PARSLEY BUTTERED POTATOES

Wash and peel medium-sized potatoes. Allow 1 potato for each serving. To prevent discoloration, place in cold water in sauce-pan as soon as each is peeled but do not soak potatoes. When ready to cook, pour off cold water. Add about 1 cup boiling water, and a pinch of salt. Cover and bring to boil. Let boil gently until potatoes are soft when pierced with two-tined fork, about 25 to 35 minutes. Pour off water and shake potatoes in pan over fire to dry. Season and serve with butter and chopped parsley or pour Cheese Sauce over potatoes.

BAKED POTATOES

Wash, scrub, and remove eyes from Maine or Idaho potatoes. Dry and place on rack in hot oven, 400° F., and bake for 45 to 60 minutes, or until tender. To test potatoes squeeze them with the hand wrapped in a towel. When potatoes are soft, break open, insert large piece of butter, and sprinkle opened part with salt and paprika. Allow 1 medium-sized or ½ very large potato for each serving.

Variations: **STUFFED POTATOES:** When potatoes are tender, place on flat side and slice off skin from top of each. Remove contents with teaspoon. Force potato through ricer. Add salt, pepper, butter, and a little hot milk. Beat well. Refill skins, leaving potato rough on top. Return to oven or broiler until potatoes are hot and delicately brown. Sprinkle with paprika and serve at once.

STUFFED POTATOES WITH CHEESE: Before refilling shells, add to potato mixture a little grated cheese and paprika. Sprinkle with grated cheese before returning to oven to heat.

ESCALLOPED POTATOES

Grease casserole well and place layer of peeled, thickly sliced, raw potatoes in bottom. Cover with thin slices of onion. Dredge lightly with flour, sprinkle with salt and pepper, and dot generously with butter. Repeat this until dish is filled to within 1 inch of top. Pour milk over potatoes and onions until top is barely covered. (Milk will be entirely absorbed by potato in baking.) Place casserole in moderate oven, 350° F., and bake for about 1 hour, or until potatoes are soft when fork is passed through them. Watch carefully that milk does not boil over.

MASHED POTATOES

Pare and boil 4 medium-sized potatoes. Drain well and shake potatoes in pan over heat until thoroughly dry. Mash or put through ricer. Be sure there are no lumps. Sprinkle potatoes with salt and pepper. Add 2 tablespoons of butter and ¼ to ⅓ cup hot milk. Beat until of soft creamy consistency. Add more milk if necessary for desired texture. Beat thoroughly to fluff and serve at once. Do not skimp on seasonings, butter, or rich milk if you desire a superior result. Allow 1 potato for each serving.

FLUFFY RICE

Preheat oven at 400° F. In an 8- by 8- by 1-inch baking pan place ½ cup unwashed rice and bake in hot oven for 20 minutes. (Don't worry if rice smokes a bit.) When it is golden brown remove from oven and pour into fine-mesh strainer. Let cold water from faucet spray over it. Then pour toasted rice into a small casserole, add ½ teaspoon salt and pour in 1½ cups boiling water. Cover and bake in hot oven, 400° F., for 25 minutes. Near the end of baking time remove cover and fluff up rice with two-tined fork. Then continue baking until rice is done. Serves 2. (This is a never-fail method of cooking rice.)

WHITE OR BASIC CREAM SAUCE *(Medium, for Creamed Foods)*

Blend in top of double boiler:	¼ teaspoon salt
	Few grains pepper. Slowly
2 tablespoons butter, melted,	add
2 tablespoons flour	1 cup milk

Stir until thick and smooth. Cook until no starchy taste remains, about 3 minutes. Stir in an egg yolk or paprika if you wish to eliminate the "white" look and have sauce of creamy color. When not serving sauce at once, cover pan tightly to prevent skin forming. Makes 1 cup of sauce.

Variations: **THIN WHITE SAUCE.** *(For Cream Soups.)* Use 1 tablespoon flour and 1 tablespoon butter to 1 cup milk.

THICK WHITE SAUCE. *(For Croquettes, Soufflés.)* Use 4 tablespoons flour and 4 tablespoons butter to 1 cup milk.

CHEESE SAUCE. Add to basic White Sauce ½ cup cheese, broken into small pieces. Stir until cheese is melted and sauce is smooth.

SPINACH *(A Typical Green Vegetable)*

Soak spinach in salted water for a few minutes to freshen. Cut off roots and wilted leaves. Wash thoroughly until no sand can be found in bottom of pan. Place in large kettle with ½ cup water. (Always cook vegetable in as little water as possible.) Cover and steam until crispness is gone. Then uncover and cook for a few minutes more. Allow no more than 12 minutes for total time. Cut through with a knife to make serving easier. Pour melted butter over it and season with salt and pepper. Allow ½-pound for each serving.

GREEN SALAD

Select salad greens. Wash thoroughly. Shake off excess water and wrap greens in wax paper or towel, or cover with cellophane bag and place in refrigerator to chill and crisp. Lettuce, endive, watercress, romaine, chickory, escarole, parsley, dandelion or tender inside spinach leaves, Chinese or celery cabbage, tender cabbage leaves, fennel and salad chervil may all be used. My favorite salad-bowl combination is composed of lettuce, curly endive, Chinese cabbage, romaine, chicory, thinly sliced onion, red cabbage, and cucumber, shredded carrots, celery strips, and wedges of tomato, with the whole garnished with watercress.

It is best to tear lettuce and cut or tear other greens just before serving time. If you like the flavor of garlic, rub the salad bowl with the cut surface of a clove garlic, or add garlic salt to dressing before turning in salad greens. Pour a generous amount of French Dressing over greens and toss lightly together with a large spoon and fork to coat greens well with dressing. Serve at once.

Variation: You may prefer to lightly marinate greens with French Dressing for 10 or 15 minutes ahead of time. Then serve with Roquefort, Thousand Island, Russian, or Chiffonade Dressing as a topping.

POTATO SALAD *(My Husband's Favorite)*

Boil medium-sized potatoes (allowing 1 potato for each person) until tender, about 20 to 25 minutes. (Do not overcook or they will be mushy when cut.) Cool and cut in ½-inch cubes. Peel onions and scrape or grate into the cubed potatoes. (Allow ½ cup onion to 2 cups potatoes.) Marinate lightly with about ⅓ cup French Dressing or just enough to be absorbed and leave no excess oil. (This seasons potatoes throughout.) Place in refrigerator until serving time. Then add mayonnaise to moisten well. Season with salt and pepper. Chopped pickle or parsley may also be added. Serve in lettuce cups garnished with quartered hard-cooked eggs and wedges of ripe tomatoes with a dot of mayonnaise for topping.

MOLDED JELLY *(for Party Salad or Dessert)*

Soften
2 tablespoons gelatin in
½ cup cold water. Add:
1 cup boiling water

¾ cup sugar. Stir until dissolved. Add
2½ cups tomato or fruit juice or either diluted with water

Pour into 8 molds and chill in refrigerator until set. The amount of sugar varies with sweetness of fruit. If lemon juice is used, it may be necessary to increase to 1 cup of sugar.

Variation: When mixture begins to cool (not before) add fresh or canned fruit—about 1½ cups berries, sliced bananas, apricot or peach halves, or melon balls. When these are used, it is a good idea first to half fill molds with them and then, when gelatin mixture has cooled and thickened slightly, to pour in enough to fill mold completely.

To unmold gelatins, fill a pan with hot water. Dip molds quickly in and out and have water deep enough to reach well up the sides. Then run a butter spreader along the sides of the mold to loosen the gelatin and break the vacuum. So treated the molded gelatin will slide out easily.

For salad, invert molds and turn gelatin out on a lettuce leaf. Serve with mayonnaise thinned with whipped cream or fruit juice.

For dessert, unmold into a sherbet cup or onto a dessert plate. Serve with whipped cream sweetened with confectioners sugar and a little vanilla.

French Dressing

Pour into a bottle:
6 tablespoons salad oil
1 teaspoon salt
¼ teaspoon pepper

Dash paprika
6 tablespoons vinegar or lemon juice

Cover bottle tightly and shake until thoroughly mixed. Makes 1 cup dressing. For a more highly flavored dressing add ½ onion or 1 clove garlic.

BAKED CUSTARD

Scald in top of double
boiler
1 quart milk. Beat
4 eggs. Add:
⅓ cup sugar

½ teaspoon salt. Mix well.
Slowly pour into scalded
milk, stirring constantly.
Add
1 teaspoon vanilla

Pour into 8 custard cups. Place them in shallow pan containing warm water. Bake in slow oven, 325° F., for about 45 minutes, or until butter spreader inserted in custard comes out clean. (Water in pan must not reach boiling point or custard will separate.) Chill and unmold, or serve, sprinkled with nutmeg, in baking cups. Caramel or Chocolate Sauce may be served with the inverted custards, or spoon maple syrup over them. The addition of a sauce makes a fancier dessert and all these combinations are delicious and easy to prepare ahead of time. Serves 8. (Custards keep well for serving at several meals or the recipe may be halved for just two of you.)

Variations: **CHOCOLATE CUSTARD.** Add 2 tablespoons cocoa mixed with sugar.

COCONUT CUSTARD. Add 1 cup grated or shredded coconut to egg and sugar mixture.

COFFEE CUSTARD. Use 2 cups strong coffee and 2 cups milk instead of 4 cups milk.

SPONGECAKE
(See Guide to Successful Baking, page 236)

Beat
5 egg yolks until light and
thick. Add
Juice and grated rind ½
lemon.
Beat
5 egg whites until very light.

Fold in:
1 cup sugar and egg yolks.
Fold in, a little at a time,
1 cup sifted flour and
¼ teaspoon salt

Turn into ungreased tube pan and bake in slow oven, 325° F., until cake has reached full height. Then increase heat to 350° for 15 minutes while cake browns. Decrease to 325° until done, 45 to 60 minutes in all. Let cake cool about 1 hour in pan inverted on cake cooler. Remove from pan by running knife around inside. Dust top with confectioners sugar. Serve cake when cool by pulling it apart with two silver forks.

STANDARD LAYER CAKE WITH MIRACLE FUDGE FROSTING *(Typical Butter Cake with Uncooked Icing)*
(See Guide to Successful Baking, page 236)

Cream well
½ cup butter or other shortening. Beat in gradually
1 cup sugar. Beat
2 egg yolks. Stir into butter mixture. Sift together:
2 cups flour

3 teaspoons baking powder. Add to egg mixture alternately with
¾ cup milk. Fold in
2 egg whites, beaten stiff, Add
1½ teaspoons vanilla

Turn into two 8-inch layer-cake pans. Bake in moderate oven, 375° F., for 20 to 30 minutes. When cool, frost with Miracle Fudge Frosting.

Miracle Fudge Frosting

Melt in top of double boiler:
6 oz. (1 c.) semi-sweet chocolate morsels
2 tablespoons butter or shortening. Stir until smooth,

remove from heat and add:
1 cup sifted confectioners sugar
1 teaspoon vanilla. Add slowly
¼ cup hot milk (about)

Beat until satin smooth. Add a little more sugar if consistency is too thin for spreading. Spread on top and sides of two 8-inch layers. Prepare half of recipe to frost top of loaf cake.

77

NUT TEA WAFERS *(Refrigerator Cookies)*
(See Guide to Successful Baking, page 236)

Cream together:
½ cup butter
1 cup brown sugar. Add
1 egg, beaten. Beat mixture well. Sift together:
1¼ cups flour

¼ teaspoon salt
½ teaspoon soda. Add to first mixture with:
½ cup meats, chopped,
½ teaspoon vanilla

Mix well and pack in greased individual bread tins, lined with heavy wax paper. Store in refrigerator overnight. Turn out on board and slice as thinly as possible with carving knife. Bake in moderately hot oven, 375° F. to 400°, for 7 to 12 minutes. Makes 3 dozen cookies. (The dough may be formed into a long roll if a round cooky is preferred to an oblong one.)

APPLE PIE WITH PLAIN OR SPICED PASTRY
(See Pie Failures and Their Causes, page 268)

Prepare
1 recipe Plain or Spiced Pastry and line 8-inch pie plate. Fill with
6 to 8 tart apples, peeled, cored, and sliced thin
Combine:

⅔ to 1 cup sugar (depending on tartness of apples)
½ teaspoon cinnamon
¼ teaspoon salt
Speck of nutmeg. Sprinkle over apples

Dot top of apples with butter. Arrange top crust and spread with a little milk. Prick crust with fork or make six 1-inch slits near center of crust to allow steam to escape. Place cooky sheet or large pan on shelf under pie to save oven from dripping fruit juice. Bake in hot oven, 425° F. for 15 minutes. Then reduce heat to moderate, 350° for rest of baking, 20 to 35 minutes.

╩ | *1. BEVERAGES ARE BASIC* | ╩

╩

Our section of New England is full of cranberry bogs. In fact, the area where you park your car when you visit Toll House was once a cranberry bog. Since we are so close to a wonderful supply, we use our native berry a great deal, particularly in punch, and in my grandmother's recipe for Fruit Shrub, our Toll House Cocktail, (page 91). We use it, too, of course, as the perfect accompaniment for poultry and we also feature it in desserts.

In the recipes that follow, you will find recipes for other kinds of punch, besides those that include cranberries. Wedding parties have enjoyed the cup that cheers and children have reveled in the ones suggested for their parties. They like this delicious chocolate too, particularly for Sunday night supper, that most intimate meal of the week.

BREAKFAST COCOA

Mix to a smooth paste:
3 tablespoons cocoa
4 tablespoons sugar
½ cup boiling water. Add

1½ cups boiling water and boil for 3 minutes. Add Few grains salt. Dilute with 2 cups hot milk

Beat to prevent scum from forming. Serves 6.

SOUTH AMERICAN CHOCOLATE

Melt in top of double boiler
6 oz. (1 c.) semi-sweet chocolate morsels.
Add slowly

1 cup strong hot coffee. Boil 1 minute. Add to 6 cups milk, scalded

Beat until thick froth forms. Let stand over hot water for 10 minutes. Serve with whipped cream sweetened and flavored, or chill and serve in tall glasses with cracked ice. Serves 8.

HOT COFFEE AND ICED
(See Primer for Brides, page 59)

HOT TEA AND ICED
(See Primer for Brides, page 60)

BASIC FRUIT PUNCH

Dissolve
3½ cups sugar in:
  2 cups lemon juice
  1 pint orange juice
  1 pint grape juice

1 pint strong tea. Add
7 quarts ice water. Pour over
  ice in punch bowl. Add:
1 pineapple, cut fine,
1 cup cherries, halved

Makes about 2½ gallons punch or enough for 100, allowing 1½ cups of punch for each guest. May be diluted with ginger ale or soda water, if desired.

CARDINAL PUNCH

Cook
1 quart cranberries in
1 quart water and strain
  through moistened cloth.
  Add:
2 cups sugar. Cook 6 minutes.

Strain, chill, and add:
1 cup orange juice
½ cup lemon juice
1 pint ginger ale. Dilute with
2 quarts water

Pour over crushed ice, and serve with green cherry in each cup. Serves 30.

PINEAPPLE AND ORANGE PUNCH

Boil for 20 minutes:
1⅔ cups sugar
  4 cups cold water'
  2 cups pineapple, chopped.

Add:
½ cup lemon juice
1 cup orange juice

Cool, strain, dilute to taste with ice water. Serves 18.

CHAMPAGNE PUNCH

Dissolve
3 cups sugar in
Juice of 12 lemons. Cube
1 pineapple and mix with
1 cup sugar. Let stand several
hours. Pour
3 quarts ice water into punch
bowl. Add sweetened lemon
juice and
1 quart strawberries, or raspberries, slightly crushed. Add
pineapple and stir. Add:
1 quart champagne
1 quart white wine. Stir again

Serve iced. Makes 6 to 6½ quarts and serves 60 guests, allowing 1½ cups of punch for each guest.

2. HORS D' OEUVRES IN THE LIVING ROOM

Serving the first course of a party dinner in the living room, on the porch, or in the garden is pleasant and informal and also a practical means to gracious entertaining for the hostess who does it all herself. Experience has taught me that it is wise to serve only a few kinds of hors d'oeuvres whether they are with cocktails, tomato juice, fruit juice, or those drinks with "spirits" added. It works out better to concentrate on just three or four unusual and delicious trifles than to attempt a diversified panorama. While a great tray of original, shapely, and colorful items may intrigue your guests, a relaxed and charming hostess pleases them even more. One rich, hot hors d'oeuvre like Alice Dixon Bond's Savories, which can be prepared ahead and popped into the oven at the last minute, one not-so-highly-caloried canapé like Easy Conscience Wafers, and one excellent dip or spread like Cottage Cheese and Chives or Wakefield Special make a cheerful enough start for any meal.

The base of a canapé may be bread, pastry, crackers, potato chips, puffs, or one of the various commercial cups or tubes offered by your grocer.

Bread canapé bases are prepared from slices of stale bread cut ¼ inch thick. Crusts are trimmed and bread is cut in oblongs, squares, rounds, crescents, diamonds, stars, or in tiny fancy holiday shapes of Christmas trees or valentine hearts. Small cooky cutters will shape them easily. Sauté the bread in butter, or toast

82

it on one side only. Use the untoasted surface for spreading or arranging a savory mixture.

When pastry is used for a canapé base, it is cut in fancy shapes but a rich or puff pastry is preferable to the plain pastry of pie crust.

FILLINGS FOR CANAPÉS

ANCHOVY CURLS

Place anchovy curls or fillets on toast fingers, dip edges in mayonnaise and then in sieved egg yolks. Garnish with strips of pimento.

CHEESE BALLS

Roll cream cheese balls in poppy seeds or chopped nuts.

CAVIAR TOAST SQUARES

Spread caviar on toast with an edging of chopped egg. Garnish center with sieved egg yolk and chopped onion.

STUFFED CELERY

Moisten well celery filled with snappy yellow cheese or with cream cheese and Roquefort mashed together. Garnish with bits of pimento and green pepper.

CHICKEN LIVER CANAPÉ

Chop cooked chicken livers and mix with chopped sautéed mushrooms, seasoned with a bit of onion. Spread on toast or crackers.

COTTAGE CHEESE BALLS

Make cottage cheese balls with a variety of seasonings. Use catsup and grated onion and roll balls in finely chopped parsley or mint; or season cheese with Worcestershire sauce, salt and pepper, and roll in grated raw carrot; or combine cheese with black caviar and onion juice, or with chutney and roll balls in chopped pistachio nut meats.

EAST INDIAN SPREAD

Mix cream cheese with chutney for a delicious spread and top with anchovy fillet.

GOLD AND BLACK SPREAD

Cream Old English Cheese with chili sauce and garnish with caviar.

CHEESE TROPICALS

Stuff dates or prunes with cream or snappy cheese mixed with nuts or ginger. Do not cook prunes but soak overnight, dry well, and pit. Prunes may be wrapped in bacon and broiled to serve hot.

DEVILED HAM TOASTIES

Combine deviled ham with chopped nuts and spread on toast with a garnish of crisp, crumbled bacon or an olive.

EASY CONSCIENCE WAFERS

For weight watchers spread Ry-Krisp with a little dressing to hold a slice of tomato; then add a bit more dressing to anchor a thin slice of unpeeled cucumber with more dressing to hold a garnish of watercress.

CRAB FLAKE BITS

Spread fresh crab flakes on toast covered with Russian Dressing. Dip edges in chopped radishes.

DEVILED EGGS

Cut hard-cooked eggs in half and mash yolks. Then mix with mayonnaise and season with a little curry powder, chopped chives, or any other seasoning you prefer. Pile lightly into the hollowed egg white and garnish with a slice of black olive or a little caviar. Salmon and chopped pickle moistened with mayonnaise make a nice filler also.

SEAFOOD MORSELS

Pierce hot fried scallops, oysters, clams, shrimps, or tiny fish balls with toothpicks and arrange on tray around a center of cabbage, eggplant, or red cabbage, which has been hollowed and filled with Russian Dressing to dip fish into.

GREEN PICKLE RINGS

Fill centers of large rings of green pickle with red caviar.

CLAM TOAST BITES

Littleneck clams may be dipped in cocktail sauce and served in tiny toast cups, made by cubing bread and hollowing out center before toasting.

STUFFED MUSHROOM CAPS

Littleneck clams may also be dipped in melted butter and then placed in hollows of partially cooked mushroom caps. Broil to finish cooking both mushrooms and clams. Garnish with parsley.

CHEESE STRIPS

Spread long strips of toast with seasoned cream cheese and place a long thin slice of green gherkin on top. Sprinkle edges of cheese with paprika.

GOLDEN PINWHEELS

Spread long thin slices of raw carrot with cottage cheese and chives, rolled like a jelly roll.

AVOCADO VARIATIONS

Mix mashed avocado with onion or lemon juice and spread on wedge of tomato pierced with toothpick, or on a tomato slice placed on toast. Spread avocado mashed with fresh crab or shrimp and moisten with Russian Dressing. Spread on toast or cracker and garnish with green pepper ring.

SARDINE CANAPÉ

Mash sardines with lemon juice, spread on crackers, or place the whole sardine on a cracker, and garnish with chopped olives or pimento.

MUSHROOMS STUFFED WITH HAM

Stuff mushroom caps, sautéed in butter, with chopped ham moistened with mayonnaise.

LOBSTER—CHEESE CANAPÉ

Spread oblongs of toast with creamed cheese and mayonnaise, seasoned with chopped chives and place meat from a whole small lobster claw on top. Dip edges of cheese in chopped chives or chopped parsley.

CHEESE SURPRISE SPREAD

Mince orange segments fine and mix with chopped chives and cream cheese.

PARMESAN TOAST

Mix Parmesan cheese with cream and spread on toast or crackers and then bake to achieve a different cheese flavor. Serve hot, of course.

YOUNGSTERS' DELIGHT

Mix peanut butter with crumbled crisp bacon and lemon juice. Garnish edges with chopped olives.

NUT-CHEESE DAINTIES

Put pecan or walnut halves together with cream cheese softened and seasoned with chopped olives, pimentos, Roquefort or snappy cheese.

PIMENTO CHEESE SPREAD

Mash pimento cheese and mix with chopped ginger and chopped crisp bacon. Garnish with olive.

BROILED FRUIT BITS

Roll in bacon strips pineapple wedges, pieces of orange or grapefruit peel, or 1-inch squares of watermelon, pear, peach, or any spiced fruit. Fasten with a toothpick and broil.

CHEESE POTATO CHIPS

Sprinkle potato chips with grated cheese and put under broiler to melt cheese and heat chips.

WAKEFIELD FAVORITE

Top potato chips with chopped lobster meat moistened with Russian Dressing.

STUFFED RADISHES

Stuff "radish roses," their centers removed, with a cheese, turkey, or chicken mixture.

SMOKED FISH

Place slices of smoked salmon on toast and, if desired, alternate with smoked herring.

MARINATED HERRING

Cut squares of marinated herring, place on small slices of raw Bermuda or Spanish onion, and arrange on crackers or toast. Garnish with tiny pickled red peppers.

DRIED BEEF PINWHEELS

Spread thin slices of dried beef with a cream cheese and horseradish mixture, roll like a jelly roll, cut in 1-inch lengths, and pierce with toothpick.

FILLED BISCUITS

Fill tiny baking powder biscuits with a chopped meat, cheese, or fish mixture and serve hot.

STUFFED PUFF SHELLS

Fill tiny cream puff shells with cheese, crab, chicken, or other mixture you prefer.

ASSORTED MEATS AND CHEESE

Arrange a plate of small frankfurters, sausage, sliced liverwurst, sliced tongue, sliced salami, and assorted cheese.

PASTRY SURPRISES

Fill small rounds or squares of pastry, like turnovers, with ham, pâté de fois gras, sausage or chicken mixture, and serve hot.

SHRIMP CANAPÉ

Place whole shrimps on small crackers which have been spread with Tartar Sauce colored green.

COTTAGE CHEESE AND CHIVES SPREAD

To 1 pound cottage cheese add enough light cream to be absorbed. Whip until light and creamy. Add 2 tablespoons chopped chives and season well with salt, Worcestershire, and tabasco sauces. Serve on crackers.

CHEESE IN PORT WINE

Put through food chopper:	Season well with:
1 pound Cheddar cheese	Onion salt
1 pound cottage cheese	Garlic salt
¼ pound Bleu or Roquefort cheese	Black pepper
	Prepared mustard. Add
¼ pound hickory-smoked cheese.	Port wine until mixture is soft

Let stand several hours before serving. Substitute dry sherry if port makes mixture too sweet. The flavor of Roquefort cheese predominates. If that is too strong, hickory salt may be substituted for hickory cheese and a smoked taste will result.

ALICE DIXON BOND'S SAVORIES

Put through food chopper:
½ pound cheese
8 slices bacon

2 small onions. Blend with:
1 teaspoon dry mustard
2 teaspoons mayonnaise

Spread on slices of bread and toast under broiler until golden brown. Cut into triangles and serve hot.

NITA'S CHEESE APPETIZER

Grind or grate
½ pound Old English Cheese.
Mix with:
2 tablespoons chopped onion
3 tablespoons olives, chopped,
2 tablespoons chopped pickle

1 tablespoon chopped
pimento
1 hard-cooked egg, chopped,
½ cup cracker crumbs
4 tablespoons salad dressing
½ teaspoon salt

Shape into long roll, wrap in wax paper, and chill overnight. Arrange on galax leaves and place on appetizer tray with crackers. Garnish with stuffed olives.

COCKTAIL CHEESE SPREAD

Mix in top of double
broiler:
½ pound processed cheese
1 small can evaporated milk

¼ pound butter
1 teaspoon scraped onion, or
1 teaspoon garlic salt, or ½
clove garlic, scraped

Stir over low heat until cheese is melted and all ingredients are well blended. Pour into bowl and chill. When cold, mixture will have consistency of cream cheese. Add a little paprika during cooking to give color. Serve with crackers.

Variations: Add chopped olives or chopped pimentoes, but this cheese has delightful flavor alone.

3 APPETIZERS
AT THE TABLE

ꗛ

Sometimes it is easier to serve hors d'oeuvres and canapés at the table as a first course. Kinds that lend themselves particularly to this service are included here, although some of these, too, might be prepared for enjoyment in the living room. The Sea-food Spread, which so many Toll House guests declare their favorite, is wonderful for a first course. It is most attractive heaped in a large clam or scallop shell crisply lined with a bright green lettuce leaf. As a really beautiful first course for a spring luncheon with a center piece of green and gold daffodils, the Party Pineapple Ring is lovely, and tastes marvelous, too. I have also served it at Christmas. Then the sherbet is arranged in a cone to look like an evergreen. A bright studding of red pomegranate seeds and tiny pieces of green cherry makes a beau-tiful trimming for a Christmas "tree" at every place. For a Halloween party you will love the Pumpkin Canapé, but for winter or summer, holiday or everyday, prepare my Grand-mother's Fruit Shrub. It's a tempting start for any meal.

COCKTAILS AND COCKTAIL SAUCES

FRAPPÉED FRUIT JUICES

Combine equal amounts of: Grapefruit juice
Orange juice Pineapple juice

Chill well. Just before serving pour into tall cocktail glasses and top with a ball of lime or lemon sherbet.

FRUIT SHRUB *(Toll House Cocktail)*

Combine:
1 cup raspberry juice
¼ cup lemon juice
½ cup orange juice
½ cup syrup from spiced peaches, spiced watermelon rind, or other sweet pickled or spiced fruit. Add
1 tablespoon rum

Chill thoroughly. Grapejuice, cranberry or loganberry juice may be substituted for raspberry juice. Add sugar if necessary. Serves 3 to 4 depending on size of glass. (May also be served away from table as a hot-weather drink. We use cranberry juice at Toll House.)

PRUNE COCKTAIL

Combine:
1 quart prune juice
1 small bottle dry ginger ale
½ cup lemon juice
⅛ teaspoon clove

Chill well. Serves 6.

TOMATO JUICE

Place in saucepan:
1 quart canned tomatoes
2 bay leaves
8 whole cloves
1 teaspoon salt
2 teaspoons sugar. Simmer 15 minutes. Remove from heat. Add:
1 tablespoon horseradish
2 tablespoons lemon juice

Strain. Chill thoroughly. Serve in fruit juice glasses. Serves 5 or 6.

CANAPÉS AT THE TABLE

ANCHOVY CANAPÉ

Boil 2 eggs until hard-cooked. Chop whites (with a silver knife to prevent discoloration). Rub yolks through a coarse strainer. Cut bread into pieces 4¼ by 2¾ inches and ¼ inch thick. Sauté in butter on one side only. Spread other side with anchovy paste. Divide bread diagonally into three sections, so that each end-section forms a triangle. Sprinkle end-sections with egg yolk. Sprinkle center section with egg white. Separate sections with narrow strips of pimento. Serves 4 to 6.

FLORENTINE CANAPÉ

Toast slices of bread and cut into fancy shapes. On each place a slice of tomato. Cover with a paste of sardines. Sprinkle grated cheese over top and put in moderate oven long enough to melt cheese.

"PUMPKIN" CANAPÉ

Toast slices of bread, or brown in moderate oven. Cut in small circles and spread evenly with yellow cheese, softened enough to spread smoothly. Then with toothpick dipped in brown color paste or with cream cheese, colored brown, mark off ridges on cheese to resemble a pumpkin. Use a strip of green pepper for stem. Serve on paper doily.

FRUIT BEGINNINGS

COMPANY BREAKFAST ORANGE

With the point of a sharp knife slit skin of orange down in eighths. Loosen skin of upper part of each section and pull it down three-fourths of the way. Remove as much as possible of the membranous portion from the outside of fruit. Then fold down skin half way, tucking it inside. Lastly loosen sections of pulp so orange may be eaten with the hands.

PARTY PINEAPPLE RING

Cut top and bottom from small pineapple. Slice crosswise into inch-thick rings. Remove center fruit, leaving whole the thick outside ring. Cube center fruit, discarding core, and sugar it.

Arrange grape or galax leaves on glass plates and place pine-apple ring on each. Fill centers with the sugared cubes of fruit. On top place a mound of pale green tart lime sherbet and around this, on top of pineapple ring, alternate sections of grape-fruit and orange. Garnish with large plump strawberry. The sherbet may be formed into a cone and "trimmed" with pome-granate seeds and green cherry slices. Serves 4 to 6, depending on size of pineapple.

GRAPEFRUIT SUPREME

Peel 2 grapefruits. Skin sections and cut in small pieces. (Canned grapefruit may be used.) Sugar to taste and chill in re-frigerator. To serve, decorate with white grapes, halved and seeded, and top with maraschino cherry. A little cherry juice may be added to grapefruit for color, if desired. Serves 4.

STUFFED CANTALOUPE

Cut a cantaloupe into 3 rings and remove outside, leaving clear golden rings of fruit. Place each ring on galax or grape leaf laid on glass plate. Fill center cavity with mound of pale green, tart lime sherbet. Around sherbet, on top of melon, al-ternate cubes of red watermelon and blackberries. Vary this with the seasons. Red cherries, large red raspberries, or strawberries can be used with large blueberries or black grapes for contrast. This may also be served as a dessert. Serves 3.

ROSE APPLE SURPRISE

Remove centers from 8 rose apples (or small toma-toes). Hard cook 2 eggs. Reserve ½ of 1 yolk. Chop remainder fine. Mix with:
2 tablespoons chopped green pepper
2 tablespoons chopped pi-mento
4 anchovies, chopped
½ teaspoon salt
Few grains pepper
Few drops onion juice. Moisten with Mayonnaise dressing.

Fill fruit with egg mixture. Cover with mayonnaise and garnish with strips of anchovy, laid crosswise. Place each serving on small plate and sprinkle with chopped parsley mixed with reserved egg yolk, rubbed through sieve. Serves 8.

SEAFOOD FIRST COURSES

GRAPEFRUIT STUFFED WITH SEAFOOD

Cut grapefruit in half and remove large core of fibre from center. Cut around each section of the fruit. Sugar slightly, if desired. Drain off excess juice and fill center core with fresh crab flakes, fresh shrimp, or a seafood mixture. Cover seafood center with Russian Cocktail Sauce.

SEAFOOD SPREAD CANAPÉ

Combine equal parts of chopped lobster and shrimp and fresh crab meat. Moisten well with Russian Dressing. Let stand 1 hour to allow dressing to flavor fish. Serve as a canapé spread or as a first-course cocktail, accompanied by crisp crackers.

MARINATED BISMARCK HERRING

Soak
6 Bismarck herring filets in a mixture of:
2 cups sweet or sour cream
Juice of 1 lemon

1 cup white wine
3 whole cloves
1 bay leaf
5 black peppers
1 thinly sliced onion

Let stand 6 days, or longer, and serve covered with this sauce to which has been added at the last minute minced fresh chives. Serves 6.

OYSTER CASINO

Wash and open
12 oysters. Leave on half shell.
On each put:
Few drops of lemon juice

1 teaspoon minced green pepper
1 square bacon. Sprinkle with
Salt and pepper

Place in hot oven, 450° F., for 10 to 12 minutes, or under broiler for 5 minutes. Serve three on a small plate as first course. Serves 4.

OYSTER COCKTAIL

Chill
24 Small oysters (or 1 pint).
Mix:
1 tablespoon prepared horse-radish
½ teaspoon tabasco sauce

1 tablespoon vinegar
3 tablespoons tomato catsup
1 tablespoon Worcestershire sauce
2 tablespoons lemon juice
½ teaspoon salt

Chill sauce for 1 hour. Then serve oysters in 6 small glasses with 1 tablespoon sauce over each. Serves 6.

COCKTAIL SAUCE

Combine:
¾ cup chili sauce
3 tablespoons lemon juice
2½ tablespoons horseradish

¼ teaspoon grated onion
1 teaspoon Worcestershire sauce
½ teaspoon tabasco sauce

Chill thoroughly and serve over seafood cocktails. Makes 1 cup sauce. (Our family likes more Worcestershire and tabasco because we prefer a hotter sauce.)

COCKTAIL SAUCE SUPREME

Blend:
1 cup mayonnaise
½ cup chili sauce
1 scant teaspoon of

Worcestershire sauce
⅛ teaspoon salt
Juice of 1 lemon

Pour over seafood cocktails. Makes 2 cups sauce.

4. SOUPS, STEWS, CHOWDERS AND ACCOMPANIMENTS

We always say that it was Toll House Onion Soup which paid our way to France the first time, for the introduction of this marvelous concoction certainly brought us hordes of new guests. We learned how to make it in an old restaurant in the wine district of Paris. A French friend took us there to try what he considered the finest onion soup in all France, high praise in a country where good soups are to be found practically everywhere. We arrived at the restaurant at 6:30, an unheard of early hour for French dinners, but it was the wee hours of morning before we left. For onion soup requires long slow cooking and in learning to make it we stayed right through!

New England has traditions of fine soup too, particularly our clam chowder which is always made with milk. We look with horror on recipes for clam chowder made only with water and vegetables, and we think that the leftover chowder which is slowly reheated the second day is best of all.

The stock kettle simmering on the back of the coal range used to offer an ever-present base for wonderful soups. Today the housewife depends a lot on canned soups. With a little imagination in combining them, a bit of unusual seasoning or garnishing, she produces from them delicious hurry-up meals. Under

Helpful Hints I pass on some soup ideas my family likes and here are the Toll House favorites that are regularly featured on our menus.

SOUPS

CLAM OR OYSTER BISQUE

Try out a
1½-inch cube salt pork, cut fine. Fry in it
1 onion, sliced. Add liquor from
1 peck clams, steamed and shucked.

Add
6 cups milk, scalded. Strain. Add clams, chopped, or put through food grinder. Add Salt and pepper to taste

Serves 8.

SOUTHERN BISQUE

Heat
1 can (1⅓ cups) tomato soup
⅛ teaspoon soda. Add:
1 cup canned or fresh stewed corn

1 cup milk
2 tablespoons butter. **Season** with
Salt and pepper

Serve very hot with Souffléed Crackers. Serves 6.

TOMATO BISQUE
(See Primer for Brides, page 61)

CLAM CONSOMMÉ

Combine in saucepan:
1 can chicken consommé
1 can water
1 cup tomato juice
1 cup liquor from steamed clams.

Add:
1 large sprig parsley
1 slice onion
Few celery leaves
2 slices lemon

Simmer about 10 minutes. Strain and season with salt and pepper to taste. Serve hot. On top, float a cracker garnished with a little salted whipped cream. Serves 6.

JELLIED CLAM BOUILLON

Soften
3 tablespoons gelatin in
¼ cup cold water. Stir into
1 quart hot liquor from steamed clams. Stir until gelatin dissolves. Dilute with a little more water, if desired.
Add
2 tablespoons tomato catsup

Pour into shallow dish. When firm, cut into cubes or chop fine and turn into bouillon cups. Serve with or without a garnish of whipped cream which may be seasoned with horseradish. Serves 4.

JELLIED TOMATO CONSOMMÉ

Combine:
1½ quarts chicken stock or bouillon
2 cups canned tomatoes
1 small onion, chopped,
½ bay leaf
6 cloves
½ teaspoon celery seed. Boil for 20 minutes. Add Speck of curry powder. Strain through colander and then cheesecloth. Add
2 tablespoons gelatin softened in
¼ cup water

Pour into bouillon cups and chill until firm, or pour into shallow dish. When firm, cut into cubes or chop fine and turn into cups. Serve with or without a garnish of whipped cream which may be seasoned with horseradish. Serves 4 to 6.

JELLIED TOMATO AND CLAM CONSOMMÉ

Prepare equal amounts of Jellied Clam Bouillon and Jellied Tomato Consommé but omit catsup from clam bouillon. Chill, chop, and combine.

CONSOMMÉ MADRILENE

Dissolve
1 tablespoon gelatin in
¼ cup cold water.
Cook together:
1 pound lean fresh shin beef

1 pound chicken bones, broken
fine
1 can (2½ cups) tomatoes
3 egg whites, beaten,
2 quarts water

Stir frequently until boiling point is reached. Reduce heat and simmer for 2½ hours. Stir in gelatin until dissolved. Strain through fine cloth and season. Add red coloring to make a rosy color. Serve in cups, iced or hot. Serves 6.

BAKED BEAN SOUP

Combine:
2 cups baked beans
1 quart water
½ cup sliced onion
½ cup diced celery. Cook slowly for 30 minutes. Rub

through strainer. Blend:
1½ tablespoons butter, melted,
1½ tablespoons flour. Add
1 cup stewed, strained tomatoes. Cook until thickened.

Combine the two mixtures. Season to taste with salt and paprika. Serves 4.

DRIED BEAN OR PEA SOUP

Pick over
1 cup dried beans or peas. Soak overnight, drain, and add:
2 quarts cold water

½ onion, sliced. Simmer until soft. Then rub through sieve. Prepare
2 cups Thin White Sauce (page 73)

Combine two mixtures. Serve with Croutons. Serves 4.

CREAM OF MUSHROOM SOUP

Sauté
½ pound mushrooms, sliced, in
¼ pound butter. Blend in
4 tablespoons flour. Add

¼ teaspoon pepper
1 tablespoon salt. Slowly add
1 quart rich chicken stock
2 cups rich milk

Allow to set awhile before serving. (If chicken stock is not available, use all milk.) Reheat. Serves 8.

OLD ENGLISH CHEESE SOUP

Blend:

½ cup butter, melted,
4 tablespoons flour
1 teaspoon salt
½ teaspoon pepper.
Add slowly
4 cups milk. Cook until thickened.

Add:

1½ pounds Old English or yellow snappy cheese
1½ tablespoons Worcestershire sauce
½ teaspoon paprika

If mixture seems too thick, thin to desired consistency with hot milk. Garnish with crumbled crisp bacon or a shredded hard-cooked egg. Serves 4.

CREAM OF CABBAGE SOUP

Put through food chopper:
1 onion
1 small head cabbage (about 3 cups after chopping). Add

Water to cover. Cook until tender. Prepare
4 cups White Sauce (page 73). Season with salt and pepper

Combine mixtures and serve hot. Serves 6.

CHICKEN SOUP

Have fowl disjointed and place in kettle or pressure cooker, cover with cold water, and cook until fowl is tender. Let fowl cool in liquid. Remove and let stock set in cold place until well chilled. Skim off fat. About 1 quart of soup stock should remain. Reheat. Blend 1 tablespoon butter, melted, with 1 teaspoon flour. Add small amount hot stock to this flour paste. When thin enough to pour, add slowly to hot stock. Stir constantly to avoid lumps. Let simmer to thicken and cook flour. Season with salt and pepper to taste. A carrot, an onion, and celery tops may be cooked with fowl for additional flavor, if desired. Serves 4.

SPINACH AND MUSHROOM SOUP

Add 2 cups raw spinach, chopped fine, to Cream of Mushroom Soup. The hot soup cooks the spinach. Serve immediately. Serves 8.

TOLL HOUSE ONION SOUP

Sauté
1 pound onions, sliced, in
4 tablespoons butter. When browned, sprinkle with
1 tablespoon flour. Stir until blended. Slowly add to
1½ quarts rich chicken or beef stock. Stir until smooth.

Season with
Salt and pepper to taste. Place on each individual serving
1 or 2 slices French bread, sprinkled with Parmesan cheese and toasted at the last moment in the oven

Serve extra cheese for sprinkling over soup at table. If soup is made in morning and allowed to stand several hours and then reheated before serving, the flavor improves. Serves 8.

CREAM OF ONION SOUP

Heat
¼ cup fat. Add
4 medium-sized onions, thinly sliced. Sauté until amber colored. Blend in
2 tablespoons flour. Add

3 pints milk. Stir until thickened. Simmer for 20 minutes. Season with
½ teaspoon sugar
1½ teaspoons salt
⅛ teaspoon pepper

Serve immediately. Serves 8.

MARJORIE MILLS' SOUP OR VICHYSSOISE CRÈME

Combine
3 onions, sliced, or the white part of 6 leek stalks, cut fine, with
3 stalks celery, diced. Cook until tender in
¼ pound butter. Add

2 cups cubed raw potatoes
1 quart chicken stock. Cook until potatoes are tender. Put through sieve. Add
1 pint cream
¼ pound butter. Season with Salt and pepper

Reheat in top of double boiler or serve chilled for a delicious summer soup. Garnish with whipped cream sprinkled with chopped chives. Serves 8 to 10.

VEGETABLE SOUP
(See Primer for Brides, page 61)

STEWS

IRISH STEW
(See Primer for Brides, page 62)

LAMB STEW

Place in pan:
2 pounds stewing lamb, cubed,
1 large onion, sliced,
3 cups cold water. Cover and simmer about 1½ hours, or until tender. Cool and skim hardened fat from surface of stock. Remove meat and re-

heat stock.
Add:
3 carrots, sliced
1 cup diced potatoes, or ¼ cup barley or ¼ cup rice. Cook until tender. Replace meat. Season with
Salt and pepper

Serves 6 to 8.

Boston's well-known food commentator, Marjorie Mills, always serves this with thin slices of floating lemon. The lemon reduces any strong muttony flavor that may exist. Lamb flanks are inexpensive but breast of lamb is preferable. Most chefs when boiling lamb, discard the first water in order to avoid a strong flavor and get rid of excess fat.

SYRIAN STEW

Dredge with flour
2 cups raw mutton or other meat, cubed. Put in spider
2 tablespoons fat. Brown meat in this, stirring constantly.

Put in kettle
2 onions, sliced,
1 can (2½ cups) tomatoes
1 can (2½ cups) string beans, cut up

Add browned meat and all the flour and fat which can be scraped from spider. Add enough water to cover. Cook slowly until meat is tender. Season to taste. Serves 8.

OYSTER STEW

Heat
1 pint oysters in their liquor.
Add:
¼ pound butter

½ teaspoon salt
⅛ teaspoon pepper. When edges of oysters curl, add
1½ quarts rich milk, scalded

Reheat just to boiling point. Remove from heat and serve at once in heated soup plates. Sprinkle with paprika and serve with tiny oyster crackers. Serves 6.

LOBSTER STEW

Melt
¼ pound butter in 2-quart kettle. Add
2 cups lobster meat, cut up. Sprinkle with:
½ teaspoon salt

¼ teaspoon paprika. Heat thoroughly. Pour over lobster:
1 quart milk and
1 pint light cream

Heat to boiling point. Remove from heat and serve at once. Serves 6.

CHOWDERS

CLAM CHOWDER
(See Primer for Brides, page 62)

CORN CHOWDER

Fry
1½-inch cube salt pork, diced. Add
1 large onion, sliced. Fry until brown. Add:
2 cups diced potatoes
1 teaspoon salt

½ teaspoon pepper
2 cups boiling water. Cook until potatoes are tender. Add:
1 can (No. 2) cream-style corn
2 cups hot milk

Reheat slowly just to boiling point. (Do not allow to boil.) If this stands awhile before serving, flavor is improved. Serves 8.

FISH CHOWDER

Procure
1 6-pound cod or haddock, cleaned. Remove head and tail. (Sometimes head is used for flavor.) Add
2 cups cold water. Boil 20 minutes. Try out
1½ inch cube salt pork. Add
1 onion, sliced. Fry until tender. Add
4 cups cubed potatoes
2 cups boiling water. Cook 5 minutes. Add liquor drained from cooked fish. Add fish after removing skin and bones. Simmer 10 minutes. Add
4 cups milk, scalded
Salt and pepper. Before serving add
3 tablespoons butter
8 Boston common crackers, split

If possible, prepare one hour before serving. Then flavor is superior. Serves 8.

VEGETABLE CHOWDER

In a hot saucepan cook slowly until crisp,
⅓ cup half-inch cubes salt pork. Remove pork. Add
1 onion, finely chopped. Cook for 5 minutes. Add:
1½ cups half-inch potato cubes
½ cup diced celery
½ cup half-inch parsnip cubes
1 cup carrots, cut in strips
½ cup chopped green pepper
1 quart boiling water. Cook until vegetables are tender, about 20 minutes. Add:
3 cups hot milk
2 teaspoons salt
¼ teaspoon pepper
¼ cup dried bread crumbs
1 teaspoon chopped parsley

Stir pork cubes into chowder and serve. Serves 6.

NEW ORLEANS CREOLE GUMBO

Melt
3 tablespoons fat. Add:
2½ cups sliced okra
1 large onion, chopped. Fry
  until soft. Sprinkle with:
2 tablespoons flour
1 teaspoon salt and mix.
  Add:
1 green pepper, chopped
2 bay leaves

2 sprigs parsley
1 teaspoon thyme
1 can (8-oz.) tomato sauce
1 cup cleaned shrimp
1 cup crab meat
1 pint small oysters with
  liquor
2 quarts hot water
3 tablespoons diced ham

Mix well and cook slowly for 1 hour. Gumbo will be thick and dark. Serve in bowl with cooked rice. Serves 10 to 12.

Variation: **BOUILLABAISSE.** Omit okra and ham, substitute in same amounts other fish such as lobster, clams, white fish or mussels, and add a pinch of saffron.

ACCOMPANIMENTS

SOUFFLÉED CRACKERS

Split Boston common crackers or water crackers. Soak in ice water to cover for eight minutes. Drain. Dot with butter and bake in a hot oven, 450° F., until puffed. When nearly brown enough, reduce heat and bake until dry inside.

CRISP CRACKERS

Split Boston common crackers or water crackers. Spread generously with butter and bake in hot oven, 450° F., until delicately browned.

CROUTONS

Cut stale bread in ⅓-inch slices. Remove crusts. Spread bread thinly with butter. Cut slices into ⅓-inch cubes or strips, or cut into triangular or fancy shapes. Bake in moderate oven, 375° F., until delicately brown, or fry in deep fat.

CRACKERS WITH CHEESE

Brush saltines or soda crackers with melted butter, sprinkle with grated cheese, and bake in a moderate oven, 375° F., until cheese is melted.

CROUSTADES

Cut stale bread in thick slices, about 2 inches, and remove crusts. Then cut in squares and remove centers to make a shell or case. Brush over with melted butter and place in oven to brown. Fill centers with creamed food, such as chicken or lobster.

5. *BREADS, SLOW AND QUICK*

Here are all the wonderful breads we serve with each meal at the Toll House. Many are made constantly, right up to the closing hour, so that our guests may always have them fresh and hot. The most popular one is Butterscotch Pecan Biscuit. Other great favorites are Rum Biscuits, Cheese Biscuits, Golden Corn Cake, a recipe made in tiny corn-stick pans, and, of course, Toll House Health Bread. We also serve Mary Jane Gingerbread on the bread tray.

At home, waffles and griddlecakes are much loved by the children because they can share in the cooking. I have happy memories too of their keen delight, when they were just tots, in dropping biscuits as they cut them into "baskets," their name for muffin pans. As a family we all also enjoy the Orange Doughnuts. I know you will like them too!

When bread making is successful there is nothing so excellent as the wholesome, home-baked loaf. But sometimes there are disappointments. To help you diagnose all possible difficulties and to answer the many questions I have been asked I have analyzed below certain problems. Baking in general is also discussed on page 20.

POINTERS ON BREAD

Bread Burns on Bottom

a. Oven too full. Proper circulation of heat shut off

b. Wrong type pans, such as granite or heavy black ones
c. Pans placed too close to bottom of oven

Bread Burns Along Sides
a. Pans placed too close to side of oven
b. Too much dough in pans—two-thirds full is enough

Bread Doughy in Center but with Heavy Outside Crust
a. Oven too hot
b. Baking too rapid. Use somewhat lower temperatures. (If trouble persists, check and service thermostat.)

Biscuits Burn on Bottom
a. Pan set on too low a rack in oven
b. Pan too long or too wide for oven
c. Black or granite pan used
d. Pan too deep

Biscuits Too Brown on Top
a. Pan set too high in oven
b. Baked too long
c. Oven flue may be obstructed

Biscuits Burn Around Edges of Pan
a. Oven too hot
b. Pans too large,—space around pan essential
c. Oven too full, cutting off proper heat circulation

Doughnuts Are Grease Soaked
a. Fat not hot enough—should start at 375° F. and not drop below 360°
b. Too many fried at once, which cools fat

Doughnuts Not Cooked Through
a. Fat too hot
b. Dough cut too thick
c. Doughnut browned before sufficiently risen

Waffles Overflow Griddle
a. Too much batter poured on griddle

Waffles Stick to Griddle
a. Waffle iron not properly heated

b. Waffle not thoroughly cooked before cover is raised—should wait until steam no longer visible

Griddlecakes Are Leathery
a. Mixture too thin
b. Too much turning
c. Not enough baking powder
d. A prepared mix might have been damp from long storing

Popovers Don't Pop
a. At beginning oven not hot enough to release steam which causes "pop"
b. Baking pans not sizzling hot when mixture poured into them
c. Ingredients not accurately measured

YEAST BREADS

HOMEMADE BREAD

Scald
1 cup milk. Add:
1 tablespoon shortening
1 tablespoon butter
2½ teaspoons salt
2 tablespoons sugar. Stir to dissolve fats. Add
1 cup cold water. When

mixture is lukewarm, add
1 yeast cake, dissolved in
¼ cup warm water. Stir in
6 to 6½ cups bread flour or enough to make fairly stiff dough which leaves a clean bowl

Turn onto a lightly floured board. Knead until ingredients are combined, mixture is smooth and elastic, and bubbles appear under the surface. Return to bowl. Cover with clean cloth. Let rise overnight or for several hours at a temperature no lower than 65° F. In the morning cut down with a knife. Knead again on lightly floured board. Shape into loaves and fill greased bread pans half full. Cover, let rise again to double its bulk. Preheat oven to 400° F. Reduce heat and bake in moderate oven, 350° F. for about 50 minutes. Makes 2 loaves of wonderful, fine-textured bread.

Variation: **WHOLE WHEAT BREAD.** Prepare 1 recipe of Homemade Bread, but use only 1 cup white flour and 5 to 5½ cups whole wheat flour. Add 3 tablespoons molasses after sugar.

CRUMB BREAD

Combine

1 pint dry bread crumbs, ground,
1 quart hot water
2 tablespoons shortening
½ cup dark molasses
2 teaspoons salt. Let cool.

Add

½ yeast cake, dissolved in
¼ cup warm water. Stir in
9 to 9½ cups flour or enough to make fairly stiff dough which leaves a clean bowl

Proceed as for Homemade Bread. Makes 3 loaves.

SHREDDED WHEAT BREAD

Pour

2 cups boiling water over
2 shredded wheat biscuits, crumbled. Add:
1 teaspoon salt
⅓ cup sugar
⅓ cup dark molasses
3 tablespoons shortening. Let

cool. Add

1 yeast cake, dissolved in
½ cup warm water. Stir in
5 to 6 cups bread flour, or enough to make fairly stiff dough which leaves a clean bowl

Let rise overnight or until double in bulk. Then cut down and add a little more flour to make a stiffer dough. Form into loaves or biscuits and let rise 1 to 1½ hours. Bake in a hot oven, 400° F., for 15 minutes; then reduce heat to 350° for remaining 30 minutes. Do not reduce temperature for biscuits which should bake only 25 to 30 minutes. Makes 2 loaves of bread or 1 loaf and 12 biscuits.

HOMEMADE ROLLS

Prepare 1 recipe of Homemade Bread but shape dough into rolls and place 1 inch apart in a shallow, greased baking pan. Cover, let rise to double in bulk, and bake in a hot oven, 400° F., for 20 to 25 minutes. Makes about 4 dozen rolls.

Variation: **CLOVERLEAF ROLLS.** Make by shaping even pieces of dough into 3 small balls for each roll. Place in greased muffin pans. Moisten tops of rolls with melted butter before baking. Bake in hot oven, 450° F. to 475°.

ICEBOX ROLLS

Crumble
1 yeast cake into a bowl with:
½ cup sugar
1 teaspoon salt and
2 cups warm water. Add
1 egg, well beaten. Sift
7 cups flour. Add half of flour to mixture. Stir well. Add
3 tablespoons shortening. Mix in remainder of flour with hands

Allow dough to rise and double in bulk, punch down, cover tightly and store. Use as desired over a period of a week. Remove desired amount of dough, shape, let rise to double in bulk and bake in hot oven, 425° F., for 20 minutes. Makes 5 dozen rolls.

SQUASH BISCUITS

Mix:
1½ cups strained squash
¼ cup sugar
1 teaspoon salt
2 tablespoons melted shortening
1 cup milk, scalded. Add
½ yeast cake, dissolved in
¼ cup warm water. Stir in
5 cups flour, or enough to make a soft dough

Let rise. Knead and shape into 2-inch biscuits. Let rise, and bake in hot oven, 425° F., for 20 minutes. Makes about 3 dozen biscuits.

BETHLEHEM SUGAR CAKE

Scald
1 cup milk. Add
½ cup riced potato. Cool to lukewarm. Add
1 yeast cake, dissolved in
¼ cup warm water. Add
2½ cups flour, or enough to make stiff drop batter.
Let stand until light. Add:
1 egg, well beaten,
2 tablespoons shortening, melted,
½ teaspoon salt
1½ cups flour, or enough to knead

Knead and turn into 8-inch-square shallow pans, spreading dough ½ inch thick. Let rise to double in height. Make deep holes 1 inch apart. Insert in each dots of butter, a little brown sugar and cinnamon, and a small cooked prune. Brush top with milk. Bake in moderate oven, 375° F., for 30 minutes. Makes 2 cakes.

SWEDISH TEA RING

Scald 1¼ cups milk. Cool ½ cup of this milk to lukewarm. Dissolve in it ½ yeast cake. Add ½ cup flour. Mix well, cover, and let rise. When light, add remaining milk and 2 cups flour. Stir until well mixed, cover, and let rise again. Stir in:

¼ cup melted butter
⅓ cup sugar
1 egg, well beaten,
⅛ teaspoon salt
½ teaspoon almond extract
¾ cup flour

Toss on floured cloth and knead, using ¼ cup flour. Cover. Let rise again. Shape, using hands, into a long roll. Turn onto unfloured board and roll as thinly as possible with rolling pin. Spread with melted butter and sprinkle with sugar and cinnamon. Roll like jelly roll. Cut ends even and join to form a ring. Place on buttered baking sheet, and cut with scissors at 1½-inch intervals, slanting from edge to within 1 inch of center. (Avoid cutting all the way through.) Spread the open points 2 inches apart. Bake in moderate oven, 375° F., for 30 minutes. Serves 6 to 8.

QUICK BREADS

BANANA BREAD

Mash 1 cup bananas. Sift together 1¾ cups flour ¾ teaspoon soda ½ teaspoon salt 1¼ teaspoons cream of tartar.

Cream together and beat until fluffy: ⅓ cup shortening ⅔ cup sugar. Add 2 eggs. Beat well.

Add flour mixture in small amounts alternately with bananas to egg mixture. Beat after each addition until smooth. Place in well-greased loaf pan and bake in moderate oven, 350° F., for about 1 hour, or until bread is done. Makes 1 loaf. (This Banana Bread has cakelike texture and flavor and can be served as cake.)

DOUBLE BOILER BROWN BREAD

Mix:
1 cup sifted white flour
1 cup rye flour
1 cup graham flour
½ cup yellow corn meal

1 teaspoon soda
Pinch of salt. Add:
1 cup sour milk
½ cup dark molasses

Pour into top of double boiler and steam 2 hours or until **done.** Place in moderate oven to dry for a few minutes. Serves 4.

GRAHAM PRUNE BREAD

Sift together:
1 cup white flour
2½ cups graham flour
1 teaspoon salt
4 teaspoons baking powder
½ cup sugar. Combine:
1¾ cups milk

1 egg, beaten,
1 tablespoon melted shortening. Combine two mixtures. Add
1 cup prunes, soaked, pitted, and chopped fine

Turn into greased loaf pan. Bake in slow oven, 325° F., for 1 hour. Makes 1 loaf. (Stewed prunes may be used. In that case substitute ¾ cup prune juice for ¾ cup of the milk.)

WINCHESTER NUT BREAD

Dissolve
½ cup brown sugar in
¾ cup cold water. Add:
½ cup dark molasses
¾ cup milk. Sift together
2 cups graham flour

1 cup white flour
1⅓ teaspoons salt
2½ teaspoons baking powder
¾ teaspoon soda. Combine mixtures and add
¾ cup chopped walnut meats

Turn into greased loaf pan. Bake in slow oven, 300° F., for 1½ to 2 hours. Makes 1 loaf.

ORANGE NUT BREAD

Sift together:
3 cups pastry flour
3 teaspoons baking powder
½ teaspoon salt
¼ cup sugar. Add:
½ cup chopped walnut meats

or grapenuts
1 tablespoon grated orange rind
½ cup orange marmalade
1 egg, well beaten,
1 cup milk

Mix well and turn into greased loaf pan. Let stand for 10 minutes. Bake in moderate oven, 350° F., for ¾ to 1 hour. Makes 1 loaf. (This is delicious for sandwiches with a cream cheese filling.)

TOLL HOUSE HEALTH BREAD

Mix together:
1 cup sifted white flour
2 cups graham flour
1 teaspoon salt
½ cup sugar. Dissolve

1 teaspoon soda in
1½ cups milk (sweet or sour). Add
1 cup dark molasses

Mix thoroughly liquid with dry ingredients. Pour into 2 greased loaf pans and bake in slow oven, 325° F., for 1½ hours. Makes 2 loaves. (Dates or raisins, ½ cup lightly floured, may be added after the molasses.)

CRUSTY BISCUITS
(See Primer for Brides, page 63)

TOLL HOUSE BISCUITS

Sift together:
2 cups flour
5 teaspoons baking powder
1 teaspoon salt. Work in with fingers or pastry cutter

3 tablespoons shortening. Add
⅔ to ¾ cup milk and water combined, or enough to make soft dough

114

Mix thoroughly and toss on lightly floured board. Pat out to ½-inch thickness. Shape with cutter and place on greased baking sheet. Bake in hot oven 450° F., for 12 to 15 minutes. Makes about 16 biscuits.

Variations: **CHEESE BISCUITS.** Prepare as for Toll House Biscuits but add ½ cup grated cheese after shortening and bake in hot oven, 500° F., for 12 minutes.

ORANGE BISCUITS. Prepare as for Toll House Biscuits. After biscuits are cut and placed on pan, indent dough, and place a little orange marmalade in each hollow. As biscuits cook, dough will rise and surround marmalade.

FRUIT MALLOW BISCUITS. Prepare as for Toll House Biscuits but place only small amount of dough in bottom of each well-greased section of muffin pan. On this place small pieces of dates, chopped nuts, and half a marshmallow. Cover with more dough, pressing edges together to seal. Brush with melted butter or rich milk and bake in hot oven, 450° F., for 15 to 20 minutes, depending on size of biscuit.

BUTTERSCOTCH PECAN BISCUITS. Prepare as for Toll House Biscuits. Pat dough out to ¼-inch thickness. Brush thickly with melted butter and sprinkle heavily with brown sugar. Cover with pecan halves and roll like jelly roll. Cut inch-thick slices and place close together, cut, not round, side up, on baking sheet which has been liberally coated with butter and sprinkled with brown sugar and pecan halves. Bake in hot oven, 450° F., for 12 to 15 minutes. Remove from pan immediately and serve, butterscotch side up. Makes 16 biscuits.

RUM BISCUITS. Prepare as for Toll House Biscuits but alter liquid requirements to scant ½ cup milk plus ¼ cup rum and 1 egg yolk. Stir well. Mix thoroughly with dry ingredients and turn onto floured board. Pat dough out to ¼-inch thickness, brush thickly with melted butter, and sprinkle with seedless raisins. Roll like jelly roll, cut into inch-thick slices, and place close together on greased baking sheet. Bake in hot

115

oven, 450° F., for 12 to 15 minutes. Allow to cool slightly. Then brush with the following frosting. Serve hot. Makes 16 biscuits.

Rum Biscuit Frosting

Combine: 2 tablespoons melted butter
1 cup confectioners sugar   2 tablespoons rum

Add more sugar if necessary to achieve a smooth spreading consistency. Spread while biscuits are hot.

BAKING POWDER PARKER HOUSE ROLLS

Sift together: 4 tablespoons butter until con-
2½ cups flour   sistency of corn meal. Beat
1 teaspoon salt   in a measuring cup
3½ teaspoons baking powder.   1 egg until light. Fill cup with
Cut in   Milk.

Combine flour and egg mixtures. Turn dough onto lightly floured board and pat out ¼-inch thick. Cut in 2-inch rounds, brush each with melted butter and crease through center with back of knife. Fold over not quite all the way. Place in greased baking pan and bake in hot oven, 450° F., for 12 minutes. Makes 2 dozen rolls.

BREAKFAST MUFFINS
(See Primer for Brides, page 63)

DARK BRAN MUFFINS

Sift together: out bran remaining in top
1 cup flour   of sifter into a mixture of:
2 cups bran   1 egg, beaten,
1 teaspoon salt   1¼ cups milk
1 teaspoon baking soda. Pour   ½ cup dark molasses

Combine two mixtures. Turn into greased muffin pans. Bake large-sized muffins in moderate oven, 375° F., for about 20 minutes. Bake small-sized in hot oven, 400° F. for about 15 minutes. Makes 12 to 18 muffins.

HEALTH MUFFINS

Cream ¼ cup shortening with ¼ cup sugar. Add: 1 egg, beaten, 1½ cups sour milk. Sift together:

1 cup whole wheat flour 1 teaspoon soda 3 teaspoons baking powder 1 teaspoon salt. Stir into first mixture. Then add 1½ cups dried bread crumbs

Beat well. Turn into greased muffin pans. Bake large-sized muffins in moderate oven, 375° F., for about 20 minutes. Bake small-sized in hot oven, 400° F., for about 15 minutes. Makes 12 to 18 muffins.

GOLDEN CORN CAKE

Sift together: 1 cup yellow corn meal 1 cup flour ¼ cup sugar 5 teaspoons baking powder

¾ teaspoon salt. Add: 1 cup milk 1 egg, well beaten, 2 tablespoons shortening, melted

Turn into 8-inch-square greased pan or corn-stick pans. Bake in hot oven, 425° F., for 15 to 20 minutes. Cut into squares and serve hot. (My grandmother called this "Johnnycake" and baked it in her iron spider.)

POPOVERS

Sift together: 1 cup flour ¼ teaspoon salt.

Add gradually to avoid lumpiness: 1 cup milk 2 eggs, beaten until light

Beat mixture 3 minutes with rotary beater. Fill hot, well-greased, iron gem pans ⅔ full and bake in hot oven, 450° F., for 25 minutes. Then decrease heat to 350° for 15 minutes. Serve at once. Makes 1 dozen popovers.

CREAM SCONES

Sift together:
2 cups flour
4 teaspoons baking powder
3 teaspoons sugar
¾ teaspoon salt. Work in
¼ tablespoon butter or other

shortening. Separate
2 eggs. Reserve part of egg white. Mix remaining eggs, beaten, with
⅓ cup cream or milk

Combine flour and egg mixtures. Toss on lightly floured board. Pat to ¾-inch thickness. Cut into squares and fold over to form triangles. Brush with reserved egg white and sprinkle with sugar. Bake in hot oven, 450° F., for 15 minutes. Makes about 16 scones.

WAFFLES, DOUGHNUTS, FRITTERS

WAFFLES

Sift together:
1¾ cups flour
3 teaspoons baking powder
½ teaspoon salt. Combine
1 cup milk

2 egg yolks, well beaten,
4 tablespoons melted butter. Stir slowly into flour mixture. Then fold in
2 egg whites, beaten stiff

Cook on hot greased waffle iron until mixture stops steaming. Serve at once with butter and syrup. Makes 8 waffles.

CORN MEAL WAFFLES

Mix:
1¾ cups flour
¼ cup yellow corn meal
½ teaspoon salt
3 teaspoons baking powder.
Combine:

1⅓ cups milk
2 egg yolks, beaten well
1 tablespoon melted butter. Add slowly to dry ingredients. Fold in
2 egg whites, beaten stiff

Cook on hot greased waffle iron until mixture stops steaming. Serve at once with butter and syrup. Makes 8 waffles.

RICE WAFFLES

Sift together:
1¾ cups flour
4 teaspoons baking powder
¼ teaspoon salt. Add
⅔ cup cold cooked rice.
Combine

1⅓ cups milk
1 egg yolk, well beaten,
1 tablespoon melted butter.
Add slowly to dry ingredients. Fold in
2 egg whites, beaten stiff

Cook on hot greased waffle iron until mixture stops steaming. Serve at once with butter and syrup. Makes 8 waffles.

GRANDMOTHER'S SOUR MILK DOUGHNUTS

Combine:
1 egg, well beaten
1 scant cup sugar. Combine:
1 scant cup sour milk, mixed with

½ teaspoon soda
Few grains salt
Few grains nutmeg
Few grains cinnamon
2 cups sifted flour

Stir into egg mixture and beat well. If necessary, add more flour to make dough stiff enough to roll. Roll ⅓ inch thick. Shape with doughnut cutter. Fry in hot fat, 360° F., turning once. Keep fat at uniform temperature. When brown, drain doughnuts on absorbent paper. Makes about 2 dozen doughnuts.

ORANGE DOUGHNUTS

Cream:
2 tablespoons shortening
1 cup sugar. Mix in well:
2 eggs, well beaten,
1 tablespoon grated orange rind. Sift together:

2 cups bread flour
2 cups pastry flour
½ teaspoon salt
2 teaspoons baking powder
¾ teaspoon soda. Prepare
¾ cup orange juice

Add dry ingredients alternately with orange juice to egg mixture. Chill 3 hours. Roll ⅜ inch thick on lightly floured board. Shape with doughnut cutter. Let stand 20 minutes. Fry in deep hot fat, 385° F., until brown, turning once. Drain on absorbent paper. Shake while warm in bag containing ½ cup sifted confectioners sugar and 2 teaspoons grated orange rind. Makes 3 dozen doughnuts.

GRANDMOTHER'S SWEET MILK DOUGHNUTS

Combine:

2 eggs
1 cup sugar
2 tablespoons melted shortening
1 teaspoon vinegar
1 cup milk. Sift together:

3 scant cups flour
1 teaspoon soda
2 teaspoons cream of tartar
Pinch salt
Few grains cinnamon and nutmeg

Proceed as for Grandmother's Sour Milk Doughnuts. Makes about 3 dozen doughnuts. (A richer recipe.)

PINEAPPLE FRITTERS

Sift together:

1½ cups flour
1½ teaspoons baking powder
2 teaspoons sugar
¼ teaspoon salt
Combine:

6 tablespoons milk
1 egg, beaten. Add to dry ingredients. Stir in:
½ tablespoon cooking oil
½ cup crushed pineapple, drained

Mix well. Drop by spoonfuls into hot fat, 370° F., and cook until well browned. Drain on absorbent paper. Serve with following sauce. Makes 12 fritters.

Fritter Sauce

Boil together:
1 cup pineapple juice

2 tablespoons lemon juice
⅔ cup sugar

When sauce thickens, remove from heat and pour around fritters or serve separately in a pitcher. Makes 1¼ cups sauce.

GRIDDLECAKES

Sift together:

2½ cups flour
½ teaspoon salt
2 tablespoons sugar

1¼ teaspoons soda. Stir in:

2 cups sour milk
1 tablespoon melted butter
1 egg, well beaten

Heat griddle or heavy frying pan. Grease with piece of fat salt pork. Rub over pan between each batch. Drop batter from tip of spoon onto griddle, being careful not to drop too much. When cakes are puffed and full of bubbles, and edges are cooked well, turn cakes and cook on other side. If no sour milk is available, add 5 tablespoons vinegar to 1¾ cups sweet milk 15 minutes ahead of preparation. Milk will then be soured enough. Serve with butter and maple syrup. Makes 12 (5-inch) griddlecakes.

---

6 MEATS AND
POULTRY

Meat cookery has always been of particular interest to me. During my senior year in college I did the experimental work for my food thesis on Tough Cuts of Meat. The knowledge gained then served me in good stead in my early homemaking years. For others who are learning to cook, certain basic information is given on page 21.

The tastes of those whose business is food are usually very simple, a fact which surprises most people who suppose that we enjoy only exotic and elaborate dishes. How often we eat hamburg and stew from preference would amaze them. We do like Curried Chicken, however, and after trying curries all over the world we have decided that the finest is made and served by an East Indian at the Plaza Hotel in Buenos Aires. We like Delmonico Chicken too. It came from Conte's in the same city and when served at Toll House is especially popular with the business men who come for luncheon with us.

On Thanksgiving and Christmas at Toll House we serve a whole turkey to large parties of guests and they take the remaining turkey and gravy home for "picking" fun later. Small groups are also given boxes of turkey meat and stuffing to take home for a night snack, and how they love it! When we served our first Thanksgiving dinner, we couldn't bear the thought of our guests missing the fun of another taste of turkey before they went to bed, so we started what has now become a most popular Toll House tradition.

BEEF AND VEAL

BROILED STEAK

(See Primer for Brides, page 66)

SPANISH STEAK

Wipe and place in pan	1 small bottle olives, chopped.
1½ pounds top of round or	Melt in saucepan
sirloin, cut 2 inches thick.	1 small piece of butter. Add
Season with	6 large mushroom caps. Cook
Salt and pepper. Over meat	for 3 minutes. Spread over
spread	steak with
1 onion, minced,	1 bottle catsup or chili sauce

Sear meat in hot oven, 400° F., for 5 minutes. Then reduce heat to 300° to 350° and bake until steak, when cut, is delicate pink, about 1 to 1¼ hours. Serves 4.

SMOTHERED STEAK

Take a 2- to 3-pound piece of round steak, cut about 1 inch thick, or the flank left from sirloin steak, and pound flour well into both sides, using edge of heavy saucer or handle of carving knife. Cut fat from edge of meat and try out in spider. Fry 1 onion, sliced, and, if you like, 1 green pepper, minced.

When brown, push onions and pepper to edge of pan. Add meat, sear on both sides, and brown well. Then add ½ cup cold water, salt and pepper. Cover and cook until water begins to boil. Then place in a moderate oven, 350° F., and cook 1¼ to 1½ hours. Add a little more water, if necessary, but none should be required as a nice thick gravy is desirable to serve with meat. Serves 4 to 6.

ROLLED STUFFED FLANK STEAK

Buy 1½- to 2-pound flank steak. Wipe with damp cloth. Score across grain with sharp knife. Rub with flour and brown on both sides in hot fat. Sprinkle with salt and pepper. Spread one side

123

with following stuffing or make a pocket for stuffing by splitting flank through middle. Roll and tie. Place in casserole with ¼ cup boiling water. Cover. Bake in moderate oven, 350° F., until tender, about 2 hours. Slice and serve with gravy made from liquid around steak. Serves 4.

Steak Stuffing

Combine:
1 cup cracker crumbs
½ to ¾ cup cold water
½ cup melted butter.

Season with
Salt and sage. Mix well. Add
1 onion, cut fine (optional)

ROAST BEEF WITH ROAST POTATOES AND GRAVY
(See Primer for Brides, page 67)

ROAST BEEF WITH YORKSHIRE PUDDING
Prepare **ROAST BEEF** (see page 67). Then pour "pudding" around it.

Yorkshire Pudding

Mix:
¼ teaspoon salt
½ cup flour. Blend in
1 cup milk, gradually, to form

a smooth paste. Add
2 eggs, beaten 2 minutes with
rotary beater

When 20 minutes remain for roasting beef, pour mixture about ½ inch deep in pan around roast. Bottom of pan should be covered with fat from roast. Bake until meat is done and pudding is firm. Serves 4.

POT ROAST OF BEEF WITH VEGETABLES
Buy 4 pounds beef cut from shin, or any other inexpensive cut. Wipe and sprinkle meat with salt and pepper. Roll in flour and sear both sides in hot fat in frying pan. Place in casserole or covered pan. Add ½ cup hot water. Cook 4 hours over low heat or in moderate oven, 350° F., adding water as needed. Turn during cooking. During last 30 minutes place around meat (or cook separately but serve together): 4 carrots, scraped and quartered,

8 small potatoes, pared and quartered, and 4 onions. (Use juices from pan, which will be slightly thickened, as gravy.) Serves 8.

PLANKED HAMBURG

Have ground together:
1 pound bottom round steak
½ pound lean pork. Add:
1 small onion, chopped fine,

Salt and pepper to taste. Add:
Milk, until meat will absorb no more,
1 egg (optional)

Form meat into flat cakes and place on cake rack for ease in handling. Preheat broiler. Place cakes on top of broiler rack and set in broiling pan. Pour ½ cup hot water into bottom of pan. Sear meat on both sides until well browned. Arrange on hot platter with border of potatoes and vegetables. Serves 4.

NEAPOLITAN MEAT LOAF

Make up and set aside
1 recipe Poultry Stuffing.
Have ground together:
1 pound bottom round steak
½ pound lean pork. Season with:

1 teaspoon salt
Few grains pepper
1 small onion, chopped fine.
Add
Milk until meat will absorb no more

In a bread pan place alternate half-inch layers of meat and stuffing, with a top layer of meat. Lay 3 strips of bacon on loaf or pour over 1 cup tomato soup. Bake in a moderate oven, 350° F. to 375°, for 1 hour. Serve hot or cold. Serves 4.

ROASTED HAMBURG STEAK
(See Primer for Brides, page 68)

HAMBURG-RICE SUPREME

Combine:
1 cup cooked rice
1 cup leftover meat or ½ pound hamburg, sautéed
1 cup gravy or 1 cup tomato soup

1 green pepper, chopped fine,
1 small onion, chopped fine,
Salt and pepper to taste
Pinch poultry seasoning (optional)

Simmer in saucepan until meat is cooked or place in baking dish, cover with buttered crumbs, and bake in moderate oven, 350° F., for ½ hour. Serves 6.

SWEDISH MEAT BALLS

Soak until soft
¼ cup grapenuts, or bread, or cracker crumbs in
½ cup milk. Add
1 pound bottom round steak ground with
½ pound lean pork. Add:

1 egg yolk
1 medium-sized cold cooked potato, grated,
½ teaspoon salt
Few grains pepper
Small amount grated onion

Knead well. Shape into small balls and fry in butter until well browned. Serves 4.

BRAISED SHORT RIBS

Buy 3½ to 4 pounds short ribs of beef, boned, rolled, and tied. Sprinkle with salt and pepper. Dredge with flour. Sear meat on all sides in roasting pan or iron pot. Add:

1 cup diced carrots
1 large onion, minced,
1 green pepper, minced,

½ cup diced celery
3 cups boiling water

Cover closely and cook slowly on top of stove or in slow oven, 250° F., for 3 to 4 hours. Serves 4.

VEAL BIRDS

Wipe with damp cloth a 1- to 1½-pound slice veal steak. Cut in pieces about 2 by 4 inches. Roll tightly and fasten with toothpicks. Dredge with flour and place in hot, well-greased frying pan. Cover and cook slowly until veal is done clear through, and entire surface is nicely browned. Season with salt and pepper. Place on hot platter. Spread with ½ cup butter creamed with 1 cup chopped parsley. Serves 4.

VEAL AND HAM LOAF

Combine:
1 pound ham ground with
1 pound veal
1 small onion, chopped,
2 green peppers, chopped,

2 teaspoons salt
½ teaspoon pepper. Mix
    lightly with 2 forks. Add:
1 egg, beaten,
⅓ cup cream

Shape into loaf. Place in roasting pan and bake in hot oven, 400° F., for 45 minutes. Serves 6.

VEAL CUTLET

Buy 1½ pounds veal steak, cut about ⅛ inch thick. Cut into 6 pieces. Dip each piece in flour, then in egg wash—made by beating 1 egg into 1 cup milk—and then into fine cracker crumbs. Coat pieces completely. Fry in hot fat, 375° F., until meat is brown and sections float to surface of fat. Serve with tomato sauce. Serves 6.

Variation: **BAKED VEAL CUTLETS.** Bread and brown as above. Then pour over meat 1⅓ cups tomato or mushroom soup. Dilute with ½ cup milk. Cover and bake in slow oven, 300° F., for 1 hour. When using this method have 2-pound veal steak cut ½ inch thick. Serves 6.

LAMB

ROAST LAMB

Select 6- to 8-pound leg of lamb. Wipe with damp cloth. Do not remove thin skin or "fell." This protects meat and makes possible a shorter roasting time. Sprinkle lamb with salt and pepper and rub well with flour. Lay meat, skin side down, on rack in roasting pan. Roast uncovered in moderately slow oven, 300° F. to 350° for 30 to 35 minutes per pound. This produces well done meat the way most people in this country like lamb. Make gravy with pan drippings following method for Roast Beef. (See Primer for Brides, page 67) or serve with Mint Sauce.

If lamb seems dry, baste occasionally during roasting with pan drippings. It is not necessary to turn meat.

A 3- to 4-pound shoulder of lamb may also be roasted and is a good choice for a small family. Have a shoulder boned (bring bones home for soup stock) and rolled and a pocket made for stuffing. Prepare Poultry Stuffing, fill pocket, fasten with skewers, and roast as suggested above.

Crown Roast of Lamb is prepared and roasted in same manner as outlined for Crown Roast of Pork. (See page 129.)

All cuts of lamb—quarter of spring lamb, loin, rack, rolled shoulder, cushion shoulder, and breast—may be roasted, for lamb is tender meat.

If mutton (full-grown lamb) is roasted, allow 5 minutes more per pound. With mutton, many chefs prefer to boil first, discard water, and then to roast.

BROILED LAMB CHOPS

(See Primer for Brides, page 66)

LAMB CHOPS WITH FRUIT DRESSING

Brown nicely in a spider
4 double-thick lamb chops. Place in baking pan and cover with mixture of:
2 canned peaches, chopped fine.
1 cup crushed pineapple
½ cup soft bread crumbs
4 tablespoons brown sugar
4 tablespoons melted butter

Bake in moderate oven, 350° F., for 20 minutes. Serves 4.

SHEPHERD'S PIE

Cover a flank of lamb with cold water. Cook until tender. Remove bones and fat. Cut meat into small pieces. Let water cool in which lamb was cooked. Remove fat. Slice 1 onion into broth and bring to boil. Add 3 potatoes, diced, and 2 carrots, cut small. Cook until vegetables are nearly done, about 12 minutes. Then add lamb. When potatoes are cooked thoroughly, thicken broth with thin paste of 1 tablespoon flour mixed with a little water. Season with salt and pepper. Turn into casserole.

Cover with a crust of Plain Pastry. Toll House Biscuit, or Mashed Potatoes. Bake in hot oven, 400° F. to 450°, until well browned. Serves 6.

MIXED GRILL DINNER

Procure:

4 lamb chops, cut thick,	2 firm tomatoes, sliced thick
4 link sausages	3 sweet potatoes, cooked, sliced
4 slices bacon	4 slices canned pineapple

Grease bottom of broiler pan. Arrange slices of sweet potato, pineapple, and tomato. (If you wish, a little creamed butter and brown sugar may be spread over potatoes to glacé them.) Place sausages on top of pineapple. Then set broiler rack over all and place well-trimmed lamb chops on rack.

Preheat broiler oven for at least 15 minutes. Place pan close to broiler flame. When chops are seared on one side, turn and sear then on other side. Then move pan down two notches and let chops cook through. Remove rack, turn potatoes and tomatoes and baste, and return rack and continue cooking. Five minutes before chops are done, lay slices of bacon on rack and cook until crisp. Remove from oven and serve. Arrange on each plate, 1 chop, 1 sausage, slices of potato and tomato, 1 ring of pineapple, and bacon. Serves 4.

PORK

CROWN ROAST OF PORK

Select 10 to 12 ribs of a young pig, about 4 pounds. Have butcher shape into crown. Sprinkle with salt, dredge with flour, and place on rack in dripping pan. Cover tip of each bone with square of salt pork to keep bone from scorching. Place in very hot oven, 450° F., for 20 minutes to brown. Reduce heat to 375°, and, including the first 20 minutes, allow 25 minutes per pound in all for cooking. Cover or else cook uncovered and baste frequently with fat in pan. When cooked thoroughly take from oven and remove salt pork from bones. Replace with a cranberry or small pickled beet.

Open center of roast may be filled with Poultry Stuffing. When this is used, place slice of bread in open crown and push to bottom to serve as base. Then fill cavity with dressing. Cook this along with meat. Or when roast is ready to serve, fill center cavity with hot mashed potato or small head of cooked cauliflower. Garnish outside of roast with parsley and Apple Circlets or with border of alternate halved rosy apples and mint jelly mounds. Serves 10 to 12.

VERMONT SPECIAL CHOPS

Place in baking dish
4 pork chops, cut thick.
Grind together:
1 green pepper
1 slice onion
4 crackers. Season with
Pinch poultry seasoning
Salt and Pepper. Moisten
with
¼ cup milk

Heap mixture on top of chops and bake in moderate oven, 375° F., for about 45 minutes. Serves 4.

BARBECUED SPARERIBS

Prepare 1 recipe Barbecue Sauce. Place in roasting pan 4 pounds spare ribs cut into serving pieces. Place in moderate oven, 375° F., to heat through. Reduce heat to 350°. Pour half of sauce over meat. Baste frequently with sauce. When half-cooked, add remaining sauce and continue to baste. Cook meat until tender and crispy, for 1 to 1½ hours. Serves 4.

BAKED HAM IN CIDER

Soak 1½-inch thick slice of ham in water for 45 minutes. Wipe dry and place in baking pan. Spread with brown sugar, a little ground clove, and a little dry mustard. Pour into pan enough sweet cider, ginger ale, or white wine almost to cover ham. Bake in hot oven, 450° F., for about 1½ hours. Serves 4. (If ham is "tenderized" soaking will not be necessary.)

HAWAIIAN HAM

Soak in warm water about 1 hour a 2-pound slice of ham, cut thick. (If ham is "tenderized" soaking will not be necessary.) Drain, and dip in flour. Brown lightly in hot greased frying pan. Place in casserole and pour over ham 1½ cups crushed pineapple, drained, and ¼ cup water. Cover and bake in moderate oven, 350° F., for 1 hour, or until tender. Time varies according to thickness of slice. Serves 4.

BAKED PICNIC OR COTTAGE HAM

(See Primer for Brides, page 68)

HAM BAKED WITH CHEESE

Place in baking dish	2 tablespoons lemon juice
4 slices cooked ham, cut ½ inch thick. Heat in top of double boiler	½ teaspoon Worcestershire sauce
½ cup light cream. Add:	½ teaspoon French mustard
½ pound American cheese, diced,	Few grains cayenne
	Few grains paprika

Stir and cook until cheese is melted. Cover ham slices with cheese sauce. Bake in moderate oven, 350° F., until cheese is slightly browned. Serves 4.

SCALLOPED HAM AND MACARONI

Cook until tender	1 cup White Sauce (page 73).
¾ cup macaroni in	Add:
1½ quarts boiling salted water. Drain, rinse in cold water, and drain again. Prepare	Pinch dry mustard
	1 cup chopped cooked ham

Combine macaroni and sauce. Turn into buttered casserole, cover with buttered crumbs, and brown in hot oven, 450° F. Serves 6.

BROILED BACON

Preheat broiler until very hot. Place strips of bacon on wire rack over broiling pan and slide into oven about 4 inches below low heat. Turn bacon, when it becomes a faint brown, and broil other side. Bacon darkens when removed from heat. Always cook bacon slowly.

LIVER SMOTHERED WITH ONIONS

Heat in spider:
1 tablespoon butter
1 tablespoon bacon drippings. Add
2 large onions, sliced, and

brown in fat. Push to side of pan. Add and brown
1 pound calf's liver, sliced thin and floured well

Stir onions around browned liver, season and serve immediately. Serves 4.

SWEETBREADS CHANTILLY WITH WILD RICE

Wash ¼ pound wild rice. Cover with cold salted water. Boil steadily for 25 minutes. Drain and dry rice in open kettle for a few minutes away from heat. (Do not stir rice and it will dry out and remain light and flaky.)

Parboil
2 pairs sweetbreads. Remove outside tissue and slice lengthwise. Sauté in
2 tablespoons butter. Blend
4 tablespoons butter, melted,
4 tablespoons flour. Stir in

2 cups milk. Cook until thickened. Add:
2 tablespoons white wine, or more,
1 cup sliced sautéed mushrooms

Place mound of hot rice on platter. Pour wine sauce over it. Arrange sweetbreads on top and serve. Serves 4.

BROILED TRIPE

Cut honeycomb tripe into individual servings, allowing ⅓ to ¼ pound for each. Sprinkle with salt and pepper. Rub with flour and dip in salad oil. Sprinkle generously with fine bread crumbs. Place on rack, 3 inches below heat, and broil slowly on each side until crumbs are brown, about 3 to 4 minutes per side. Mustard Sauce served with this is delicious.

SAUSAGE AND OYSTER LOAF

Combine:

1 pound sausage meat
1 pint raw oysters, ground,

2 cups soft bread crumbs
2 eggs, slightly beaten

Mix well, place in loaf pan, and bake in moderate oven, 350° F., until loaf leaves edges of pan but meat remains moist, about 45 minutes. Drain occasionally to remove excess fat. Serve with hot Hollandaise Sauce. Serves 6. (Loaf shrinks considerably in baking due to loss of fat.)

POULTRY

ROAST STUFFED CHICKEN WITH GIBLET GRAVY

(See Primer for Brides, page 69)

CHICKEN SUPREME

For each person use a medium-thick slice of hot ham—preferably Virginia or southern-cured. On top of each slice arrange a breast of chicken. Cover with sauce made by blending:

4 tablespoons melted butter
4 tablespoons flour. Add
2 cups rich chicken stock.

Season with:
1 teaspoon salt
Few grains pepper

Top with large plump mushrooms, broiled or sautéed in plenty of butter. This amount of sauce serves 4.

DELMONICO CHICKEN

Slice meat of 6-pound cooked chicken into long sliverlike pieces. Boil 1 package (6-oz.) egg noodles in 2 quarts boiling salted water for 8 minutes. Drain. Place in a shallow buttered baking dish alternating layers of noodles and chicken. Prepare a sauce by melting:

2 cups American cheese in
2 cups hot milk. Blend:
4 tablespoons butter, melted,

2 tablespoons flour
1 teaspoon salt
¼ teaspoon mustard

Stir until thickened. Combine with melted cheese. Pour sauce over chicken and noodles, sprinkle with paprika, and brown in hot oven, 450° F. Serve bubbling hot and at table sprinkle with grated Parmesan cheese. Serves 6.

CHICKEN PIE

Disjoint a 6-pound chicken. Place in pan with small amount of water and few stalks of celery and a carrot or two. Cover and cook until meat is ready to drop from bones. Remove chicken from liquid and remove skin and bones. Cut chicken into good-sized pieces and arrange in baking dish, alternating white and dark meat. Prepare the following sauce.

Blend:
4 tablespoons butter, melted,
4 tablespoons flour
1½ teaspoons salt

Few grains pepper. Add to
2 cups hot chicken stock and
cook until thickened. (Add
additional seasoning to taste.)

Pour sauce over chicken, cover with crust of Plain Pastry, and bake in hot oven, 450° F., until sauce is brown and bubbles. Serves 6.

SMOTHERED CHICKEN

Brown halves of 2- to 2½-pound broilers in frying pan with generous ½ cup fat and butter. Meanwhile simmer giblets in 3 cups water. When chicken is browned, place in shallow baking pan. Add 3 tablespoons flour to fat in pan, brown it and pour giblet stock in slowly, stirring carefully so that mixture will not lump. Add more water if necessary. Add chopped giblets, season, and pour this gravy over chicken in pan. Add 1 cup sliced mushrooms, if you wish. Let chicken cook slowly in oven, 350° F., about 1½ hours, until meat separates easily from bones. Allow ½ chicken for each serving.

PARISIAN BAKED CHICKEN

Split and sauté	24 small white onions
3 2- to 2½-pound broilers in	24 mushrooms
4 tablespoons butter with:	Salt and pepper

When chicken is slightly browned, cover pan and bake in moderate oven, 350° F., for 45 minutes. Remove chicken from pan and make following sauce:

Pour over onions and mushrooms in pan	1 tablespoon flour with a little Water. Stir into
2 cups red wine. Simmer a few minutes. Blend	1 cup chicken stock

Bring to boil and add thickened stock to onions and mushrooms. Add more seasoning, if necessary. Pour over chicken before serving. Serves 6.

BROILED CHICKEN

Buy 1½-pound broilers, allowing ½ chicken for each serving. Cut in half down the back. Wash and dry well. Brush thoroughly with butter or oil, sprinkle with salt and pepper, and place skin-side down on rack in broiling pan. Place 2 to 3 inches below broiler unit and allow to cook at 450° F. for about 10 minutes, or until brown. Turn, brush with fat, and allow to cook from 10 to 20 minutes more at 350°, or until skin is crisp and brown. (Smaller chickens may take only 20 minutes in all to cook through. If a less well browned skin is desired, reduce temperature, or move rack farther from heat, and allow to cook more slowly.) Remove to hot platter, brush with butter, or serve with Hollandaise Sauce or Creamed Mushrooms.

CHICKEN DIVAN

Place 5-pound fowl in large kettle, add 2 teaspoons salt, and about 5 cups water. Bring to boil. Lower heat and simmer until tender, about 3 hours. Let cool in broth. (In pressure cooker, use only 2 cups water and cook at 15 pounds pressure for about 25 minutes.) When chicken has cooled in broth, remove skin, slice breast, and leg meat.

Prepare
2 cups White Sauce (page 73).
Blend in:
¼ teaspoon nutmeg
½ cup mayonnaise
½ cup cream, whipped,

3 tablespoons sherry
1 teaspoon Worcestershire sauce. Boil for 15 to 20 minutes
1 large bunch broccoli or asparagus

Drain and arrange on deep ovenproof serving platter. Arrange chicken over vegetable and cover with sauce. Sprinkle generously with 1 cup grated Parmesan cheese. Place in broiler about 5 inches below flame, until brown and bubbly. Serves 4 to 6.

CHICKEN FRICASSEE

Have butcher disjoint a small 4- to 5-pound fowl. (Ask him to use knife, not cleaver.) Rinse pieces with cold water and place in pan with about 3 cups boiling water. Cover and simmer until tender, about 1½ hours for year-old fowl.

About 1 pint of strong broth will result. Drain chicken in colander over pan of chicken broth. Dust each piece lightly by shaking it in paper bag containing small amount of flour, seasoned with salt and pepper. Fry in spider in which butter has been melted to sizzling point. Brown each piece quickly on both sides. Remove from pan, place meat where it will keep warm while gravy is being made. Skim fat off broth. Make gravy as follows:

Heat in spider
3 tablespoons butter. When sizzling, blend in
4 tablespoons flour. Add

1 pint chicken broth (about) and
½ cup cream or rich milk

Stir and cook until gravy is thickened and smooth. Pour onto platter and arrange chicken on top. Serve immediately. Serves 4. Toll House Biscuits and Mashed Potatoes are a must with this dish.

FRIED CHICKEN WITH CREAM GRAVY
(See Primer for Brides, page 70).

FRIED BONELESS CHICKEN

Allow half of a 2½-pound boiler per person. Place halves, skin side up, in baking pan, with breasts overlapping somewhat. Sprinkle with salt and pepper. Place in moderate oven, 375° F., until chicken is heated through but not cooked or browned. (This is to soften joints so that tendons and joints may be easily removed.) Cool enough to handle. Then remove breast bones. Make small slits on underside of chicken and twist leg and thigh joints to remove those bones. Save liquor in pan in which chickens were heated.

In a paper bag place small amount of flour with ample seasoning of salt and pepper. Dip chicken in cold milk, then drop into bag of flour and shake to coat well. Fry in drippings made up of about 4 tablespoons salt pork and the same amount of butter, having fat deep enough to reach well up on sides of chicken while browning on each side. Let fat reduce in amount until at end of frying there is just enough left to use in the making of cream gravy.

Add chicken liquor (about 1 cup) from baking pan and 1 cup cream or rich milk. Thicken with about 4 tablespoons flour mixed with a little water. Serve on platter with chicken resting on top of gravy.

CHICKEN SOUFFLÉ

Prepare
1⅓ cups White Sauce (page 73). Add
½ cup fine stale bread crumbs. Cook 2 minutes. Remove from heat. Add:

1½ cups finely chopped chicken
2 egg yolks, well beaten, Salt and pepper. Fold in
2 egg whites, beaten stiff

Turn mixture into baking dish. Set in pan of warm water and bake in slow oven, 325° F., for 35 minutes, or until puffed and brown. Serves 6. This is delicious baked in ring molds (which must be buttered). Unmold and serve with center filled with Creamed Mushrooms.

CURRIED CHICKEN

Cook a 4-pound chicken until tender. Allow to cool in its own broth. Then skim fat from top of broth. Remove chicken and disjoint into leg, thigh, breast, and wing sections. Cut breast meat into serving-sized pieces and for ease in eating remove all bones possible from other parts. If stock does not measure at least 1 quart, add milk to make up difference. Prepare the following sauce:

Blend:
½ cup butter, melted,
½ cup flour
1 small onion, finely chopped,
1 teaspoon curry powder
¼ teaspoon salt
Small piece of ginger root, chopped (optional)
Few grains pepper

Mix well. Then slowly add chicken stock, stirring over low heat until smooth and well thickened. Serve over chicken with hot Fluffy Rice. Pass a tray containing grated fresh coconut, seedless raisins, chutney, Bombay duck, or crumbled crisp bacon. Serves 4.

This recipe can be elaborated but it is the simplest and best recipe I have found for the average housewife to use with success. In some sections you may be able to get Pappadums (bean wafers) to eat with curry. Another common variation in serving includes saffron, raisins and almonds mixed with the rice before it is brought to the table.

ESCALLOPED CHICKEN AND NOODLES

Disjoint a 6-pound chicken and cook in small amount of water until meat drops from bones. Remove skin and bones and cut meat into large pieces. Prepare the following sauce and noodles:

Blend:
4 tablespoons butter, melted,
4 tablespoons flour
1½ teaspoons salt
Few grains pepper. Add to
2 cups chicken stock. Cook
1 package (6-oz.) egg noodles in
2 quarts boiling salted water

138

Drain noodles and arrange in baking dish in alternate layers with chicken. Pour sauce over all to cover. Spread soft buttered bread crumbs over top and bake in hot oven, 400° F., until nicely browned. Serves 6.

HAWAIIAN CHICKEN

Blend:
2 tablespoons butter, melted,
4 tablespoons flour. Add
2 cups milk, scalded. Cook until thick. Add:

1½ cups cooked chicken, cubed,
1 cup pineapple, cubed,
1 tablespoon pimento, cut in strips
Salt and pepper to taste

Cut top from coconut and reserve as a cover. Cut slice from bottom so that shell will stand erect. Fill center of coconut with chicken mixture, sprinkle with toasted almonds, and place top, cut from coconut. Set in oven to heat well. A subtle flavor from the coconut meat results. Serves 6.

Variation: This may also be served in Croustades or Patty Shells, omitting coconut. In that case sprinkle mixture generously with chopped almonds.

CHICKEN TERRAPIN

Hard-cook
3 eggs.
Mash yolks and add:
5 tablespoons flour
1 teaspoon prepared mustard
¼ teaspoon white pepper
3 tablespoons melted butter. Stir into
2 cups milk, scalded, and cook in top of double boiler until

thick. Add:
3 egg whites, finely chopped,
1½ cups cooked chicken,
1 to 2 tablespoons sliced pimento
1 to 2 tablespoons sliced green pepper
6 ripe olives, sliced,
½ teaspoon salt
Juice of 1 lemon

Serve in Patty Shells. Serves 8.

CHICKEN À LA KING

Heat
2 cups chicken stock or milk.
Blend:
4 tablespoons flavor
1 teaspoon salt with a little
Cold water. Add to stock and
cook until thickened. Add:

3 cups cooked chicken, cubed,
1 pimento, cut fine,
1 cup mushrooms cooked a
few minutes in
Butter. Stir in
¾ cup cream

Mix well and serve hot on toast or in Patty Shells. Serves 6 to 8.

SWEDISH STUFFING

Combine:
2 cups stale bread crumbs
½ cup melted butter
½ cup seedless raisins, chopped
Makes 4 cups stuffing.

½ cup broken English walnuts
Season with
Salt, pepper, and sage

POULTRY STUFFING

(See Primer for Brides, page 69)

7. MEAT SUBSTITUTES

Memories of Sunday night suppers in the home of my girlhood are of the delicious Ring-Tum-Diddy my mother used to make. Our children enjoy it too. It is a cheese dish which your family will find a pleasant change from Rarebit. And, of course, we New Englanders could not enjoy Saturday night supper without our traditional Baked Beans, Brown Bread, and Fish Cakes with enough beans baked to warm over for Sunday breakfast. Our family prefers the recipe made without tomatoes, but people outside New England seem to enjoy the added flavor which tomatoes give.

GOLDENROD EGGS

Prepare
1 cup Thin White Sauce (page 73).
Chop whites of
3 hard-cooked eggs. Combine with sauce. Cut
4 slices toast in halves lengthwise

Arrange toast on platter or on individual plates and pour sauce over it. Force yolks through strainer or potato ricer, letting them fall on sauce to make a yellow mound. Garnish with parsley and toast points. Serves 4.

FOAMY OMELETTE

Separate
4 eggs. Beat yolks until lemon-colored. Add:
½ teaspoon salt
Few grains pepper. Beat egg
whites until stiff with
4 tablespoons water. Melt
1 tablespoon butter in frying pan

Fold yolk mixture carefully into egg whites. Turn into pan. Cook over low heat until underside is brown. Then place pan in warm oven for a few minutes to allow mixture to dry and stiffen. Crease through the middle, fold over, and serve immediately on hot platter. Serves 4.

Variations: Grated cheese, chopped meat, chopped cooked vegetables, or jelly may be spread over half of omelette just before folding over.

SOFT- AND HARD-COOKED EGGS
(See Primer for Brides, page 64)

FRIED BACON AND EGGS
(See Primer for Brides, page 64)

SCRAMBLED EGGS
(See Primer for Brides, page 65)

SAVORY CHEESE MILK TOAST

Combine 2 cups Thin White Sauce (page 73) and 1 cup cheese, broken in pieces. Stir over low heat until blended and smooth. Toast 6 slices of bread and lay on hot platter. Pour sauce over toast and serve. Serves 6. (Excellent for a supper dish with Cole Slaw.)

CHEESE FONDUE

Combine:
1 cup stale bread crumbs
1/4 pound cheese, finely cut,
1 cup milk, scalded. Separate
2 eggs and beat yolks well.

Add:
1/2 teaspoon salt
Few grains pepper
1 tablespoon melted butter

Combine crumb and egg-yolk mixtures. Beat egg whites until dry and fold in. Turn all into buttered baking dish and bake in moderate oven, 375° F., for 20 minutes. Serve immediately. Serves 4.

CORN AND CHEESE FONDUE

Combine:
1 cup milk
1½ cups stale bread crumbs
1 cup canned corn
1 cup grated American cheese

1 tablespoon butter. Season with
Salt and pepper
Few grains paprika. Add
3 egg yolks, well beaten. Fold in
3 egg whites, beaten stiff

Turn into buttered dish and bake in moderate oven, 350° F., until firm. Serves 6.

CHEESE SOUFFLÉ

Melt in saucepan
¼ cup butter. Blend in
¼ cup flour. Add:
1 cup warm milk
½ cup American cheese, cut fine. Cook, stirring until thick. Add slowly:

3 egg yolks
½ teaspoon salt
Few grains paprika
1 teaspoon onion juice. Carefully fold in
3 egg whites, beaten stiff

Turn into ungreased baking dish and set in pan of warm water. Bake in hot oven, 400° F. to 450°, until firm, about 1 hour. (Depth of dish determines time of baking. A deep dish requires a lower temperature and longer cooking period.) Serve immediately. Serves 4.

CHEESE CROQUETTES

Prepare
1 cup Thick White Sauce (page 73). Stir in
2 egg yolks. Add:
1 cup grated mild cheese

1 tablespoon Parmesan cheese. When cheese melts, remove from heat. Add:
⅛ teaspoon salt
Few grains cayenne

Spread in shallow pan and let cool. Shape into croquettes, roll in crumbs, dip into egg whites beaten with a little water, and then roll in crumbs again. Place in frying basket and fry in deep fat, 390° F., until brown. Drain on absorbent paper. Serve immediately. Serves 4.

Variation: **VEGETABLE-CHEESE CROQUETTES.** Incorporate with this cheese base 1 cup cooked mixed vegetables such as peas, carrots, string beans, corn, celery, and Lima beans.

RING-TUM-DIDDY

Melt in top of double boiler
2 tablespoons butter. Blend in
1 tablespoon flour. Add:
1 cup tomato soup
1 teaspoon salt

1 teaspoon Worcestershire sauce
2 cups finely cut cheese. Stir until melted. Add
1 egg, beaten

Cook until thickened, about 4 minutes. Before removing from heat, add pinch of soda. Pour over squares of toast or crisp crackers. Serves 4.

TOLL HOUSE BAKED BEANS *(A Favorite Family Recipe)*

Pick over and wash 1 pint pea beans. Cover with cold water and soak overnight. In the morning drain, cover with fresh water, heat slowly, and simmer until skins burst. (This is determined by taking a few beans on tip of spoon and blowing on them. When sufficiently cooked, skins will burst.) Drain.

Scald rind of
½ pound salt pork. Scrape off a piece and put in bottom of bean pot. Cut through rind of remaining pork at ½-inch intervals, making cuts 1 inch deep. Turn beans into pot, filling only ¾ full, and bury section of pork in them, leaving rind exposed. Mix:

½ tablespoon salt
1 tablespoon dark molasses
1½ tablespoons sugar
1 teaspoon dry mustard (optional)
Add:
1 cup hot water
1 can (2½ cups) tomatoes. Pour over beans and bury
3 small onions in top of bean pot

If beans are not covered with liquid, add boiling water. Cover bean pot and bake in a moderate oven, 275° F., for 6 to 8 hours. Uncover during last hour so that rind may become brown and crisp. Watch the cooking and add water as needed. Tomatoes may be omitted and 2½ cups water used instead. Serves 12. (Better plan these, reheated, for Sunday breakfast, too, when your family will appreciate them even more.)

ESCALLOPED MACARONI AND CHEESE
(See Primer for Brides, page 65)

CHEESE-CUSTARD MACARONI RING

Cook for 20 minutes
1 cup macaroni in
2 quarts salted boiling water.
Drain and add:
1 cup hot milk
2 tablespoons butter
1 cup bread crumbs. Soak for
a few minutes. Add:

1 cup grated cheese
½ cup pimentos, cut fine,
1 large onion, cut fine,
2 tablespoons chopped parsley
2 eggs, well beaten

Pour into greased ring mold. Set in pan of warm water and bake in moderate oven, 350° F., for 40 minutes, until firm. Unmold and fill center with peas, creamed mushrooms, creamed oysters, ham, lobster, shrimp, or any food you enjoy combined with cheese. Serves 8.

NOODLE RING

Cook and drain
1 package (6-oz.) noodles.
Combine:
1½ cups milk, scalded,
1 cup soft bread crumbs
1 teaspoon salt

Few grains pepper
¼ teaspoon paprika
3 eggs, well beaten,
1 teaspoon grated onion
2 tablespoons chopped pimento

Add noodles to milk mixture and pour into buttered ring mold. Place in pan of warm water and bake in moderate oven, 350° F., for 30 minutes. Unmold and fill center with creamed chicken and mushrooms, creamed lobster, or any fish, vegetable or meat mixture. Serves 6.

Variation: **CHEESE NOODLE RING**. Add 1 cup grated American cheese to hot milk.

PEA TIMBALES WITH TOMATO SAUCE

Beat	1 small onion, minced,
2 eggs. Add:	½ green pepper, minced,
1 can (1⅓ cups) pea soup	¾ teaspoon salt
1 pimento, chopped fine,	⅛ teaspoon pepper

Mix well and turn into greased molds or custard cups and bake in slow oven, 300° F., about 20 minutes, until firm. Turn onto ovenproof platter and pour 1 can (1⅓ cups) hot tomato soup or purée over hot timbales. Cover with grated cheese and place under broiler to melt cheese. Serves 6.

PINWHEEL ASPARAGUS CASSEROLE (page 164) is also an excellent meat substitute.

FRENCH TOAST

Beat slightly	In this mixture dip
2 eggs. Add:	6 to 8 slices bread. Melt
1 cup milk	2 tablespoons butter in frying
¾ teaspoon salt.	pan

Brown bread on each side in butter. Serve very hot with maple syrup or jelly or sprinkle with cinnamon and sugar. Serves 6 to 8.

8. SEAFOOD, WITH EMPHASIS ON LOBSTER

No one comes to New England without looking forward to eating lobster and lots of it. At Toll House we serve two to three tons of lobster a week and it comes to us only thirty minutes out of the ocean. Lobster is certainly a favorite with our guests and so you will find many lobster dishes here.

Among the other fish dishes are some which I recommend especially to you. The Molded Salmon with Cucumber Dressing was one of my grandmother's pet summer-day dishes. Sole Fouquet is wonderful too. We spent a lot of time working out this recipe for fish connoisseurs since the Fouquet Restaurant in Paris did not care to part with its secrets. We find that our local guests prefer the fish recipes we brought from Germany. People in our section are not especially fond of sauces. It was in Germany that we found how to make a delicious butter to rub into sautéed fish. It is absorbed into the crust and gives the fish a subtle and delicious flavor.

FISH

COURT BOUILLON FOR POACHING FISH

Heat together:

½ cup diced celery
½ cup diced carrot
1 onion, sliced,
1 bay leaf
4 peppercorns

3 cloves
2 slices lemon
2 tablespoons lemon juice or mild vinegar
1 tablespoon salt
3 quarts cold water

Simmer for 15 to 20 minutes. Then place halibut, haddock, salmon, or other fish in this mixture and simmer or "poach" until fish is done. Allow about 10 minutes per pound, according to thickness of fish. (If large fish is to be cooked whole, use shallow fireproof baking pan instead of kettle.) When fish is done, remove from liquor. Then strain liquor and thicken slightly, adding 1 teaspoon flour mixed with a little cold water for each cupful of liquor. Season with additional lemon juice, salt and pepper, and pour over fish.

Variations: Serve poached fish with White Sauce or Egg Sauce instead of thickened Court Bouillon. The fish will retain its delicious flavor from the bouillon it was poached in.

BROILED FISH

Heat broiler as for steak. Clean fish and remove head, tail, and fins. (Also remove backbone from cod or haddock.) Cut large fish into 1-inch pieces. Broil small fish whole or halved. Wipe fish dry. Sprinkle with salt and pepper and dot with butter. Place in broiling pan with skin side next to pan. Place 2 inches below broiler heat until brown, then turn skin side toward heat and broil until crisp. If not cooked through thoroughly after browning, place in upper oven for 5 minutes to finish cooking. Time required depends upon thickness, but 10 to 20 minutes usually suffices. To serve, brush with melted butter and garnish with lemon and parsley.

BAKED HALIBUT STEAK
(See Primer for Brides, page 65)

BAKED FILLETS OF FLOUNDER

Wipe fillets dry. Wrap "tails" of each about fleshy portion and fasten with toothpicks. Butter baking pan and lay fish on it. Sprinkle each with salt, pepper, and chopped green pepper. Over this lay a thin slice of onion and solid piece of canned tomato. Pour 1 teaspoon tomato juice over each fillet. Cover with fine buttered bread crumbs and grated cheese. Bake in hot oven, 450° F., about 30 minutes. Serve at once. Allow 1 fillet for each serving.

BAKED HALIBUT

Rub
1 2-pound halibut steak with:
2 tablespoons butter
⅛ teaspoon pepper

½ teaspoon salt. Place in baking pan and pour over
1½ cups milk

Bake in moderate oven, 350° F., for 45 minutes, basting frequently. Serve with Rarebit Sauce. Serves 4.

BAKED STUFFED HADDOCK

Select 2- to 3-pound haddock. Clean fish, remove head, tail, fins, and wipe thoroughly with damp cloth. Rub over both outside and inside with salt. Slit almost whole length of fish. Lay in greased pan, and fill it until it bulges with following stuffing. Fasten fish together and gash crosswise on top in four places. Insert strips of fat salt pork. Bake in hot oven, 450° F., for about 15 minutes to the pound. Serves 6 to 8.

Rice-Tomato Stuffing

Wash and cook
½ cup rice in boiling salted water for 15 minutes. Drain. Turn into top of double boiler. Add:
2 cups canned tomatoes

1 small onion, minced,
¾ teaspoon salt
⅛ teaspoon pepper
½ teaspoon curry powder
1 tablespoon sugar

Cook until rice is tender and liquid absorbed. Then use as stuffing. Makes 2½ to 3 cups stuffing.

FISH SPENCER

Wash and wipe dry 1 pound haddock fillets. Cut in pieces for individual servings. Dip in milk and then in fine cracker crumbs. Place in buttered pan. Pour melted butter over fillets, place pan in broiling hot oven, 550° F., and cook about 10 minutes. Serve with Egg Sauce. Serves 4.

SOLE FOUQUET

Place in shallow baking dish
4 fillets lemon sole. Add:
2 cups water
1 small onion, sliced,
2 bay leaves
Pinch thyme
Salt and pepper. Boil a few
minutes until fish is done.
Pour off liquor and strain.
Cook

½ cup sliced mushrooms in
4 tablespoons butter. Blend in
4 tablespoons flour. Add hot
liquor, stirring until thick.
Add:
½ cup chopped peeled tomato
1 tablespoon Parmesan cheese
White wine
Salt and pepper to taste

Pour sauce over fish in baking dish, place under broiler flame
and brown. Serve at table from baking dish. Serves 4.

HADDOCK À LA KING

Prepare in double boiler
2 cups White Sauce (page
73). Add:
1½ cups cooked haddock,
flaked,

½ green pepper, parboiled 5
minutes and cut in strips
4 slices pimento
½ cup mushrooms, skinned
and boiled 15 minutes

Let stand over hot water for 10 minutes to allow flavor to
permeate sauce. Serves 6.

FISH BALLS

Wash
1 cup salt codfish in cold water.
Break in small pieces, or cut
with scissors.

Prepare
2½ cups raw cubed potatoes

Cook fish and potatoes in boiling water to cover until potatoes
are nearly soft. Drain well through strainer. Return to saucepan
in which they were cooked. Mash until no lumps remain and
add ½ teaspoon butter, 1 egg, well beaten, and ⅛ teaspoon
pepper.

Beat mixture with fork 2 minutes. Add salt if necessary. Take

up by spoonfuls and put in frying basket. Fry 1 minute in deep
fat, 375° F., allowing 6 fish balls for each frying. Drain on absorbent paper. Reheat fat after each frying. Serves 6.

CODFISH SOUFFLÉ

Cook
½ green pepper, chopped fine,
½ onion, chopped fine, in
2 tablespoons butter, until
  onion is transparent. Add:

2 cups mashed potato
1 cup cooked codfish, flaked,
2 egg yolks, well beaten.
  Fold in
2 egg whites, beaten stiff

Turn into casserole and bake in hot oven, 400° F., for 20 minutes. Serves 6.

FISH TIMBALES

Combine:
2 tablespoons butter, melted,
¼ cup fine bread crumbs
⅔ cup milk. Cook 5 minutes,
  stirring occasionally. Add:

1 cup chopped haddock, or
  other cooked fish
½ teaspoon chopped parsley
2 eggs, slightly beaten,
  Salt and pepper to taste

Turn mixture into custard cups, set in pan of hot water and
bake in moderate oven, 350° F. to 375°, until firm to touch,
about 30 minutes. Serve with Medium White Sauce (page 73)
and peas. Garnish with paprika. Serves 4.

EPICUREAN FINNAN HADDIE

Soak 2 pounds finnan haddie in water for 1 hour. Boil, or bake
in moderate oven, 350° F., for 30 minutes. Separate into flakes.
Prepare following sauce:

Mix:
1 tablespoon minced onion
2 tablespoons minced green
  pepper

2 tablespoons minced red pepper or pimento. Add
2 cups Thin White Sauce
  (page 73)

Stir in finnan haddie. Serve with toast or in potato nests.
Serves 6.

CURRIED SALMON SPECIAL

Mold 2 cups Fluffy Rice into small cups or tins and heat on top of stove in pan of boiling water.

Heat in saucepan
3 tablespoons oil. Stir in
4 tablespoons flour
½ teaspoon curry powder, and cook together. Add:
1 cup hot milk
1 cup hot fish stock or milk

Few grains salt and pepper
Few drops lemon juice.
Stir until smooth. Add:
2 cups whole boiled salmon
½ cup cream or rich milk
2 tablespoons butter

Unmold rice to form a ring on platter. Pour salmon into center. Decorate with sliced hard-cooked eggs and parsley. Serves 6.

TUNA FISH PIE

Combine:
1 can (7-oz.) tuna fish
2 teaspoons minced onion
1 pimento, chopped,
1 teaspoon salt
1 tablespoon Worcestershire sauce

⅛ teaspoon pepper. Make
2 cups Thick White Sauce (page 73). Pour over mixture. Prepare
1 recipe Toll House Biscuits

Turn fish mixture into baking dish. Place biscuits on top. Bake in hot oven, 450° F., for 12 to 15 minutes. Serves 4 to 6.

CALIFORNIA "CHICKEN" PIE

Boil in salted water
2 carrots, diced
2 potatoes, diced
1 medium-sized onion, chopped,

1 cup peas. Prepare
1 cup White Sauce (Page 73)
Add
¼ teaspoon paprika
1 can (7-oz.) tuna fish, flaked

Fill baking dish with alternate layers of fish mixture and vegetables. Cover with an upper crust of Plain Pastry, Toll House Biscuits, or buttered crumbs and bake in hot oven, 450° F., until brown. Serves 6.

SALMON AND RICE DELIGHT

Line casserole with cooked rice. Flake fine 2 cans (each 7-oz.) salmon. Put in dish on top of rice. Pour salmon liquor over fish.

Cover with more rice. Pour in: 1 egg, well beaten ¼ cup milk. Season with Salt and pepper

Dot with butter. Bake in a moderate oven, 375° F., for 30 minutes. Serves 4.

LOBSTER

When you are selecting lobsters, pick out live ones that are a good dark green color and show signs of activity. (If you are buying boiled ones, make sure of freshness by straightening out the tail. It should spring back quickly.)

To kill a lobster which you intend to broil, place it on its back and insert a sharp knife between the eyes. Then split from head to tail.

If you are boiling live lobsters, grasp lobster body from behind and plunge head first into a large kettle of actively boiling salted water. (Add 2 tablespoons salt to 1 quart water.) Cover and boil hard for 5 minutes. Then simmer 15 to 20 minutes more, depending on size, and until shell turns bright red. A 1½-pound lobster will take about 20 minutes. After cooking, plunge at once into cold water. Drain, cool, split, and clean. If you are near the ocean, by all means cook lobsters in sea water.

LOBSTER, TOLL HOUSE

Allow a whole 1-pound boiled lobster for each serving. Split from head to tail and lay open. Remove claw meat, keeping it whole. Discard contents of body cavity except liver or "tomali." Leave tail meat intact, but remove intestinal tract. Place claw meat in body cavity to fill well. Cover with following sauce. Be sure that both body and tail meat are sufficiently covered for sauce to run down under meat and fill cavity so as to moisten

153

throughout. Place lobsters close together in baking pan, so as to stand upright. Brown quickly in hot preheated oven, 450° F., and serve immediately. (If prepared ahead and sauce is cold, heat in moderate oven, 375° F. Do not cook long enough for sauce to boil out.)

Blend:
½ cup butter, melted,
1¼ cups flour
1 teaspoon prepared mustard
¼ cup vinegar
¼ teaspoon Worcestershire sauce
Juice of ¼ lemon

1 cup grated cheese. Slowly stir in
6 cups hot milk. Continue stirring until all is thickened. Add:
1 cup white wine
1 cup sliced mushrooms sautéed in butter
1 sup soft bread crumbs

Makes enough sauce for 8 servings.

BAKED STUFFED LOBSTER

For each serving allow half of a 1½-pound boiled lobster. Split lobster from head to tail through the middle, remove meat, and cut into pieces. Stand shells on sides in baking pan, allowing tails to curl around slightly. Fill each shell with following mixture and cover with soft, buttered bread crumbs mixed with grated American cheese. Sprinkle with paprika and brown in hot oven.

For each lobster, blend in top of double boiler:
2 tablespoons butter, melted,
4 tablespoons flour
½ teaspoon salt

¼ teaspoon prepared mustard
½ teaspoon paprika. Add:
2 cups hot milk
½ cup grated cheese. Cook until thick and smooth

BROILED STUFFED LOBSTER

Procure a whole 1-pound live lobster for each serving. Hold large claws firmly. With sharp pointed knife begin at mouth to make incision. Then split shell entire length of body and tail. Remove stomach and intestinal canal, and small sac at back of head. Crack large claws and lay lobster open as flat as possible. Brush meat with melted butter. Season with salt and pepper and stuff.

Stuffing

For each lobster crumble enough soda crackers to fill body cavity, about 5 or 6. Blend in lobster "tomali" and juice of ¼ lemon. Add enough melted butter to moisten well. Stuff lobster cavity and cover with inverted pan while lobster is broiling. Remove cover when meat shrinks from shell. Allow crumbs to brown. Broiling usually takes 20 to 25 minutes, 500° F., depending on size of lobster. Serve hot with melted butter flavored with sherry if you like, and wedge of lemon. At Toll House we allow ¼ pound butter for each lobster—about half to moisten crumbs before cooking and half to serve melted as a sauce.

LOBSTER IMPERIAL

Split four 1-pound lobsters lengthwise. Remove meat from tail and claws. Clean inside of shell. Cut meat into good-sized chunks. Mix with following sauce and refill shells. Place in hot oven, 400° F., to heat through and brown. Serves 4.

Blend together:
2 cups White Sauce (page 73)
2 cups mayonnaise
½ onion, cut fine,
½ cup sliced, sautéed mush-rooms. Season with:
2 teaspoons lemon juice
1 teaspoon prepared mustard
½ teaspoon Worcestershire sauce
Salt and pepper to taste

LOBSTER À LA NEWBURG

Remove meat from
1 2-pound boiled lobster and cut into good-sized pieces. In top of double boiler blend:
¼ cup butter
½ teaspoon paprika
½ cup Newburg Sauce or cooking sherry. Stir in lobster meat. Cook 1 to 2 minutes. Sprinkle with
2 tablespoons flour, and stir lightly. Combine:
2 cups thin cream
2 egg yolks, and beat

155

Add egg-yolk mixture to lobster. Fold over and over until well blended. Cook until thickened and smooth. Serve with toast or in Patty Shells. Serves 4.

LOBSTER THERMIDOR

Split two 1½-pound boiled lobsters lengthwise. Remove all meat. Clean shell and wash well. Prepare Lobster à la Newburg and add 1 cup mushrooms, sliced and sautéed. When Newburg has thickened, put mixture into the 4 half shells, packing well. "Button" tops with whole sautéed mushrooms. Sprinkle with grated American cheese. Brown well under broiler or in oven. Serves 4.

ESCALLOPED LOBSTER

Remove meat from 6 pounds boiled lobster. Cut into good-sized pieces. Blend:

4 tablespoons butter, melted,
½ cup flour

1 teaspoon salt
1 teaspoon paprika. Add
1 quart hot milk, stirring constantly until thickened. Add lobster meat.

Fill large scallop shells with mixture and cover with well-buttered soft bread crumbs. Brown in hot preheated oven, 400° F., and serve immediately. (If shells tend to tip in baking pan, keep upright by wedging crusts of bread between them.) Serves 6.

MERRYMOUNT LOBSTER

Prepare
1½ cups boiled lobster meat
Heat
1 cup milk. Add:
½ cup soft bread crumbs
1 egg, well beaten,

½ teaspoon prepared mustard
Few drops onion juice
1 teaspoon lemon juice
1 tablespoon melted butter
½ teaspoon salt
Pepper to taste

Stir lobster into sauce. Turn into scallop shells, ramekins, or casserole and cover with buttered bread crumbs. Bake in hot oven, 400° F., for 10 minutes until brown. Serves 6.

OTHER SHELLFISH

CRAB DE LUXE

Prepare
1 cup crab meat. Cook to-
gether for 3 minutes:
3 tablespoons butter
1 small onion, chopped,
1 small green pepper,
chopped.

Blend in
2 tablespoons flour. Stir and
add
1 cup hot milk. Bring to boil
and season with
Salt, pepper, and paprika

Stir crab meat into sauce. Serve on crackers, rounds of toast, or in Patty Shells. Serves 4.

CRAB SOUFFLÉ

Pick over
1 can (7-oz.) crab meat or 1
cup fresh cooked crab.
Prepare
1 cup Thin White Sauce (page
73) and when thickened, remove from heat. Add

1 teaspoon lemon juice. Stir in
crab meat. Add
1 egg yolk, well beaten. Add
Salt and pepper to taste.
Fold in
1 egg white, beaten stiff

Pour mixture into greased baking dish, set in pan of warm water, and bake in hot oven, 400° F., for about 20 minutes. Serves 4.

Variations: Salmon, shrimp, or lobster may be substituted for crab meat.

CRAB MEAT PIE

Combine:
2 cups cooked crab meat
3 eggs, beaten,
⅓ cup melted butter
¾ teaspoon prepared mustard
Speck of cayenne pepper

½ teaspoon Worcestershire
sauce
1 teaspoon salt
1½ cups rich milk
1 tablespoon chopped
green pepper
½ cup cracker crumbs

Turn mixture into greased baking dish. Sprinkle with buttered bread crumbs. Bake in a slow oven, 325° F., until set and a delicate brown, about 45 to 60 minutes. Avoid overcooking. Serves 6.

CRAB DELIGHT IN CROUSTADES

Prepare
1 cup cooked crab meat. Melt
2 tablespoons butter. Cook in it for 5 minutes
2 tablespoons chopped green pepper. Blend in:
2 tablespoons flour
½ teaspoon prepared mustard
½ teaspoon salt

½ teaspoon Worcestershire sauce
Few grains cayenne pepper
1 cup stewed, strained tomatoes
1 cup grated cheese
1 egg, slightly beaten. Cook 3 minutes. Heat
¾ cup milk

Stir green pepper mixture into milk. Then add crab meat. Cook until thickened. Serve in croustades. Serves 8.

SEAFOOD SAVORY

Prepare
1 cup shredded crab meat or other shellfish. Scald
1 pint oysters. Drain and reserve liquor. Heat:
1 cup milk
½ cup cream. Add oyster liquor. Blend

2 tablespoons butter, melted,
3 tablespoons flour. Stir into hot liquid. Cook until thick and smooth. Add:
½ cup tomato catsup
1 teaspoon Worcestershire sauce
Few grains salt and paprika

Stir oysters and crab meat into sauce. Serve hot on buttered toast or toasted crackers. Serves 6.

PORTUGUESE SHRIMP

Shell and clean
2 pounds raw fresh shrimp
Combine in saucepan:
8 tablespoons catsup
1½ teaspoons salt
1½ teaspoons dry mustard
Small amount boiling water

1½ tablespoons prepared horseradish
½ onion, cut fine
1 bay leaf
¼ teaspoon pepper
1 teaspoon allspice
1 clove garlic, cut fine

Place shrimp in mixture and simmer 15 to 20 minutes, adding a little more water if necessary to keep shrimp from burning. Let cool in sauce. Reheat or serve cold. Serves 8.

SHRIMP LOUISIANA

Clean and break into small pieces
⅔ cup canned shrimp. Cook
1 tablespoon chopped onion in
2 tablespoons butter, stirring constantly. Add:
⅔ cup hot boiled rice

⅔ cup milk or cream. When hot, add:
½ teaspoon salt
¼ teaspoon celery salt or minced stalk of celery
3 tablespoons tomato sauce
Few grains paprika

Stir shrimp into sauce and simmer until heated through. Turn into serving dish and garnish with parsley. Serves 4. (This is also attractive served in Patty Shells.)

SHRIMP WITH RICE SNOW

Boil in salted water
1 cup rice. When tender and flaky mix lightly with
3 tablespoons butter
½ cup rich milk
2 egg yolks, slightly beaten. Pour into oiled mold and set in pan of boiling water. Bake in moderate oven, 350° F., for 20 minutes, or

until firm. In top of double boiler blend
3 tablespoons butter, melted,
3 tablespoons flour
⅛ teaspoon salt. Beat until frothy. Mix with
1 cup grated Parmesan cheese
1 cup milk. Clean and wash
2 cups cooked shrimp

Stir shrimp into cheese sauce and cook over boiling water until well heated. When ready to serve, turn rice out onto a platter. Pour shrimp over it. Serves 8. (If ring mold is used for rice and center filled with shrimp, a very pretty dish results.)

CURRIED SHRIMP

Clean and wash
2 cans (each 7-oz.) shrimp or 1
pound fresh, cooked shrimp.
Melt in saucepan
1 tablespoon butter. Add
1 onion, finely chopped.
Sauté until golden brown

Blend in:
1½ teaspoon curry powder
1 tablespoon flour
2 cups chicken or meat
stock. Cook until thick-
ened. Add
½ cup rich milk

Simmer sauce about 20 minutes. Then strain and add shrimp. Keep on stove just long enough to heat shrimp. Pour over a mound of Fluffy Rice or serve rice in separate dish. Serves 6. (Chutney is the usual accompaniment.)

SHRIMP AND MUSHROOMS

Clean and cut in halves
1 can (7-oz.) shrimp. Melt in
saucepan
1½ tablespoons butter. Add:
½ teaspoon salt
¼ teaspoon pepper
¼ teaspoon Worcestershire
sauce
Few grains paprika
¾ pound mushrooms, peeled
and quartered,

2 teaspoons minced onion
1 teaspoon chopped parsley
2 teaspoons minced green
pepper
1 tablespoon grated cheese.
Simmer 10 to 15 minutes,
or until mushrooms are
tender. Blend in
2 tablespoons flour. Add
¾ cup rich milk.

Stir until smooth and add shrimp. Fill buttered ramekins with shrimp mixture and cover with buttered bread crumbs or crumbled cornflakes. Brown in hot oven, 450° F. Serves 6.

PANNED OYSTERS

Drain and wash 1 pint oysters. Place in very hot frying pan without liquor. Shake pan while oysters cook until edges curl. Add salt, pepper, and butter. Serve on hot toast. Place 1 slice of crisp bacon over oysters on each slice of toast and garnish with parsley. It is important to fry bacon first and then cook oysters at the last minute before serving. Serves 4.

OYSTER FRICASSEE

Drain and wash 1 quart oysters. Heat liquor to boiling point. Add oysters and cook until plump and edges curl. Remove with skimmer. Strain liquor through double thickness of cheesecloth. Add enough milk to oyster liquor to make 2 quarts of liquid. Prepare the following sauce.

Melt
4 tablespoons butter. Add
4 tablespoons flour. Add
2 quarts oyster liquor and milk. Cook until thickened. Add:

Few grains cayenne pepper
½ teaspoon salt
2 teaspoons chopped parsley. Pour mixture over
2 eggs, slightly beaten

Stir in oysters. Cook 1 minute. Serve in border of Mashed Potatoes. Serves 8.

OYSTERS AND MUSHROOMS

Drain 1 cup oysters. Reserve liquor. Cook oysters in very hot frying pan until edges curl. Remove to hot dish. Cook 1 cup chopped mushrooms. Drain, and reserve juice. Prepare following sauce.

Blend in top of double boiler:
3 tablespoons butter, melted,
3 tablespoons flour. Stir in
1 cup milk. Add
1 cup oyster liquor and mushroom juice. Cook 2 to 5

minutes. Add mushrooms and:
1 teaspoon onion juice
½ teaspoon lemon juice
½ teaspoon salt. Beat
1 egg

Slowly add hot mixture to beaten egg. Then add oysters and cook over hot water 1 minute, stirring constantly. Serve at once. Serves 4.

LITTLE PIGS IN BLANKETS

Season 12 oysters with salt and pepper. Wrap each oyster in thin, short slice bacon, and fasten with a toothpick. Heat a saucepan and put in the "little pigs"; cook just long enough to crisp the bacon. Quarter slices of toast and place one pig in its blanket on each small piece. Serve immediately, garnished with parsley. Serves 4. (These may also be served without toast as an hors d'oeuvre.)

ESCALLOPED CLAMS

Cut into small pieces
2 cups clams or 2 cans (7-oz.) clams. Add:
4 soda crackers, crushed,
1 egg, ·slightly beaten,

¼ cup milk
1 tablespoon melted butter
¾ teaspoon poultry seasoning
Salt and pepper to taste

Turn into greased baking dish and cover with ½ recipe Plain Pastry. Bake in hot oven, 450° F., for 20 minutes. Serves 6. (A rich, luscious dish.)

SHIRRED CLAMS

Place in shallow baking dish
8 large mushroom caps, curved side down. Dip
8 clams in mixture of:

5 tablespoons butter, melted,
½ teaspoon salt
⅛ teaspoon paprika

Place clams in mushroom caps and pour over remaining butter. Bake in hot oven, 400° F., about 15 minutes, or until tender. Serve on toast with Anchovy Sauce poured over all. Serves 4.

FRIED SHELLFISH (Clams, Scallops, Oysters, Lobster, Shrimp)

Remove shell from fish, dipping lobster and shrimp into hot water to kill quickly. Do not precook any shellfish before frying, if you desire superior results. Rinse scallops. Pinch stomach contents out of clams. Remove black intestinal tract from lobster

tail and from shrimp. Drain fish and dry between folds of absorbent paper.

Flour each fish individually and then dip in egg wash made
by adding ½ cup water to 1 beaten egg. Roll in half-and-half
mixture of crumbs made of finely ground cracker crumbs and
fine corn meal seasoned with salt and pepper. Place in frying
basket and fry in deep fat, 375° F. to 380° for 2 to 3 minutes, or
until golden brown. Drain on absorbent paper. Salt and serve.

Allow for each average serving: meat of 1 lobster; 6 to 8 large
shrimps; 4 to 6 oysters; 12 to 15 scallops; 12 clams. Serve Tartar
Sauce or Chili Sauce as an accompaniment.

At our New England roadside stands featuring Fried Clams
thinned condensed milk is often used instead of egg with water
for the "wash." This produces the sweet taste so many people
like, but very few New Englanders cook these foods in this manner in their own homes. They are of the same type as frankfurters elsewhere, an outdoor "finger food" of today.

9 VEGETABLES, NEW WAYS AND OLD

Have you ever wished for just one more new vegetable? I have. Yet in serving our guests, we find that 80 per cent prefer fresh peas! Still we are constantly trying to think up new ways to tempt them with other vegetables too. Spanish Eggplant is popular, especially with men who would never eat eggplant otherwise, my husband included. Cheese Spinach, Cheese Beans, Lyonnaise Carrots, Hot Red Cabbage are other recipes which seem to appeal the year round. Soufflé Potatoes are a real challenge to prepare, so don't be surprised if every one doesn't puff. Even the chefs I've seen fry them miss out on some. Probably the Escalloped Potatoes are the most popular version of the tuber at Toll House.

PINWHEEL ASPARAGUS CASSEROLE

Make a paste of:
1/4 pound American cheese, grated,
1 tablespoon milk

2 tablespoons chopped pimento or use 1 glass (5-oz.) pimento cheese spread

Cut 3 lengthwise slices of bread, remove crusts. Spread with cheese mixture. Roll like jelly roll and wrap in wax paper. Place in refrigerator while preparing asparagus in the following way:

Drain, reserving liquor,
1 can (2½ cups) asparagus or use 1 package frozen asparagus. Cook over low heat
2 teaspoons chopped onion in
3 tablespoons butter. Blend in

3 tablespoons flour. Add
1 cup milk, or milk and asparagus liquor combined. Add asparagus and
1 cup diced cooked ham

Pour mixture into greased baking dish. Cover top with pinwheels made by slicing cheese rolls into 1-inch sections. Bake in hot oven, 400° F., to heat through and brown top. Serves 6.

Variations: Other vegetables such as peas, carrots, string beans, Lima beans, or a package of frozen mixed vegetables may be used instead of asparagus.

CHEESE BEANS

Wash 1 pound green beans and slice lengthwise. Cook in small amount salted boiling water, about 20 minutes, until nearly done. Then place in shallow casserole and pour in enough light cream to nearly cover them. Grate American cheese over top. Bake in moderately hot oven, 375° F., until cheese is melted and brown. Serves 4.

HARVARD BEETS

Blend:
2 tablespoons butter, melted,
2 tablespoons flour. Add
¼ cup boiling water. Cook until thickened, stirring constantly. Add:

¼ cup sugar
½ cup vinegar. Season with Salt and pepper. Add
1 can (2½ cups) diced beets or 12 small beets, sliced

Heat thoroughly before serving. Serves 6.

ORANGE BEETS

Cook, peel, and slice
12 small beets. Blend:
2 tablespoons butter
2 tablespoons cornstarch

¼ cup lemon juice
2 cups orange juice
¼ cup sugar. Add
Salt and pepper to taste

Cook sauce until slightly thickened. Pour over hot sliced beets. Serves 6.

CABBAGE AU GRATIN

Remove outer leaves from small head of cabbage. Cut head into sections, remove core, wash, and drain. Place cabbage in large kettle, ⅔ full of salted boiling water. Boil, uncovered, for 20 minutes, or until tender. Drain and cut cabbage somewhat fine. Turn into buttered baking dish in alternate layers with Cheese Sauce. Cover with buttered crumbs and bake in hot oven, 450° F., until brown. Serves 6.

TEN-MINUTE CABBAGE

Remove outer leaves from small head of cabbage. Cut head in slices ¼ inch thick across leaves so they will fall in shreds. Place in salted boiling water and cook 10 minutes only. Serve with melted butter, salt, pepper, and top milk, if desired. Serves 6.

HOT RED CABBAGE

Melt in bottom of kettle
2 tablespoons butter. Add:
1 medium-sized red cabbage, shredded, (about 4 cups)
2 medium-sized apples, pared, and ·chopped,

½ cup vinegar
2 cups hot water
½ teaspoon salt
3 tablespoons sugar

Cover and steam until apples and cabbage are tender, about 20 to 25 minutes. Serves 6.

BAKED CARROTS

Wash and scrape raw carrots and cut in strips. Place in casserole, add a little water, dot with butter, sprinkle with salt and pepper, and bake in hot oven, 400° F., for about 45 minutes. If you like carrots browned, do not cover; otherwise, cover for entire cooking period. Allow 2 carrots per serving.

LYONNAISE CARROTS OR ZUCCHINI

For every cup of sliced hot carrots sauté in butter 1/4 cup sliced onions until lightly browned. Add carrots to onions and sauté together until carrots are nicely browned. Salt and pepper to taste. Allow 1/2 cup carrots for each serving. Or substitute sliced cooked zucchini for carrots.

GINGERED CARROTS

Cook, peel, slice lengthwise	1 1/2 teaspoons powdered ginger or 2 tablespoons preserved
8 carrots. Blend:	ginger with syrup
2 tablespoons sugar	2 tablespoons butter
1/4 cup water	1/4 cup light corn syrup

Cook sauce until thickened. Pour over hot carrots. Serves 4.

CAULIFLOWER HOLLANDAISE

Remove leaves from cauliflower. Cut off stalk and soak, head down, in cold water for 1/2 hour. Then cook, head up, in salted boiling water for 20 minutes, or until tender. Remove from water, drain, and put in serving dish. Serve with 1 tablespoon Hollandaise Sauce beside each portion. Serves 4 to 6.

STUFFED CELERY

Cut tender outside stalks of celery in pieces 4 inches long. Remove all green leaves, retaining yellow leaves on inner stalks. Mix a few chopped stuffed olives with a package of Philadelphia cream cheese. Or use 1 teaspoon chopped green pepper and 1 teaspoon chopped pimento with the cheese. Season with salt and paprika. Fill celery with mixture. Serve as an hors d'oeuvre or instead of salad with a hearty meal. Processed cheese makes a delicious and easily prepared filling.

ESCALLOPED CELERY AND CARROTS

Scrape and cut small	1 cup diced celery. Prepare
3 medium-sized carrots (about	1 cup White Sauce (page 73).
2 cups). Cook in small	Add
amount salted water with	1/2 cup grated yellow cheese

Stir sauce until thickened. Place layer of vegetables in casserole, then layer of sauce, repeating until all are used. Cover with buttered bread crumbs and bake in hot oven, 450° F., until brown. Serves 6.

CORN AND TOMATO CASSEROLE

Place in a casserole:
2 cups corn, drained,

1 can (1⅓ cups) tomato soup
1 slice stale bread, crumbled

Mix all ingredients and cover with buttered bread or cracker crumbs. Sprinkle with paprika. Bake in hot oven, 450° F., for about 30 minutes. Serves 4.

SAUTÉED CORN WITH PEPPERS

Melt in saucepan
2 tablespoons shortening. Add
1 medium-sized green pepper, chopped fine. Cook until

nearly tender. Add
1 can (2½ cups) corn
¾ teaspoon salt

Cook until tender and very lightly browned, about 5 minutes. Serve at once. Serves 4.

SPANISH EGGPLANT

Peel good-sized eggplant and cut into 1-inch cubes. Cook in salted boiling water until tender, 10 to 15 minutes. Prepare following sauce:

Melt in spider
2 tablespoons butter. Add
1 green pepper, cut small,
1 small onion, sliced thin.
Cook until tender. Add:
1 small bottle stuffed olives, cut fine
½ bunch celery, sliced and

parboiled until tender.
Heat
1 can (2½ cups) tomatoes.
Add drained eggplant, celery, and pepper mixture.
Season with:
½ cup sugar
1 tablespoon salt

Turn mixture into casserole and bake in moderate oven, 350° F., until brown and thick. Serves 8.

Variation: Substitute sliced cooked zucchini for eggplant.

CREAMED MUSHROOMS

Wash and slice ½ pound mushrooms. Cook for about 3 minutes in 3 tablespoons butter. Avoid overcooking. Sprinkle with 2 tablespoons flour. Blend in. Pour in slowly 1 cup cold milk. Stir until thickened. Season with Salt and pepper

If you prefer more sauce in proportion to mushrooms, use 4 tablespoons flour, 4 tablespoons butter, and 2 cups milk. Serves 4.

OVEN-COOKED ONIONS

Peel onions, allowing 1 or 2 for each serving, and place in casserole. Add ½ teaspoon salt and ¼ cup cold water. Cover and bake in slow oven, 275° F., for 3 hours. Pour melted butter over onions before serving.

STUFFED ONIONS

Peel 8 onions. Cook in salted boiling water until slightly soft. Rinse with cold water to make firm. Push out centers. Place onion shells in well-buttered baking dish. Fill each onion with a mixture of:

1 cup bread crumbs
2 tablespoons tomato pulp
2 tablespoons butter
2 teaspoons chopped parsley

2 tablespoons chopped pimento
2 egg yolks
½ cup diced cooked celery
1 teaspoon salt

Bake in hot oven, 400° F., for 20 minutes. Serves 4 to 6.

GLAZED ONIONS

Boil until tender 6 to 8 small onions in 4 cups water seasoned with 1 teaspoon salt. Drain.

Melt in frying pan 4 tablespoons butter. Add 4 tablespoons sugar

Place onions in mixture. Cook over low heat until well glazed, turning to glaze evenly. Sprinkle with minced parsley and serve at once. Serves 4.

Variation: Carrots and turnips are also delicious cooked this way.

BAKED PEAS

Brown in frying pan
6 slices bacon, chopped.
Pour off fat and add:
4 cups fresh peas, cooked,
1 teaspoon salt

$\frac{1}{8}$ teaspoon pepper
1 cup rich milk. Turn into casserole and cover with
$\frac{1}{2}$ cup buttered bread crumbs

Bake in a hot oven, 400° F., for 20 minutes. Add additional Broiled Bacon for a delicious luncheon dish. Serves 6.

STUFFED PEPPERS

Wash green peppers, remove tops, and scrape seeds from inside. Parboil in salted water for about 15 minutes. Place peppers in greased baking dish. In each pepper place some soft bread crumbs and a bit of butter. Drop an egg on crumbs and sprinkle with salt and pepper. Cover with more crumbs and bits of butter. Bake in moderate oven, 375° F., until egg is firm, about 10 minutes. Serve with Cheese Sauce and strip of cooked bacon. Allow 1 pepper for each serving. A very delicious luncheon dish.

BAKED POTATOES

(See Primer for Brides, page 71)

BAKED POTATOES EN CASSEROLE

Wash potatoes, place in baking dish, cover, and bake in slow oven, 275° F., for 3 hours, or at 250° for 4 to 5 hours. Peel and serve as border for Baked Picnic Ham.

POTATOES BAKED WITH BACON OR SAUSAGE

Wash, pare potatoes, and remove centers with apple corer. Insert in each potato a slice of bacon or section of sausage. Place in pan and bake in moderate oven, 375° F., until potatoes are brown. Baste with fat while baking. Sprinkle with salt and pepper. Allow 1 potato for each serving.

CHEESE POTATO BALLS

Peel, boil, and mash potatoes. Season well with butter, salt and pepper and beat in enough hot milk to make smooth and creamy. Allow mixture to cool slightly for ease in handling and to stiffen somewhat.

Between palms of hands roll a heaping tablespoon of potato around a cube of American cheese. Then roll ball in rather finely crushed corn flakes and dip in melted butter.

Place in baking pan and bake in moderate oven, 350° F., until brown. Or make ahead and reheat in hot oven just before serving time. Serve at once. (Two small balls make a more attractive serving than one large one.)

POTATO CHEESE PUFF

Prepare
3 cups mashed potatoes. Heat in top of double boiler
½ cup milk. Add
¼ pound cheese, grated. Stir until smooth. Beat
2 egg yolks with
2 tablespoons cream. Stir into cheese mixture. Then add mashed potatoes, whipping until light and fluffy. Add:
3 tablespoons butter
2 egg whites, beaten stiff.
Season with
Salt and paprika

Pile roughly into buttered baking dish, sprinkle lightly with grated cheese, and bake in hot oven, 400° F., for 25 minutes. Serve at once. Serves 6 to 8.

PIMENTO AND CHEESE POTATO

Prepare
2 cups cooked, diced potatoes. In top of double boiler scald
1 cup milk. Make paste of:
2 teaspoons cornstarch
1 teaspoon mustard
Salt and pepper, mixed with cold water. Add to milk and stir well. Add
1 cup grated cheese. Cook until thick

171

Line bottom of casserole with diced potatoes, sprinkle with ¼ cup sliced pimento, and pour in half of cheese mixture. Add remaining potatoes, sprinkle with additional pimento, and pour remaining cheese mixture over top. Cover with buttered bread crumbs. Bake in moderate oven, 375° F., for ½ hour to brown crumbs. Serves 4.

DUCHESS POTATOES

Prepare
2 cups hot, riced potatoes.
Add:

2 tablespoons butter
½ teaspoon salt
3 egg yolks, slightly beaten

Using pastry tube or fork, make border of potatoes around Broiled Steak. Brush over with 3 beaten egg whites, diluted with 1 teaspoon water. Brown in hot oven. Serves 4. These potatoes may be prepared on cooky sheet, browned in oven, and served with other foods.

ESCALLOPED POTATOES
(See Primer for Brides, page 72)

DELMONICO POTATOES

Place alternating layers of cold boiled cubed potatoes, White Sauce (page 73), and grated cheese in buttered baking dish. Cover with buttered crumbs. Bake in moderate oven, 375° F., about 15 minutes until well-heated and browned. Allow 1 medium-sized potato for each serving.

FRANCONIA POTATOES

Wash and pare medium-sized sweet or white potatoes. Parboil for 10 minutes. Drain and place in pan in which meat is roasting. Bake until soft, about 40 minutes, basting with fat when basting meat. Prepare 1 potato for each serving.

MASHED POTATO AND CARROT

Peel and boil potatoes and carrots in salted water. When cooked thoroughly, mash each separately. Season to taste. To potatoes add hot milk and butter as for mashed potatoes. Then combine vegetables and mix well. Allow 1 carrot and 1 small potato for each serving.

MASHED POTATOES
(See Primer for Brides, page 72)

PAN FRIED POTATOES

Melt ½ cup bacon fat in spider. Slice raw potatoes ½ inch thick, allowing 1 medium-sized potato for each serving. Turn into pan and cover. Fry slowly in fat, about 30 to 45 minutes, turning occasionally. Drain on absorbent paper. Sprinkle with salt and pepper. Serve hot.

PARSLEY BUTTERED POTATOES
(See Primer for Brides, page 71)

POTATO CROQUETTES

Combine:

2 cups riced potatoes	½ teaspoon salt
1 tablespoon melted butter	Few grains cayenne
⅛ teaspoon white pepper	1 teaspoon chopped parsley
¼ teaspoon celery salt	Few drops lemon juice
	1 egg yolk

Shape mixture into croquettes, roll in crumbs, and then in egg white, beaten with a little water. Roll in crumbs again. Chill. Place in frying basket and fry in deep fat, 390° F., for about 1 minute, until brown. Drain on absorbent paper. Garnish with parsley. Serve at once. Serves 4.

Variation: **SURPRISE POTATOES.** Prepare above mixture but form into small round shells. Fill with finely minced ham moistened with Yellow Béchamel Sauce. Cover with potato. Roll, dip, and fry same as croquettes.

POTATO NESTS

Cook and mash potatoes. Add hot milk, butter, and seasonings. Heat until smooth. Then, using a pastry tube, arrange

173

potatoes on platter in "nests" about 2 inches across with round pieces for bottoms and sides piled about 1½ inches high. If no pastry tube is available, arrange potatoes with fork, leaving edges rough. Brush with melted butter or egg white, beaten stiff, and place in hot oven, 400° F., to brown for a minute. Fill centers with any small vegetables like carrots and peas, either mixed or separate, or string beans. Serve with meat or fish. Allow 1 nest for each serving.

POTATOES À LA MAÎTRE D'HÔTEL

Wash and pare potatoes. With French cutter or melon scoop carefully cut into balls, or use very small new potatoes. Cook until tender in salted boiling water. Drain and pour Maître d'Hôtel Butter over potatoes. Allow 1 medium-sized potato for each serving.

POTATOES À LA SUISSE

Bake medium-sized potatoes. When done, remove slice from top of each. Scoop out centers. Mash and season. Break 1 egg into each potato shell, refill with mashed potato, leaving it fluffy on top. Bake in moderate oven, 375° F., for 10 minutes to set egg and brown potato. Serve with a strip or two of cooked Bacon on plate with potato. Allow 1 potato for each serving. This is an excellent luncheon dish.

Variations: Substitute for egg, creamed chipped beef or creamed fish.

SOUFFLÉ POTATOES

Peel potatoes to oval shape. Do not wash, but wipe with towel. Cut lengthwise in flat slices about ⅛ inch thick. Turn into melted fat that is just warm and place over heat. When potatoes are nearly done, they will swim on top of fat, and swell like little cushions.

Have another deep pan of very hot fat ready. When all potatoes have come to top, remove from first pan and place in very hot fat in second pan. When nicely browned, remove, salt well, drain on absorbent paper, and serve on a napkin.

This is given exactly as a chef in one of the oldest restaurants in Paris gave it to me. He used both white and sweet potatoes and they were excellent. Allow 1 potato for each serving.

SWEET POTATO BALLS WITH PINEAPPLE

Boil and peel sweet potatoes. Mash and season well with butter, salt and pepper. Add enough pineapple juice to soften. Roll about 1 tablespoonful potato at a time between palms with 1-inch piece of pineapple as center of ball. Cover with rather finely crumbled corn flakes and dip in melted butter.

Place on baking sheet in hot oven, 400° F., to brown. Or make ahead and reheat in hot oven just before serving time. Serve at once. Allow 1 for each serving.

CANDIED SWEET POTATOES

Select 6 sweet potatoes of uniform size and cook in salted boiling water until tender. Drain and peel. Make a syrup of:

1 cup sugar	⅓ cup butter
¾ cup water	

Bring mixture to boiling point and pour over potatoes, which have been placed in baking pan. Bake in hot oven, 400° F., for 20 minutes, or until sweet potatoes are well glazed and slightly brown. Serves 6.

GLAZED SWEET POTATOES

Select 6 sweet potatoes of uniform size and boil in salted water until tender. Peel and cut in half lengthwise. Place in oiled baking pan and sprinkle with:

½ cup brown sugar	4 tablespoons butter. Add
½ teaspoon salt.	¼ cup water
Dot with	

Bake, turning often, in hot oven, 400° F., until brown, about 20 minutes. Serves 6.

STUFFED SWEET POTATOES

Bake medium-sized potatoes in hot oven, 450° F., until done, about 40 to 45 minutes. Remove from oven, cut off top of one side and scoop out insides. Mash, and moisten with butter and cream. Season with salt and pepper. Refill skins and place ½ marshmallow on top. Place in hot oven again for 5 minutes. Serve hot. Allow 1 potato for each serving.

SHERRIED SWEET POTATOES WITH PECANS

Select 6 medium-sized sweet potatoes or yams and boil in salted water until tender. Peel and cut in thick slices. Place layer of potato in baking dish.

Combine:
½ cup brown sugar
1 cup orange juice
1 tablespoon grated orange rind
⅓ cup sherry

Pour a little of this mixture over potatoes. Sprinkle generously with coarsely cut pecans. Repeat layers of potatoes, liquid, and pecans until casserole is filled. Pour remaining juice over top, sprinkle with nuts, and dot with butter. Cover and bake in moderate oven, 350° F., for 30 minutes or until juice has been absorbed by potatoes and top is browned. Serves 6.

APPLES STUFFED WITH SWEET POTATOES

Core large red apples and cut crosswise to make two circles. Place in shallow baking pan with cut side of circle up. Fill centers and cover with brown sugar. Bake slowly in moderate oven, 350° F., about 10 to 15 minutes, or until soft.

Prepare well-seasoned and smoothly mashed sweet potatoes. Pile on top of apple, swirling potato into attractive peaks. Cover with melted butter and place in hot oven, 400°, long enough to reheat and brown lightly. Allow ½ apple and about ½ sweet potato for each serving.

Variation: Substitute pineapple rings for apple and flavor sweet potatoes with pineapple juice.

FLUFFY RICE

(See Primer for Brides, page 72)

SPINACH

(See Primer for Brides, page 73)

CHEESE SPINACH

Trim and wash spinach. Cook in covered kettle with only the water which drips from leaves. When crispness is gone, drain and place in baking dish. Cover with grated cheese or Cheese Sauce. Bake in moderate oven, 350° F., until cheese is melted and brown. Allow ½ pound spinach for each serving.

HARVEST SCALLOPED TOMATOES

Brown and crisp in oven	1 large onion, cut fine
2 cups bread cubes in	2 tablespoons sugar
2 tablespoons hot fat.	½ teaspoon salt
Combine:	Few grains pepper. Add
1 can (2½ cups) tomatoes	bread cubes
1 cup diced celery	

Turn mixture into large greased casserole. Bake in moderate oven, 375° F., for 45 minutes. Serves 6.

Variation: Add ½ cup grated cheese and make this a main-course dish.

ZUCCHINI (ITALIAN SQUASH) WITH CHEESE

Wash 3 small zucchini and cut into ¼-inch slices. Cook in small amount salted water until soft. Place in casserole and cover with a mixture of:

¼ cup milk	⅔ cup grated cheese. Dot with
1 egg, beaten,	4 tablespoons butter

Cook in hot oven, 400° F. to 450°, until cheese is melted and top nicely browned. Serves 4.

```
┌─────────────────────────────────────────┐
│                                          │
│        10. ATTRACTIVE                    │
│  ॐ    SALADS AND          ॐ             │
│        SALAD DRESSINGS                    │
│                                          │
└─────────────────────────────────────────┘
```

ॐ

Here is where the womenfolk will shine. As I look around our dining room at noon most of them are enjoying the Bouquet of Salads. This is composed of chicken or shrimp in a lettuce cup, a vegetable salad, (perhaps Puffed Tomato Salad), and usually a molded fruit salad served on watercress. These three are arranged on dark green salad plates with lime sherbet in a lemon cup resting in the center. When men select salads, they usually want mixed greens with Roquefort Dressing. They also enthuse over our Condensed Milk Salad Dressing with molded fruit salads. As you prepare salads at home, remember to wash the greens before you start your cooking. That allows time for you to return greens to the refrigerator to crisp before serving time.

BEET, CABBAGE, AND PINEAPPLE SALAD

Sprinkle with water and drain
2 cups finely sliced cabbage. Let stand in refrigerator 15 minutes to crisp.

Combine with 1 cup diced pineapple, drained.
Moisten with
Mayonnaise. Season with
Salt.

Serve on lettuce or cabbage leaves. Garnish with 1 cup ground raw beets and serve at once. Serves 6.

CABBAGE SALAD

Melt
Butter size of egg and add:
1 cup mild vinegar
1 tablespoon dry mustard
1 tablespoon salt

2 tablespoons sugar
2 eggs. Cook until mixture thickens, stirring constantly, and pour over
4 cups shredded cabbage

Chill before serving. Serves 6. (This is a standby recipe used at New England Baked Bean Suppers.)

COLE SLAW

Mix together:
1 small cabbage, sliced fine,
1 green pepper, sliced thin,
3 pimentos, sliced thin,

10 stuffed olives, sliced,
Pour over all
1½ cups French Dressing

Mix well. Let stand a few hours to marinate. Serve as salad course or as relish with beans or meat. Serves 8.

"CARROT" SALAD

Season cottage or cream cheese with salt and pepper, and soften with a little cream. Shape into small "carrots." Roll in grated raw carrot and insert a carrot leaf or two in large end. Serve on lettuce with French or Mayonnaise Dressing. Allow 2 "carrots" for each serving.

POTATO SALAD
(See Primer for Brides, page 74)

GREEN SALAD
(See Primer for Brides, page 74)

SPRING TONIC SALAD

Sprinkle with water and drain
2 cups finely sliced cabbage. Let stand in refrigerator for 15 minutes to crisp. Combine with

1 cup grated raw carrot
1 cup chopped tart apple (unpeeled)
½ cup chopped green pepper
1 small onion, grated. Season with salt

Moisten mixture with a little salad dressing. Serve on lettuce or cabbage leaves. Serves 8.

TOMATO SURPRISE

Scoop out centers of small tomatoes, or use canned Rose Pepper Apples. Mix removed tomato pulp with Piccalilli, mayonnaise, salt and pepper. A few finely cut pieces of cucumber also add flavor. Fill tomatoes with mixture and garnish tops with a little mayonnaise, dash of paprika and a tiny lettuce leaf stuck on top. Serve on lettuce leaves. Allow 1 tomato for each serving.

PUFFED TOMATO SALAD

Slice off stem end of a small tomato. Gash tomato at ½-inch intervals, cutting well down into center. Into each gash insert thin slice cucumber or hard-cooked egg. Place in cup of lettuce and garnish with mayonnaise. Allow 1 tomato for each serving.

VEGETABLE SALAD

For each serving arrange on crisp lettuce 2 or 3 flowerets of cauliflower, small amount of diced cooked or raw carrots, and small amount of peas or string beans. Garnish center of salad with a bit of beet. Serve with French Dressing.

CORNUCOPIA SALAD

Dice
3 medium-sized cooked potatoes

2 medium-sized cooked beets.
Add
½ cup cooked peas

Mix well with generous quantity of salad dressing and season. (A teaspoon of horseradish may be used in the dressing, if you like.) Roll large thin slices of boiled ham into cornucopias. Fasten each with a toothpick. Fill with vegetable mixture and place on crisp lettuce leaves. Garnish with olives and parsley. Serves 6.

AUTUMN DELIGHT

Cut red apple into very thin crosswise slices. Remove core from each slice. Arrange very thin, small round slices raw carrots on top of apple. Heap minced dates and nuts in center. Serve on lettuce with French or Mayonnaise Dressing.

PINEAPPLE WALDORF SALAD

Combine:
1 red apple, unpeeled, and cubed,
1 slice pineapple, cut up,
2 tablespoons walnut meats.
Marinate in
French Dressing

Before serving moisten with mayonnaise. Serve in apple cup or on lettuce garnished with 2 strips of red apple, set on end. Sprinkle with broken walnuts. Serves 1.

PINEAPPLE SUPREME SALAD

Combine:
1 cup diced celery
1 cup cubed pineapple
½ cup pimento, cut small

Mix with mayonnaise. Arrange in small mounds on lettuce leaves. Serves 4.

GINGER AND PEAR SALAD

Cut peeled pears lengthwise in thin slices. Arrange in circles on lettuce bed, so that the slices form petals of a flower. Put a little chopped ginger in center of each. Use strips of green pepper for stems. Serve mayonnaise separately. Allow 1 pear for each serving.

SPICED PEACH SALAD

Cook for 3 minutes:
½ cup mild vinegar
6 cloves
1 stick cinnamon
½ cup sugar. Pour
mixture over
6 halves peaches or pears,
drained

Chill several hours. Drain and arrange fruit, with curved side down, on lettuce. Fill hollows with cream cheese. Garnish with mayonnaise. Serves 6.

PEACH MELBA SALAD

Pipe softened and seasoned cream cheese through pastry tube over cut surface of each peach. Fill hollows with fresh raspberries. Serve with French or Boiled Dressing. Allow 1 large half peach for each serving.

HARVEST SALAD

Cut unpeeled red apple into thin wedges and dip in pineapple juice, lemon juice, or salt water to prevent darkening. Arrange on chopped endive in triangles, using 3 slices of apple. On top of each slice of apple place a section of grapefruit and then arrange sections of orange. Build up sides but allow red apple skin to show and keep center open. Fill centers with seasoned cottage cheese. Pour French Dressing over all.

BACON SALAD

Mix:

½ cup diced apples
½ cup diced celery
¼ cup mayonnaise. Let stand for 5 to 10 minutes.

Shred

1 small head lettuce. Add
1 cup cold cooked bacon, cut in short strips

Combine mixtures and toss lightly together with fork. Serve at once. Serves 6.

CHICKEN AND WHITE GRAPE SALAD

Combine:
2 cups cubed chicken
1 cup white grapes, seeded. Add
French dressing to moisten

well and let stand. Before serving, stir in:
½ cup buttered, toasted almonds
½ cup mayonnaise

Garnish with additional toasted almonds and place on each serving a grape sliced part way open and stuffed with a slice of pimento. Serves 4.

PINEAPPLE AND CHICKEN SALAD

On cup of lettuce place a slice of pineapple. Cut white meat of chicken into thin slices and then cut into long slivers. Cut celery in the same way as thinly as possible. Heap these on pineapple or pack log-cabin style. Garnish with mayonnaise which has had whipped cream and a little pineapple juice added to it.

HAWAIIAN CHICKEN SALAD

Combine:
2 cups cubed chicken
1 cup pineapple, cut up. Add French dressing to moisten.

Let stand and stir in before serving:
½ cup mayonnaise
Salt and pepper to taste

Place on pineapple rings. Garnish with watercress and stuffed olive slices. Serves 4.

AVOCADO AND FRESH CRAB SALAD

Cut avocados (alligator pears) in half and peel. Place each half in a lettuce cup and fill cavity with fresh flaked crab. Cover with Russian Dressing and garnish with pimento strips and caviar. Allow ½ avocado for each serving.

JELLIED SALADS

After combining all essential ingredients chill them until slightly congealed. Then turn into one large mold or several individual ones. Chilling first will avoid, to a great extent, the "floating" or "sinking" of solids. You will soon discover which foods float and which sink. For instance, cabbage and banana slices float as will almost all fresh fruit. Canned fruit sinks. If you wish to achieve a certain design in a mold, pour a small amount of gelatin on the bottom of the pan, arrange the design of fruit or vegetable over it, and then allow this small amount of mixture to set or harden before filling mold with the remainder. Fresh pineapple, because of the enzyme it contains, can never be added to gelatin salads. Always use this fruit cooked or canned.

To unmold salads, fill a pan with hot water. Dip molds quickly in and out and have water deep enough to reach well up the sides. Then run a butter spreader along the sides of the mold to loosen the gelatin and break the vacuum. So treated the molded gelatin will slide out easily. At Toll House we use aluminum muffin pans as molds and serve the salads in lettuce cups. With molded fruits we serve Condensed Milk Salad Dressing.

JELLIED CABBAGE SALAD

Soften
2 tablespoons gelatin in
½ cup cold water. Add
1½ cups boiling water and cool. Shred:
2 cups cabbage

2 green peppers. Add:
1 pimento, sliced,
1 teaspoon salt
½ cup sugar
¼ cup lemon juice
½ cup vinegar

Mix gelatin and cabbage mixture until thoroughly blended. Turn into quart-sized square mold. Chill. When firm cut into 2-inch cubes. Place on lettuce leaves. Serve with Boiled Dressing or mayonnaise. Serves 6.

ASHEVILLE SALAD

Dissolve over hot water
½ pound cream cheese in
1 can (1⅓ cups) tomato soup.
Soften
2 tablespoons gelatin in

½ cup cold water. Combine mixtures. Add:
¼ teaspoon salt
1½ green peppers, cut fine,
½ cup chopped celery

When gelatin is completely dissolved, remove from heat and add 2 tablespoons mayonnaise. Pour into molds and place in refrigerator. When firm serve on lettuce leaves with mayonnaise. Serves 6.

TWOPENNY SALAD

To
1 package lemon gelatin, add:
1¾ cups hot water
¾ teaspoon salt

¾ teaspoon celery salt
⅛ cup tomato ketchup
⅛ cup vinegar. Pour over
2 cups finely shredded cabbage

Mix well. Pour into molds. Chill and serve on lettuce leaves. Garnish with salad dressing. Serves 6.

MOLDED JELLY SALAD
(See Primer for Brides, page 75)

MOLDED MEXICAN SALAD

To
1 package lemon gelatin, add:
1 cup boiling water
¾ cup cold water or fruit juices
2 tablespoons mild vinegar
½ teaspoon salt

1 teaspoon chili powder
1 cup shredded cabbage
½ cup diced celery
1 green pepper, chopped,
2 pimentos, chopped,
½ cup diced apple

Mix well. Pour into molds. Chill and serve on lettuce leaves. Garnish with salad dressing. Serves 3.

Variation: Substitute lime gelatin for lemon and ½ cup diced beets for apple. Add 1 tablespoon horseradish for a different combination. Pour into molds. Chill and serve on lettuce leaves. Garnish with Condensed Milk Salad Dressing.

FROZEN TOMATO SALAD

Strain into saucepan
3 cups canned tomato. Add:
1 tablespoon chopped onion
4 tablespoons chopped pimento
4 tablespoons chopped green pepper. Cook 5 minutes. Remove from heat. Add:
2 teaspoons gelatin,

softened in
2 tablespoons cold water, and
3 tablespoons vinegar
1 tablespoon lemon juice
1 teaspoon grated horseradish
¾ teaspoon salt
Few grains cayenne

Turn into refrigerator trays and let stand 3 hours. Serve on lettuce with rings of green pepper. Garnish with mayonnaise. Serves 8.

185

JELLIED BEET AND CELERY SALAD

Soften
1 tablespoon gelatin in
⅓ cup cold water for 10
minutes. Dissolve in
½ cup hot water or beet water.
Add:
¼ cup sugar

2½ tablespoons lemon juice
1½ teaspoons horseradish
Few grains pepper
½ teaspoon salt. When mixture begins to thicken, add
¼ cup diced, cooked beets
½ cup celery, cut fine

Turn into molds. Chill and serve on lettuce with Boiled Dressing. Serves 6.

TOMATO JELLY SALAD

Soften
2 tablespoons gelatin in
½ cup cold water. Cook
1 can (2½ cups) tomatoes with
½-inch piece bay leaf
½ teaspoon mixed spices

1 rounded teaspoon celery salt
2 tablespoons sugar
½ small Bermuda onion, chopped. When vegetables are soft, add gelatin and stir until dissolved

Pour into ring molds. Chill. Serve on bed of shredded endive. Fill center with Cottage Cheese and Chives Spread. Serves 6.

RED CREST SALAD

Dissolve
1 package strawberry gelatin in
2 cups hot canned tomatoes. Mix well. Add:
⅔ tablespoon prepared horseradish
½ tablespoon scraped onion

½ tablespoon salt
Dash cayenne. Force through sieve. Add:
¼ cup pickles, chopped,
1 cup shredded cabbage
½ teaspoon celery seed
1 pimento, chopped

Pour into molds. Chill. Serves 6. (A wonderful salad!)

JELLIED WALDORF SALAD

To
1 package lemon gelatin, add:
1 pint boiling water
1 cup diced apple
½ cup diced celery, salted,
½ cup broken walnuts or pecans

Pour into molds. Chill. Serves 6.

AMBER SALAD

To
1 package orange gelatin, add:
½ cup boiling water
1½ cups dry ginger ale
⅔ cup unpeeled apple, thinly
sliced in 1-inch lengths
¼ cup celery, cut fine,
½ cup grapes, halved and seeded,
½ cup crushed pineapple

Pour into molds. Chill. Serves 6.

CRANBERRY SALAD

Cut in half
2 cups cranberries. Cook in
1 cup water for 20 minutes. Soften
1 tablespoon gelatin in
½ cup cold water. Add
1½ cups sugar and gelatin to
cranberries. Stir well and remove from heat. Cool. Add:
½ cup diced celery
½ cup diced apples
3 tablespoons broken nutmeats

Pour into molds. Chill. Serve on crisp lettuce leaves and garnish with mayonnaise. Serves 6.

TOLL HOUSE FROZEN FRUIT SALAD

Beat until stiff
⅔ cup heavy cream. Gradually beat in:
⅓ cup mayonnaise
1 teaspoon gelatin, soaked in
3 tablespoons pineapple syrup and dissolved over hot water,
1 teaspoon powdered sugar
2 tablespoons lemon juice
1 tablespoon maraschino syrup. Then fold in:
½ cup cubed bananas
¾ cup pineapple, diced,
½ cup maraschino cherries, sliced

187

Turn into refrigerator trays and freeze, stirring occasionally over a period of 4 to 5 hours. (May also be frozen like ice cream.) Remove from pans when frozen and serve on lettuce hearts. Garnish with pieces of cherry cut to make rose petals. Serves 6.

SAVORY GRAPEFRUIT SALAD

Remove sections from 2 grapefruit. Slice 1 pimento. Soften 2 tablespoons gelatin in ¼ cup cold water. Dissolve in ½ cup boiling water. Add: ¼ cup sugar ½ cup lemon juice Juice of grapefruit ½ cup minced celery ¼ cup chopped olives

Arrange grapefruit sections and pimento in cold, wet mold. Pour over them the gelatin mixture. Chill. Serve on lettuce leaves with mayonnaise. Serves 6.

CARDINAL PEAR

To 1 package cherry gelatin, add: 1½ cups hot water ½ cup canned pear juice 1 tablespoon chopped ginger ½ teaspoon salt 2 tablespoons lemon juice 4 pears, quartered, 1 cup white grapes, seeded

Pour into molds. Chill. Serves 6.

MACAROON PEAR SALAD

Frost each half of pear with softened cream cheese. Roll in crushed dry macaroon crumbs. Place tablespoon salad dressing on lettuce and cover with pear placed hollow side down.

For a main-course salad put pear halves together by filling hollows with cream cheese and standing pears up in lettuce cups. Garnish with rings of cherry at stem end of pear.

Variation: Bananas may be substituted for pears. The bananas are then "frosted" with the cream cheese and rolled in macaroon crumbs.

PERSIAN PEACH SALAD

Combine:
1 cup canned peach juice
¼ cup vinegar
½ cup sugar
12 whole cloves
3 small sticks cinnamon.
Bring to a boil. Add

1 cup canned sliced peaches.
Simmer for 10 minutes.
Strain syrup and add water
to make 2 cups liquid. Dissolve in this
1 package orange gelatin

Chill gelatin mixture and when slightly thickened, fold in peaches. Chill until firm. Served with a ham entrée, this makes a delightful luncheon. Serves 4 to 6.

Variation: Pears, apricots, or pineapple may be used instead of peaches to give variety.

TROPICAL SALAD

To
1 package mint gelatin add:
1 cup boiling water
1 cup cold water. Stir and

mix well. Add:
1 apple, diced,
1 banana, sliced,
3 slices pineapple, diced

Pour into mold. Chill and serve with mayonnaise flavored with pineapple juice. Serves 6.

ORIENTAL SALAD

To
1 package lemon gelatin and
½ package cherry gelatin add:
1 cup boiling water
1 cup cherry juice
2 tablespoons vinegar

½ teaspoon salt. When mixed, add:
¾ cup pitted red cherries
½ apple, diced,
3 slices pineapple, diced

Pour into mold. Chill. Serve on lettuce with mayonnaise. Serves 6.

189

LIME SALAD

To
1 package lime gelatin add:
1 cup boiling water
1 cup pineapple juice
2 tablespoons vinegar

½ teaspoon salt. Stir well. Add:
3 slices pineapple, diced,
1 pimento, finely cut,
1 orange, in sections,
½ cup finely cut celery

Pour into mold. Chill. Serve with mayonnaise. Serves **6.**

BLACK RASPBERRY SALAD

To
1 package orange or lemon
  gelatin add:
1 pint boiling water

Juice from 1 can (2½ **cups)**
black raspberries
1 tablespoon vinegar
Dash of salt

Place raspberries, cubed pineapple, orange slices or sliced peaches in individual molds. Cover with gelatin mixture and chill. Serves 6.

Variation: For a delicious layer salad, mold this in a thin layer. When firm, spread with softened cream cheese. Cover cheese with layer of Golden Glow Salad mixture. Allow to harden. Then cut in slices and serve on lettuce with the layer side up.

EAST INDIA SALAD

Work until smooth
2 packages cream cheese.
  Moisten with
2 tablespoons milk
2 tablespoons cream. Add:
½ cup grated American cheese
1 cup whipped cream
1 tablespoon gelatin,

softened in
1 tablespoon cold water and
  dissolved in
2 tablespoons boiling **water.**
  Add:
½ teaspoon salt
¼ teaspoon paprika

Turn into individual molds. Chill. Serve on lettuce leaves, sprinkle with chopped green pepper and pimento and garnish with mayonnaise. Serves 6.

190

Variation: Turn mold out on slice of pineapple and omit green pepper and pimento.

DELICIOUS SALAD

To
1 package lemon gelatin add
1 pint hot water. Beat in:
1 can (2½ cups) crushed pineapple
3 packages cream cheese

Salt and pepper
Speck prepared mustard
Dash of spices. Add:
¼ cup chopped pimento. As mixture thickens, beat in
½ cup whipped cream

PINEAPPLE MINT SALAD

To
1 package lime gelatin add:
1 cup boiling water
1 cup canned pineapple juice and water combined

1 cup crushed pineapple
⅛ teaspoon peppermint extract
1 cup finely cut cabbage

Pour into molds. Chill. Serves 6.

Variation: To make a layer salad, pour into shallow pan. Chill and cover with layer of Red Crest Salad.

GOLDEN GLOW SALAD

Dissolve
1 package lemon gelatin in
1 cup boiling water. Add
1 cup canned pineapple juice
½ teaspoon salt
1 tablespoon vinegar. When

mixture thickens add:
1 cup pineapple, diced and drained,
1 cup carrots, ground,
⅓ cup nuts, cut fine

Pour into mold. Chill. When firm serve on lettuce. Garnish with mayonnaise. Serves 8.

SALAD DRESSINGS

BOILED DRESSING

Heat in saucepan:
3/4 cup vinegar
1/4 cup water. Mix together:
1/3 cup sugar
1 teaspoon salt
2 tablespoons cornstarch
1 teaspoon dry mustard. Combine mixtures and cook until
thick. Add:
1 egg, beaten, or 2 egg yolks
1 tablespoon butter. Cook until clear. Cool. Thin with
Milk when ready to serve

Makes 1 pint dressing after thinning. (This dressing will keep for weeks without milk.)

Variation: Beat in 3 to 4 tablespoons of soft peanut butter to make a delicious dressing for fruit salads.

FRUIT SALAD DRESSING

Cook for about 4 minutes:
1/4 cup orange juice
3 tablespoons lemon juice
1/4 cup sugar. Add:
2 eggs, beaten, and cook until
custard consistency. Chill.
Add
1/2 to 1 cup whipped cream

Makes 2 cups of dressing. Serve with fruit salad.

CONDENSED MILK SALAD DRESSING

Beat until thick and lemon-
colored
1 egg. Add
1 tablespoon dry mustard
1 tablespoon salt
1/4 teaspoon pepper
1/2 teaspoon paprika. Add
3/4 to 1 cup vinegar, according
to strength
1 can condensed milk
1/4 cup melted butter

Beat thoroughly, but do not cook. Chill and serve on shredded cabbage or cole slaw.

Variation: Beat 2 tablespoons soft peanut butter into this mixture to make delicious dressing for fruit salads.

FRENCH DRESSING
(See Primer for Brides, page 75)

TOMATO FRENCH DRESSING

Combine:

1 can (1⅓ cups) tomato soup
¾ cup vinegar
½ cup sugar
1½ cups salad oil
1 teaspoon salt

½ teaspoon pepper
1 teaspoon paprika
2 tablespoons Worcestershire sauce
1 tablespoon prepared mustard

Beat with rotary beater until blended. Store in covered jar in refrigerator. Makes 1 quart of dressing. (Keeps well).

Variation: Chopped onion, green pepper, or clove of garlic may be added.

ROQUEFORT DRESSING

Mash Roquefort cheese well with fork and slowly work in well-shaken French Dressing until of thin creamy consistency. Serve over hearts of lettuce or with any green salad. Especially nice with fruit salads.

THREE-MINUTE MAYONNAISE DRESSING

Break

1 egg into a bowl. Add
1 tablespoon salad oil. Beat vigorously until thoroughly mixed. Add 1 tablespoon oil and continue beating. Then add 2 tablespoons oil, then 3 tablespoons oil, beating after each addition until mixture begins to thicken. Add 4

tablespoons oils at a time until dressing is as stiff as desired. Add:

½ teaspoon salt
1 teaspoon sugar
1 teaspoon dry mustard
1 generous pinch paprika
1½ tablespoons lemon juice or vinegar

Beat dressing until seasonings are well blended into mixture. If this thins dressing too much, add more oil until of desired stiffness. (A deep narrow bowl is best for making mayonnaise.)

Chill and use at once or store in covered jar in refrigerator. Makes 2 cups of mayonnaise.

CHIFFONADE DRESSING

Shape up in jar:
½ cup salad oil
3 tablespoons vinegar
½ teaspoon salt, or more
¼ teaspoon paprika
1 tablespoon finely cut, hard-cooked egg

1 tablespoon finely chopped red pepper
1 tablespoon finely chopped green pepper
1 tablespoon finely chopped onion

Place on ice until ready to serve. Shake thoroughly before using. Serve on hearts of lettuce, sliced cabbage, or over any green salad. Makes 1 cup of dressing.

THOUSAND ISLAND DRESSING

Mix well:
1 cup mayonnaise
1 chopped pimento
2 tablespoons chopped sour

and sweet pickles or chow-chow
⅓ cup chili sauce or ketchup
⅓ cup whipped cream

Serve on hearts of lettuce. Makes 2 cups of dressing.

Variation: One chopped hard-cooked egg makes a nice addition.

RUSSIAN DRESSING

Combine:
1 cup mayonnaise
3 tablespoons chili sauce
3 tablespoons finely chopped green pepper
2 tablespoons finely chopped

red pepper or pimento
2 drops tabasco sauce
1 sour cucumber pickle, chopped,
½ teaspoon grated onion

Mix well and serve over lettuce. Makes 2 cups of dressing.

HEAVENLY DRESSING

Combine:
1 cup mayonnaise
½ cup whipped cream

4 tablespoons beaten Bar-le-Duc jelly

Serve with fruit salads. Makes 1½ cups dressing.

11. DESSERTS, IN VARIETY

Here are our famous desserts, the ones you've heard or read about and those our guests enjoy the most. Here too are the desserts every family depends on. Well cooked and attractively served, the plain ones also are excellent.

The special Mary Jane dessert is named for my daughter (who was named for my grandmother). Other outstanding favorites are the Frozen Cake Balls, Ice Cream Clowns, especially with the children, and our New England Indian Pudding, and Toll House Special.

If church suppers are one of your responsibilities, do try Scotch Pudding. It is splendid. My Red Cross canteens served pan after pan of it during war days with great success. You will really have fun with this chapter and where is the family that doesn't adore the maker of marvelous desserts?

DUTCH APPLE CAKE

Sift together:
- 2½ cups flour
- 3 teaspoons baking powder
- ½ teaspoon salt
- 3 tablespoons sugar. Cut in
- 4 tablespoons butter. Beat
- 1 egg and add enough
  Milk to make 1¼ cups liquid. Stir into first mixture. Turn batter into shallow buttered pan. Core, pare, and slice
- 2 apples. Place apples on dough in pattern, pressing edges into dough. Sprinkle with:
- ¼ cup sugar mixed with
- ½ teaspoon cinnamon

Bake in moderate oven, 375° F., for 25 to 30 minutes. Serve with Lemon Sauce. Serves 8.

ROSY APPLES

Pare and core
8 apples. Combine
1 cup sugar
1 cup water
1 cup red cinnamon candies.

Boil until candies dissolve. Add whole apples and cook in syrup until tender, but not mushy

Remove apples from syrup and chill. For dessert, fill centers with whipped cream. For salad, fill centers with cream cheese and chopped nuts. Serves 8.

SCOTCH BETTY

Cover bottom of greased baking dish with buttered Bread crumbs. Slice thinly
1 apple. Arrange over crumbs. Cover with syrup made of
1 cup sugar
½ cup water, boiled until quite thick. Add small pieces of orange peel. Cook until syr-up turns brown. Cover with more crumbs, another apple, sliced thin, and more syrup. Top with more crumbs and add
½ cup water combined with
1 teaspoon lemon juice or extract

Cover and bake in moderate oven, 350° F., until apples are soft, about 35 minutes. Remove cover and brown for a few minutes. Serve hot with Hard Sauce or whipped cream. Serves 6.

SCOTCH PUDDING

Pare, core, and cut into eights
4 large apples. Combine:
½ cup sugar
⅛ teaspoon cinnamon
¼ teaspoon salt. In buttered baking dish place half the apples. Sprinkle with half the sugar mixture. Dot with
1 tablespoon butter. Sprinkle
½ cup rolled oats over all. Arrange another layer of apple, sugar mixture, butter, and oats. Over all pour
1½ cups milk

Cover dish and place in moderate oven, 350° F., and bake for 45 minutes. Remove cover and bake 15 minutes more. Serve hot or cold. Serves 6 to 8.

BUTTERSCOTCH PUDDING

Soak in baking dish
4 slices bread in
½ cup milk. Cook until dark
1 cup brown sugar
½ cup butter. Add
2 cups hot milk. Let stand

over low heat for about 5 minutes. Add:
2 eggs, beaten,
1 teaspoon vanilla. Pour over bread in baking dish

Bake in slow oven, 325° F., for 45 minutes. Serve hot or cold with whipped cream. Serves 4.

BAKED CUSTARD

(See Primer for Brides, page 76)

CARAMEL CUSTARD

Caramelize in spider
½ cup sugar. Add
3 tablespoons boiling water.
In top of double boiled heat
2 cups milk. Add sugar mix-

ture and let stand until sugar melts. Add
2 eggs, beaten,
Pinch of salt
1 teaspoon vanilla

Pour into baking dish and set in pan of hot water. Bake in moderate oven, 325° to 350° F., for 25 to 30 minutes, until done. To test, insert a silver knife. If it comes out clean, custard is done. Serves 4.

COCONUT CUSTARD

Soak until soft
½ cup bread crumbs
½ cup grated or shredded coconut in
2 cups milk. Mix and add:

3 tablespoons sugar
½ teaspoon salt
½ tablespoon melted butter. Add
1 egg, beaten until light

Pour into greased baking dish. Set in pan of hot water and bake in slow oven, 325° F., for about 30 minutes, or until a silver knife inserted in custard comes out clean. Serves 4.

CARAMEL CORNFLAKE RING

Cook in spider until bubbly	6 cups cornflakes. Pour hot
1⅓ cups brown sugar	hot sugar mixture over corn-
⅓ cup butter. Place in large	flakes
buttered bowl	

Stir until each flake is coated. Pack into 10 small buttered ring molds or into one large mold. Chill, unmold, and serve with ice cream. Serves 10.

TOLL HOUSE CHOCOLATE ICEBOX CAKE

Melt in top of double boiler	1 cup confectioners sugar
2 squares chocolate. Add:	1 cup butter. Add chocolate
½ cup sugar	mixture and fold in
¼ cup water	4 egg whites, beaten stiff
4 egg yolks. Cook until thick	
and smooth. Cool. Cream	
together:	

Line mold with lady fingers and turn mixture into mold. Chill thoroughly. Unmold. Decorate with whipped cream or with pistachio nuts and candied cherries, cut fine. Serves 6.

SPICY CHOCOLATE BREAD PUDDING

Cook in top of double	late morsels. Beat together
boiler until smooth:	and add:
1 cup soft bread crumbs	1 egg
2 tablespoons butter or short-	½ cup milk
ening	¼ teaspoon salt. Cook until
½ cup sugar	mixture thickens. Add:
1½ cups milk	½ teaspoon cinnamon
3 oz. (½ c.) semi-sweet choco-	¼ teaspoon ginger

Turn into greased baking dish. Bake in moderate oven, 350° F., for 20 minutes. Serve hot or cold with light cream. Serves 6 to 8.

CHOCOLATE CAKE CRUMB PUDDING

Cook in top of double boiler:
1 pint cake crumbs
1 pint milk
1 square melted chocolate. Stir often and when crumbs are soft add:
2 egg yolks

½ teaspoon vanilla. Turn into buttered baking dish. Bake 10 minutes in hot oven, 375° F. Top with
2 egg whites, beaten with
2 tablespoons sugar

Brown in hot oven or under broiler. Serves 4.

Variation: Mix egg whites in with pudding before baking and bake in moderate oven, 350° F., for 20 minutes. Serve hot with Hard Sauce.

CHOCOLATE MOUSSE

In a 1-quart bowl place
3 oz. (½ c.) semi-sweet chocolate morsels. Place bowl in pan of hot water to melt chocolate. In another bowl break, one at a time,
3 egg yolks. Beat after each

addition. Add to chocolate. Add:
1 teaspoon vanilla or 1 tablespoon rum and fold in
3 egg whites, beaten stiff but not dry

Spoon chocolate mixture into sherbet glasses. Chill well. Serve with cream or soft Vanilla Ice Cream. Serves 4 to 6.

CHOCOLATE SOUFFLÉ

Blend in top of double boiler:
3 tablespoons butter, melted,
3 tablespoons flour. Cool. Add
1 cup milk. Cook until thick. Add
1 square chocolate, melted. Beat well

3 egg yolks. Add:
¼ teaspoon salt
⅓ cup sugar. Mix well. Pour chocolate mixture over egg mixture. Mix well and cool. Add
1 teaspoon vanilla. Fold in
3 egg whites, beaten stiff

Turn into baking dish and bake in moderate oven, 350° F., for 30 minutes. Serve at once with Sunshine Sauce. Serves 6.

MAGIC PUFF SOUFFLÉ

Heat in top of 2-quart double boiler:

3 oz. (½ c.) semi-sweet chocolate morsels.

1 cup milk. Beat with rotary beater until smooth. **Add:**

3 tablespoons sugar

Pinch of salt

1 teaspoon vanilla

3 eggs

Beat mixture with rotary beater for 1 minute. Cover and cook over boiling water for 20 minutes, without lifting cover. Remove from heat and serve immediately with whipped cream. Serves 6 to 8. (If the 20-minute cooking period is started when main course is served, the finished soufflé will probably be just about ready for dessert. This recipe is easy and exceptionally delicious. Like any soufflé, do not let it stand after removing from heat.)

SUNSHINE SOUFFLÉ

In top of double boiler melt

3 tablespoons butter. Stir in:

½ teaspoon salt

4 teaspoons flour

½ cup milk. Remove from heat when sauce is thick. Beat in

3 egg yolks. Fold in

3 egg whites, beaten stiff. Add

¼ cup seedless raisins. Pour into baking dish

Bake in moderate oven, 375° F., for 25 minutes. Serve topped with orange marmalade. Serves 6.

Variation: Before baking, top with meringue, made of the egg whites beaten with 3 tablespoons sugar, and brown in hot oven.

CRANBERRY PUDDING

Beat

2 egg yolks slightly. Add:

1 cup sugar

½ cup milk

3 tablespoons melted butter. Sift

1½ cups flour

1 teaspoon cream of tartar

¾ teaspoon soda. Stir into egg mixture. Stir in

2 cups cranberries

Bake in moderate oven, 350° F., for 45 minutes. Serve hot with Fluffy Sauce. Serves 8.

CRÈME BRÛLÉE

Scald in top of double boiler 2 cups cream with 3 tablespoons brown or maple sugar, shaved. Stir ½ cup of mixture into 4 egg yolks, beaten. Return to double boiler. Cook until slightly thickened and mixture coats spoon. (Overcooking causes curdling.)

Pour mixture into 6 custard cups, cool, and set in refrigerator. When set, sprinkle tops with 3 tablespoons maple sugar, about ½ inch thick. Place under broiler until sugar caramelizes. Watch carefully lest sugar scorch. Cool again before returning to refrigerator. Chill. Serve with heavy cream. Serves 6.

COCONUT DATE SURPRISE

Heat in top of double boiler 1 quart milk. Combine and Add: 4 tablespoons minute tapioca 2 tablespoons corn meal 1 cup brown sugar 4 tablespoons grated coconut 1 cup dates, pitted and cut fine, ½ teaspoon salt

Turn into greased baking dish. Cover and bake in moderate oven, 350° F., for 45 minutes. Remove from oven and cover with marshmallows. Return to oven to brown marshmallows. Serve hot. Serves 8.

RICH DATE PUDDING

Bring to boil ⅓ quart water. Add: ¾ cup sugar 1 teaspoon salt. Sift in ½ cup graham flour, a little at a time. Boil until mixture thickens. Add 1 pound dates, pitted and cut up. Cook 2 to 3 minutes. Remove from heat. Add: ¼ pound walnut meats, broken, 1 teaspoon vanilla

Serve cold with cream. Serves 6. (Small portions are enough of this very rich dessert.)

DAFFODIL PUDDING

Heat in top of double boiler 1¾ cups milk. Combine: ½ cup sugar 4 tablespoons cornstarch ⅛ teaspoon salt. Dissolve in ¼ cup milk. Add slowly to hot milk, stirring constantly. Cook for 12 minutes. Remove from heat. Pour slowly over 2 egg whites, beaten stiff. Add 1 teaspoon vanilla

Pour into 1 large mold or 4 individual molds. Chill. Serve with Custard Sauce. Serves 4.

ENGLISH FRUIT PUDDING

Remove crusts and cut in 1½-inch strips 8 slices buttered bread. Line a buttered pudding dish with strips, buttered side up. Add 4 cups canned blueberries, sweetened to taste. Add ¼ teaspoon salt

Cover with bread strips. Place a plate on top and on it a weight. Let stand in cool place 24 hours. Turn out and serve with whipped cream. Serves 8.

Variation: Heat blueberries and place in alternate layers with bread strips in pudding dish. Serve immediately.

GINGER PUDDING

Beat 2 eggs until light. Add: 1 teaspoon salt 2 tablespoons sugar 2 tablespoons melted butter ⅔ cup fine bread crumbs 1½ tablespoons finely chopped ginger ½ cup milk 1 teaspoon vanilla

Mix thoroughly and turn into individual molds. Set molds in pan of boiling water. Bake in moderate oven, 350° F., about 30 minutes or until centers are firm. Serves 4.

GRAPENUT PUDDING

Bring to a boil
1 quart milk with
1 cup grapenuts. Cool and add
2 egg yolks, mixed with:

4 tablespoons sugar
Pinch of salt. Fold in
2 egg whites, beaten stiff

Turn into buttered baking dish. Bake in slow oven, 325° F., for 45 minutes. Serves 6. This pudding may be served hot or cold with light cream, whipped cream, or an ice cream topping.

INDIAN PUDDING

Scald
3 cups milk. Combine:
3 tablespoons corn meal
⅓ cup dark molasses. Stir into
hot milk and cook until
thickened. (Stir constantly
to prevent scorching.)

Remove from heat. Add:
½ cup sugar
1 egg, beaten,
Butter, size of walnut,
¼ teaspoon salt
½ teaspoon ginger
½ teaspoon cinnamon

Mix thoroughly. Pour into buttered baking dish and bake in slow oven, 300° F., for 30 minutes. Then pour in ½ cup milk. Continue baking at 300° for 2 hours more. Serve hot with whipped cream or an ice cream topping. Serves 8. (A favorite dessert in New England.)

LEMON RICE PUDDING

Combine:
1 cup cooked rice
1 pint hot milk
2 egg yolks, beaten,

Few grains salt
Butter, size of egg,
Grated rind of 1 lemon
4 tablespoons sugar

Turn into baking dish and set in pan of warm water. Bake in moderate oven, 350° F., for 30 minutes. When done, spread with the following topping.

Combine:
2 egg whites, beaten stiff,

8 tablespoons sugar
Juice of 1 lemon

Spread topping over pudding and return to hot oven to brown. Serves 4 to 6.

MOTHER'S FLOATING ISLAND

In top of double boiler scald

3 cups milk. Mix in a bowl:

¼ cup sugar

1 tablespoon cornstarch

¼ teaspoon salt. Gradually add a little hot milk and pour mixture into rest of milk.

Cook for 15 minutes, until mixture thickens. Beat

2 eggs with additional

2 egg yolks. Add a little hot milk mixture, stir, and add to remaining milk mixture. Cook 2 minutes more. Add

1 teaspoon vanilla

Pour into serving dish and chill. Serve with meringue "islands" floating on top. Make meringues as follows:

Beat until stiff

2 egg whites with

Pinch of salt. Add

¼ cup sugar and beat well

Drop by tablespoonfuls into shallow spider of simmering water. Cover and cook 5 minutes. Place meringues on custard.

Variations: Drop on each island a spoonful of strawberry or raspberry jam, or sprinkle with sweet chocolate. Serves 6.

ORANGE SPONGE PUDDING

Cook in top of double boiler:

2 cups bread crumbs

1 pint milk. When crumbs are soft add:

2 tablespoons butter

Juice and grated rind of ½ orange

¼ teaspoon salt

¼ cup sugar. Fold in

2 egg whites, beaten stiff

Turn into buttered baking dish and bake in slow oven, 325° F., for 25 minutes, or until firm. Serve hot with Orange Sauce. Serves 8.

ORANGE FAIRY FLUFF

Beat
4 egg yolks. Add:
4 tablespoons sugar
Grated rind and juice 1 orange
Grated rind and juice 1 lemon.

Cook in top of double boiler until thick, stirring constantly. Cool slightly. Fold in
4 egg whites, beaten stiff with
2 tablespoons sugar

Line sherbet glasses with thin layers of spongecake or with lady fingers. Fill with orange mixture. Chill and serve. Serves 8.

FRUIT COBBLER

In bottom of a greased custard cup place 1 heaping tablespoon of canned fruit. On this drop baking powder biscuit dough. Bake in a hot oven, 500° F., for 15 minutes. Invert, turn out, and garnish with whipped cream and additional fruit. Serve hot. (Muffin tins may be used instead of custard cups.)

JIFFY PRUNE WHIP

Combine in top of double boiler:
2 egg whites
½ teaspoon grated lemon rind
2 teaspoons lemon juice
⅓ cup sugar. Cook over boil-

ing water and beat with rotary beater until mixture fluffs up and holds its shape. Fold in
1 jar (½ cup) strained prunes

Cool. Serve with Custard Sauce, using egg yolks. Serves 4.

Variation: Other strained fruit pulps (baby food variety) may be used to make this an excellent simple dessert, especially for small children.

RHUBARB DESSERT

Cover bottom of a buttered baking dish with rhubarb cut in 1-inch pieces. Sprinkle generously with sugar, then with buttered bread crumbs to which has been added a small amount of sugar.

Place rhubarb and crumbs in alternate layers to fill dish, finishing with crumbs. Dot with small pieces of butter. Cover and bake in moderate oven, 375° F., for about 40 minutes, or until rhubarb is tender and juice has penetrated crumbs. Serve hot with whipped cream.

SHREDDED WHEAT PUDDING

Crumble in baking dish
2 shredded wheat biscuits.
Mix in a bowl:
2 eggs, slightly beaten,

2 cups milk
¾ cup dark molasses
1 teaspoon cinnamon
¼ teaspoon salt

Pour mixture over shredded wheat. Dot with butter. Bake in moderate oven, 350° F., for 45 minutes. Serve with Hard Sauce or whipped cream. Serves 4.

INDIAN TAPIOCA PUDDING

Combine:
3 tablespoons corn meal
3 tablespoons minute tapioca
2 tablespoons sugar
¼ teaspoon salt

⅛ teaspoon cinnamon
⅛ teaspoon ginger. Add:
3 cups hot milk
½ cup dark molasses

Stir well and pour into buttered baking dish. Bake in slow oven, 325° F., for about 45 minutes. Stir frequently while baking. Serve hot. Serves 6.

APRICOT AND PINEAPPLE TAPIOCA

Let stand overnight in water to cover
½ cup dried apricots, washed and cut small. Drain and reserve liquid. Add enough boiling water to make 2½ cups. Gradually add
½ cup minute tapioca. Cook

until thickened, stirring occasionally. Turn into baking dish. Add apricots and:
¾ cup sugar
½ teaspoon salt
2 slices canned pineapple, cut up

Mix well. Cover and place in pan of warm water. Bake in moderate oven, 350° F., for 45 minutes. Cool slightly before serving. Serves 4.

TAPIOCA CREAM

Beat in a 1-quart bowl
1 egg white. When foamy, add
2 tablespoons sugar. Continue
    beating until mixture forms
    soft peaks. Mix in saucepan:
1 egg yolk

½ cup milk. Add:
3 tablespoons minute tapioca
2 tablespoons sugar
⅛ teaspoon salt
1½ cups milk

Cook over low heat until mixture reaches boiling point, stirring constantly. (Mixture will be thin.) Remove from heat and gradually fold into egg white. Add ½ teaspoon vanilla. Cool for 15 minutes. Then carefully stir. Chill and serve plain or with cream. Serves 4.

Variations: Add sliced bananas or peaches, or other fruit after mixture has cooled and is ready to stir. Chocolate morsels, shredded coconut, broken nut meats may also be added or the pudding may be served with cubed fruit gelatin. It is easy to vary flavors and add interest to this delicious stand-by pudding.

TOLL HOUSE SPECIAL

Grind or crush
¼ pound or 12 graham
    crackers.
    Reserve ½ cup crumbs.
    Combine:
¼ pound or ¾ cup dates,
    pitted and cut fine

¼ pound or 14 marshmallows,
    cut fine
¼ pound or 1 cup nut meats,
    broken
½ cup thin cream or
    evaporated milk

Mix all ingredients thoroughly. Form into roll and cover with reserved crumbs. Chill in refrigerator. Slice and serve with cream. Serves 8

AMBER PUDDING

Mix: Few grains salt with
4 tablespoons tapioca   2 cups cold water.
1 cup brown sugar

Place in top of double boiler. Cook until clear and soft, about
10 minutes. Cool and add ½ teaspoon vanilla. Serve either warm
or cold with whipped cream. Serves 4.

CONCORD GRAPE DELIGHT

Bake Hot Milk Spongecake in individual Mary Ann pans.
When cool, cover with mixture of equal parts Lemon Meringue
Pie filling (make only ½ recipe) and whipped cream. Add crushed
pineapple until mixture is of desired consistency. On top and
in hollow of cake place large mound of Concord Grape Sherbet.
Serve at once. Serves 6.

Variation: **ORANGE BLOSSOMS.** Omit crushed pineapple and substitute Orange Ice for the Concord Grape Sherbert.

ANGEL OR HEAVENLY PIE

Beat until frothy   1 hour. In top of double
4 egg whites. Add   boiler beat until thick
¼ teaspoon cream of tartar.   4 egg yolks. Slowly beat in
Beat until stiff. Slowly   1 cup sugar. Add
beat in   Juice and grated rind of 1
1 cup sugar. Spread mixture   lemon. Cook until thick.
in deep well-greased 9-inch   Cool and spread over baked
pie plate. Bake in slow   meringue. Cover with
oven, 250° F. to 275°, for   1 cup heavy cream, whipped

Chill in icebox until ready to serve. (This dessert is good the
second day.) Serves 6.

MARY JANES

Bake Hot Milk Spongecake in individual Mary Ann pans. Turn
out on individual plates. Cover with Hot Chocolate Sauce. Fill

hollows of cake with pink peppermint or other ice cream. Cover ice cream with whipped cream colored a soft green and flavored slightly with almond extract. Let chocolate show.

BABA AU RHUM

For the American version of this French dessert, we use Hot Milk Spongecake baked in individual Mary Ann pans, or a large cupcake hollowed out in center. Soak cake in Buttered Rum Sauce. Then place on serving dish. Fill center with frozen pudding ice cream. Garnish with whipped cream. Serve at once.

STEAMED PUDDINGS

If you do not have a covered mold, you may use a coffee can or other type of tin can without a cover. Tie a double thickness of paraffin paper tightly over top. Let it extend down over outside of tin. Fill greased molds, two-thirds full, place on rack, and set in deep kettle with about 2 inches of water in bottom. Cover kettle tightly, keep water boiling until time required for pudding to cook is over. Many good steamed puddings can be made in top of double boiler. Just make sure top sets well down into bottom of lower section. All types of double boilers are not suited to steaming.

STEAMED CHOCOLATE PUDDING

Combine:
1 teaspoon melted butter
1 square melted chocolate
½ cup sugar
½ teaspoon salt
1 egg, beaten slightly. Sift

1 cup flour
1 teaspoon baking powder. Add flour alternately with
1 cup milk to chocolate mixture

Turn into greased mold or 1-pound coffee tin. Steam for 1 hour. Unmold and serve hot with Mock Maple Sauce. Serves 6.

NUT PUDDING

Sift together:
1 teaspoon soda
1 teaspoon salt
1 teaspoon grated nutmeg
2½ cups flour. Mix
  thoroughly:
1 cup seeded raisins
½ pound chopped figs

½ pound chopped English
  walnuts
1 cup chopped suet. Add
1 cup dark molasses. Add
  flour mixture alternately
  with
1 cup milk

Turn into greased mold. Cover and steam for 2½ hours. Or use individual molds and steam for 1 hour. Unmold and serve hot. Serves 6.

HOLIDAY PLUM PUDDING

Beat
2 egg yolks. Mix well with
¾ cup brown sugar
2 tablespoons lemon juice.
  Add
¾ cup chopped suet.
  Combine:
1¾ cups soft bread crumbs
1½ teaspoons baking powder
¾ teaspoon salt

1½ teaspoons cinnamon
¾ teaspoon nutmeg. Add to
  egg mixture. Combine
  and add:
¾ cup seeded raisins
½ cup currants
½ cup nut meats
1½ tablespoons flour. Fold in
2 egg whites, beaten stiff

Grease and sprinkle with flour a 2-quart covered pudding mold with tube. Turn in mixture. Cover and steam for 3 hours or bake in slow oven, 250° F., for 3 hours. Individual molds may be used if desired. (This pudding may be kept for several weeks before using.) Unmold and serve with Sunshine Sauce. Serves 6.

STEAMED SPICE PUDDING

Sift together:
2½ cups flour
2 teaspoons cinnamon
2½ teaspoons soda. Add:
1 cup seedless raisins

½ cup broken nut meats. Mix
1½ cups dark molasses with
1 cup warm water. Stir into
  mixture. Add
2 egg yolks, beaten

Turn into buttered mold, cover and steam for 2 hours. Or use individual molds and steam for 1 hour. Unmold and serve hot. Sunshine Sauce is excellent with this pudding. Serves 6.

JELLIED DESSERTS

We used to think it essential to use the juices of fresh fruit in desserts made with gelatin. Today our prepared fruit gelatins are of delightful flavor, but I almost always add a little lemon juice or substitute a fruit juice for half the water called for. I find too that it saves a good deal of time when using prepared fruit gelatins if only half the required liquid is hot. When the gelatin and sugar are dissolved, I add the other half of the liquid, cold, and then proceed, usually adding solid fruits also. In preparing gelatins remember that most fresh fruits float, while canned or cooked fruits and vegetables sink. Never use fresh pineapple in gelatin. Its enzyme kills the jelling process. And it is not necessary to rinse molds with water, as we once considered essential. The simplest way to unmold a gelatin dessert is to immerse the outside or dip it quickly in and out of hot water. Slip a butter spreader around the inside to allow air to slide under the gelatin. Then the vacuum is broken and the dessert slips out clean and whole—and very pretty!

CHOCOLATE SPANISH CREAM

Mix well:
½ cup sugar
3 egg yolks, beaten. Add
2 squares chocolate, melted. Soften
1 tablespoon gelatin in
¼ cup cold water. Fill up cup with boiling water. Stir into chocolate mixture. Add
1 teaspoon vanilla. Fold in
3 egg whites, beaten stiff

Turn into a bowl or spoon into sherbet glasses. Chill and serve with whipped cream. Serves 4.

211

CHOCOLATE ICEBOX CAKE

Melt over hot, not boiling water

3 oz. (½ c.) semi-sweet chocolate morsels. Add:

¼ cup sugar

⅛ teaspoon salt

½ cup hot water. Stir until smooth and sugar dissolves

Soften

2 tablespoons gelatin in

1 tablespoon cold water. Add to chocolate mixture. Stir until dissolved. Remove from heat. Beat in, one at a time,

4 egg yolks. Add

1 teaspoon vanilla. Cool. Fold in

4 egg whites, beaten stiff, and

½ cup cream, whipped

Chill mixture and turn into mold first lined with wax paper and then with split lady fingers (about 3 dozen). Pour in chocolate mixture. Chill thoroughly in refrigerator. Unmold and serve with whipped cream. Serves 8.

COFFEE JELLY

Soak

2 tablespoons gelatin in

1½ cups cold water. Add

1 cup boiling water. Stir

until dissolved. Add:

½ cup sugar

2 cups boiled coffee

Stir until all sugar is dissolved. Turn into mold and chill. Serves 6.

Variation: **COFFEE CREAM.** As it begins to stiffen, beat 2 cups Coffee Jelly with rotary beater until light and foamy. Beat 1 cup heavy cream and add 2 tablespoons sugar. When cream is stiff, fold into jelly. Pour into mold and chill.

COFFEE SOUFFLÉ

Soften

2 tablespoons gelatin in

2 tablespoons cold water. Beat

2 egg yolks and add

Few grains salt.

Add slowly to:

1½ cups hot milk

1½ cups strong coffee. Cook mixture for 5 minutes. Stir in gelatin. Fold in

2 egg whites, beaten stiff with

½ cup sugar. Add

1 teaspoon vanilla

Turn into mold. Set in cold place to stiffen. Serve with whipped cream. Serves 8.

COFFEE WHIP

Dissolve
1 pound marshmallows, cut up, in
1¾ cups strong, hot coffee.

When marshmallows are dissolved, let cool. When mixture starts to jell, fold in
1 cup heavy cream, whipped

Turn into mold and chill. Serve with thin cream poured over jelly. Serves 6.

Variation: **MOUSSE.** Turn mixture into a refrigerator tray and let stand 2 hours. For a less rich dessert omit whipped cream.

HARLEQUIN JELLY

Soften
4 tablespoons gelatin in
1 cup cold water. Add
5 cups boiling water. Stir

until dissolved. Add
2 cups sugar. Stir until dissolved. Add
1 cup lemon juice

Divide mixture into 3 parts. Color one green; another, violet; and the third, yellow. Turn the yellow mixture into a mold and let harden in a cold place. Add the green mixture. Chill. When this is firm, add the violet mixture. Pour each layer in very carefully, letting it run down the side of the mold and spread out over the layer of jelly. When all have hardened, turn onto a plate and serve with whipped cream. Serves 12.

MAPLE CHARLOTTE

Heat in top of double boiler
1 pint milk. Pour slowly over
2 egg yolks, beaten. Return to heat and cook 5 minutes. Add
2 tablespoons gelatin, soaked in
2 tablespoons cold milk for 5 minutes. Add
⅛ teaspoon salt. Remove

from heat and add
1 cup maple syrup. Cool. When mixture begins to jell, add
½ cup blanched almonds, chopped, or shredded coconut
½ teaspoon almond extract. Fold in
2 egg whites, beaten stiff

Turn into a mold. Chill. Serve with or without whipped cream. Serves 8.

ORANGE CHARLOTTE

Soak for 20 minutes
1⅓ tablespoons gelatin in
1⅓ cups cold water. Add:
1⅓ cups boiling water
1 cup sugar
Juice of 1 lemon. Add:
1 cup unstrained orange juice

1 tablespoon grated orange rind. Cool. When mixture begins to stiffen, beat until light. Add
3 egg whites, beaten stiff and continue to beat until mixture is stiff. Line a mold with Sections of 1 orange

Pour mixture into mold. Chill. Serve plain or with whipped cream. Serves 6.

PINEAPPLE ICEBOX CAKE

Heat in top of double boiler
2 cups milk. Add
1 cup sugar, mixed with
2 tablespoons cornstarch. Stir until thickened. Add
2 eggs, beaten. Remove from heat and stir in

1 tablespoon gelatin, softened in
1 tablespoon cold water. Add
¾ cup pineapple juice with Juice and grated rind of 1 lemon

Line a mold with lady fingers or thin pieces of spongecake. Turn in mixture and let stand overnight or until well set. Unmold and cover with whipped cream and decorate with halves of canned pineapple slices. Garnish with maraschino cherries. Serves 6.

PINEAPPLE TRIFLE

Cook for 2 to 3 minutes
1 cup crushed pineapple
1 cup hot water
½ cup sugar. Add to
1 package strawberry gelatin.

Cool and add
½ teaspoon orange extract. Let stand. When mixture begins to jell add
½ pint cream, whipped

Pour into mold and chill. Garnish with whipped cream and serve. Serves 6.

RASPBERRY APPLE WHIP

Dissolve
1 package raspberry gelatin in
1 cup boiling water. Add
1 cup cold water. Pour half
of mixture into 6 individual
molds. Chill. When remaining gelatin begins to jell,
add
½ cup strained applesauce.
Whip until frothy. Fold in
¼ cup cream, whipped

Pour mixture over the firm gelatin already in molds. Chill until top layer is firm. Unmold. Serve with plain or whipped cream. Serves 6. (Small children love this.)

RICE PARFAIT

Soften for 5 minutes
2 tablespoons gelatin in
1 cup cold water. Dissolve in
3¾ cups hot milk. Add:
1 cup brown sugar
½ teaspoon salt
4 tablespoons chopped nut
meats
2 cups cooked rice. Mix well.
Chill, and add
1 cup cream, whipped

Turn into molds. Let stand in refrigerator for 2 hours. Serve with whipped cream, if desired. Serves 8.

BUTTERSCOTCH RICE PUDDING

Cook in top of double boiler
⅓ cup rice in
2 cups milk, scalded, until
tender. Caramelize
1 cup brown sugar with
2 tablespoons butter. Add to
rice and cook until caramel
dissolves. Soften
1 tablespoon gelatin in
½ cup cold water. Dissolve in
1 cup hot milk.

Pour gelatin into rice mixture. Turn into mold and chill. Unmold and serve with whipped cream. Serves 6.

Variation: One cup pitted and chopped dates may be added before pouring into mold but then omit using ½ cup brown sugar.

STEPHANIE PUDDING

Soften
1 tablespoon gelatin in
¼ cup cold water. Dissolve in
1 cup hot grape or loganberry
  juice. Add:
½ cup sugar

¼ cup lemon juice. Strain
and cool. Stir occasionally.
When thick, beat until
frothy. Fold in
3 egg whites, beaten stiff, and
continue to beat until stiff

Pour into sherbet glasses and chill. Serve with Custard Sauce. Serves 4 to 6.

SOUFFLÉ PARISIENNE

Beat until thick
3 egg yolks. Beat in
⅔ cup sugar and
  Grated rind of ½ lemon.
Soften
1 tablespoon gelatin in

1 tablespoon cold water. Dissolve over hot water. Add
4 tablespoons lemon juice.
Stir into egg mixture.
Fold in
3 egg whites, beaten stiff

Pour into glass serving dish. Chill. Serve spread with whipped cream, sweetened with confectioners sugar. Serves 4. (This is an excellent hot weather dessert, both to prepare and to eat.)

FROZEN DESSERTS

Few of the younger generation own ice cream freezers so common before automatic refrigeration. Those of us who can look back on the happy days of "licking the dasher" are fortunate. Homemade freezer ice cream was indeed a marvelous Sunday treat!

If you use a freezer, be sure the ice cream mixture is cool before you pour it into the can and fill this only two thirds full. After fitting the can into the freezer tub, adjust the dasher and cover with top bar and handle, ready for turning. Pack chopped ice and ice cream salt in alternate layers around the can, using 1 part salt to 4 parts ice. Turn handle slowly at first and then more briskly until it is really hard to turn it. When you have finished churning, carefully remove ice and salt from around the top of the can so you can take off the cover and dasher without letting salt drop into the ice cream. Plug the hole in the cover and allow the ice cream to "ripen" for a few hours before serving, if your family will let it be that long.

When ice cream is made in the automatic refrigerator, the mixture must have air incorporated in it. The addition of whipped cream or beaten egg white or the beating of the mixture half way through the freezing process will accomplish this. To obtain body and smoothness in refrigerator ice cream, we use evaporated or condensed milk, gelatin, prepared mixes, eggs, marshmallow, or cornstarch. Keep in mind that freezing lessens the sweetness of ice cream. The smoothest ice cream seems to result if freezing is done fast at first by setting the temperature control high. Then after about 1 hour, set the control back to normal temperature to ripen the ice cream.

"Store" ice cream also has interesting possibilities. Broken bits of fruitcake may be stirred into vanilla ice cream which is then hardened and ripened in the tray of an automatic refrigerator. Or you can add broken chocolate mint wafers, Nestle's Semi-Sweet Chocolate Morsels, or such a fruit as banana which has little water content. This is an easy way to have unusual and delicious kinds of ice cream. (Unless otherwise indicated all the recipes which follow are for automatic refrigerators.)

VANILLA ICE CREAM

Scald in top of double boiler
1½ cups milk. Combine and add:
⅓ cup sugar
3 tablespoons light corn syrup
⅛ teaspoon salt
1 tablespoon flour. Cover

and cook 10 minutes. Add mixture to
1 egg yolk, well beaten. Cook 1 minute. Cool and turn into freezing tray. Freeze 2 hours. Turn into bowl, add:
½ cup heavy cream, whipped,
1 egg white, beaten stiff
2 teaspoons vanilla

Mix well. Return to freezing tray and freeze. Stir every 20 minutes while mushy to keep ingredients well mixed and creamy. Makes about 1 quart.

Variations: **CHOCOLATE ICE CREAM.** Add ¼ cup ground chocolate to dry ingredients. You may also like to substitute 1 teaspoon lemon extract for the vanilla.

STRAWBERRY ICE CREAM. Add 2 cups sweetened crushed strawberries along with the whipped cream and egg white. Stir in well.

PEPPERMINT STICK ICE CREAM. Add ½ cup ground peppermint stick candy to dry ingredients.

JIFFY ICE CREAM

Soften
1 tablespoon gelatin in
⅓ cup cold water. Melt
over hot water. Beat
1 egg. Add:
1 large can (14½ oz.)
evaporated milk
⅔ cup sugar
1 teaspoon vanilla
¼ cup cream or rich milk
(optional)

Add dissolved gelatin. Turn mixture into freezing tray. Twice during freezing period scrape down sides, and beat mixture with egg beater. This is an excellent quick inexpensive ice cream for children or as a base for sundaes. Other flavorings may be added. Will freeze in 1 hour if temperature control is set at coldest point. Makes about 1 pint.

PINEAPPLE-MINT ICE CREAM

Scald in top of double
boiler
1 cup milk. Add
1 tablespoon gelatin softened
in
2 tablespoons cold water.
Combine:
3 tablespoons flour
½ teaspoon salt
½ cup sugar
½ cup pineapple juice. Add to
milk. Add
1 egg, slightly beaten. Strain
into freezing tray. Fold in
½ pint heavy cream, whipped
but not stiff,
2 drops oil of peppermint or
½ teaspoon peppermint
extract
½ cup crushed pineapple

Freeze, stirring occasionally until mixture is firm. Makes about 1 quart.

ANGEL PARFAIT

Soak

½ teaspoon gelatin in
1 tablespoon cold water 5 minutes. Boil:
1 cup sugar
½ cup water to soft ball stage, 238° F.

Pour slowly over

3 egg whites, beaten stiff. Add gelatin. Beat until cool.

Fold in

1 pint heavy cream, whipped.

Add

1 teaspoon vanilla

Pour mixture into freezing tray and freeze without stirring until mixture is firm. Makes 2 pints.

Variation: **GOLDEN PARFAIT**. Substitute egg yolks, well beaten, for egg whites.

FROZEN CRANBERRY SPONGECAKE

Beat until smooth:

1 can (2 cups) cranberry sauce
½ teaspoon grated orange rind
2 tablespoons honey or sugar
1 teaspoon vanilla
2 egg yolks. Beat until stiff

2 egg whites. Gradually add
2 tablespoons sugar. Fold in cranberry mixture and then fold in half of
1 cup heavy cream, whipped

Line freezing tray with wax paper and then with slices of spongecake. Pour in cranberry mixture. Garnish top with remaining half of whipped cream. Freeze. Serves 6 to 8.

CONCORD GRAPE SHERBET

Dissolve:

2 cups sugar
2 teaspoons gelatin in
1 cup hot water. Add:
3 cups cold water

2 teaspoons tartaric acid
¼ cup light cream
¾ cup puréed Concord grapes
¼ cup crushed pineapple

Pour mixture into freezing tray and freeze. Makes 1½ pints.

LIME SHERBET

Dissolve:
2 cups sugar
2 teaspoons gelatin in
1 cup hot water. Add:
3 cups cold water

¼ cup light cream
2 tablespoons lime emulsion
8 drops green coloring
1 tablespoon citric acid

Pour mixture into freezing tray and freeze. Serves 6 to 8. (Your home candy store can usually supply the lime emulsion but if you have difficulty in finding it I will gladly send you a bottle.)

LIME MOUSSE

Combine:
1 cup heavy cream, whipped,

¼ cup powdered sugar
4 drops oil of lime

Color delicately with green color paste. Freeze in refrigerator or pack in ice and salt and leave until frozen, about 3 to 4 hours. Makes 1 pint.

Variation: **COUPE ESPÉRANCE.** Fill sherbet glasses two thirds full of chilled diced pears and diced bananas. Place Lime Mousse on top and garnish with whipped cream.

PEACH MOUSSE

Mix well:
1 cup peaches, mashed,
⅓ cup sugar
3 tablespoons light corn syrup

Few grains salt.
½ teaspoon almond extract.
Chill until firm. Stir in
½ pint heavy cream, whipped

Turn mixture into freezing trays and freeze without stirring. Makes 1½ pints.

WILD ROSE MOUSSE

Combine:
2 cups pineapple juice
¼ cup lemon juice
⅓ cup sugar (or to taste)
Color delicately with pink

color paste. Pour into large freezing tray. Combine:
½ pint heavy cream, whipped,
¼ cup confectioners sugar
1 teaspoon vanilla

Pour whipped cream over pineapple mixture and freeze for 4 hours. Makes 1 quart. If desired, ½ cup chopped nuts may be added. (A very refreshing dessert after a heavy dinner.)

ORANGE ICE

Boil for 20 minutes:	2 cups orange juice
2 cups sugar	¼ cup lemon juice
4 cups water. Add:	Grated rind of 2 oranges

Cool. Strain. Pour into freezing trays and freeze. Makes 2 quarts.

RASPBERRY ICE

Boil for 5 minutes:	squeezed through a double
2 cups water	thickness of cheesecloth.
⅔ cup sugar. Cool. Add:	Add
1 cup juice from raspberries,	2 tablespoons lemon juice

Strain mixture. Pour into freezing tray and freeze. Makes 1½ pints. May be served alone or combined with Italian Meringue.

ITALIAN MERINGUE

Boil to soft ball stage,	mixture until cold. Soften
240° F.,	¼ teaspoon gelatin in
½ cup sugar	1 tablespoon cold water. Dis-
¼ cup water. Pour over	solve over hot water. Strain
3 egg whites, beaten stiff,	into mixture. Fold in
beating constantly. Place	1 cup heavy cream, whipped,
pan in ice water and beat	½ teaspoon vanilla

Thoroughly chill a melon mold, line with Orange or Raspberry Ice by spoonfuls. Spread evenly ¾ inch thick with back of spoon. Fill center of mold with the meringue, cover with Orange or Raspberry Ice. Pack in ice and salt and freeze for 5 to 6 hours. Serves 8.

MANHATTAN PUDDING

Combine:

1½ cups orange juice
¼ cup lemon juice
⅓ cup sugar (or to taste)
Pour into deep freezing tray.

Combine:

½ pint heavy cream, whipped,
¼ cup confectioners sugar
1 teaspoon vanilla
⅔ cup chopped walnut meats

Pour whipped cream mixture over fruit juices to fill tray. Freeze for 4 to 5 hours. Serves 8. (Finely crushed macaroons may be used instead of walnut meats.)

MAPLE FANGO

Cook until it threads
¾ cup maple syrup. Pour over
3 egg whites, beaten stiff.
Beat until cold. Fold in

1 to 2 cups heavy cream,
whipped, depending on
strength of maple flavor
desired

Pour into freezing tray and freeze without stirring. Serves 6 to 8.

FROZEN ORANGE-PRUNE WHIP

Beat
1 egg white until stiff.
Beat in
½ cup sugar. Add
½ cup puréed prunes, made
by rubbing pitted cooked
prunes through sieve or

chopping them fine.
Combine:
1 cup heavy cream, whipped,
½ cup orange juice
½ teaspoon grated orange peel
1 tablespoon lemon juice

Combine the two mixtures and pour into deep freezing tray. Freeze. Serves 6.

FROZEN CAKE BALLS

Cover a scoop or ball of any flavor of ice cream with soft cake crumbs. Place on serving plate and cover with sauce. Vanilla Ice Cream with hot Uncooked Fudge Sauce and a generous sprinkling of chopped pecans is the favorite at Toll House. Other delicious combinations are raspberry or strawberry ice cream rolled in grated fresh coconut instead of cake crumbs and covered with fruit sauce of the same flavor as the ice cream. Many unusual combinations can be used, substituting chocolate cake or spicecake crumbs with various sauces.

ICE CREAM CLOWN

On a plate arrange a circle of colored whipped cream to look like a ruff or collar. In the middle of the cream set a ball of ice cream, preferably vanilla or strawberry. On top invert and securely set an ice cream cone. Decorate the ball of ice cream with pecan ears, raisin eyes, and cherry nose and mouth. This is easily handled by a child who simply picks up the cone and eats it like an ordinary ice cream cone. We make thousands of these clowns at Toll House each year for our younger guests.

JACK FROST'S SURPRISE CAKES

Cover a board with wax paper. Cut heart-shaped pieces from a thin sheet of Spongecake. Place on top of each heart a serving of ice cream, allowing about half an inch of cake to extend beyond the ice cream. Cover with meringue made by slowly adding 4 egg whites, beaten stiff, to 4 tablespoons powdered sugar. Brown quickly under broiler flame and serve immediately.

12. SAUCES OF ALL KINDS

ॐ

We have gone from the sublime to the very plainest of sauces in this chapter. The Sunshine Sauce recipe may be made for Holiday Christmas Plum Pudding *before* you go to the table. Then when you are ready to serve, just run the beater through it for a minute. I remember my grandmother never had a sauce but that it separated on standing, so she waited to make the whole thing between courses. But that is a great bother. It's much nicer to have everything really ready at the beginnnig of a meal, if it is at all possible. We flavor Sunshine Sauce with rum at Toll House on the great day and some guests even take Sunshine Sauce plus Hard Sauce on their plum pudding.

The making of sauces is an art. Even a simple white sauce can be good or bad and taste like wallpaper paste or be really marvelous. It all depends on the care you give its preparation and the length of time you cook it. It is well worth perfecting.

A good hollandaise is another challenge. What a delectable dish it makes of plain boiled asparagus or broccoli. How different chicken or fish tastes with this velvet-textured lemon-flavored sauce poured over it. Fine hollandaise is certainly well worth learning to achieve.

MAIN-DISH SAUCES

ANCHOVY SAUCE
(For Shirred Clams, mushrooms, or broiled whole white fish)

Blend
2 tablespoons butter, melted,
4 tablespoons flour. Add slowly
1 cup milk. Cook over low heat, stirring until thick.

Add:
½ teaspoon grated onion
½ teaspoon anchovy paste
Season further if desired

Makes 1 cup of sauce.

BARBECUE SAUCE
(For spareribs, frankfurters, hamburg)

Sauté until brown
2 onions, sliced, in
2 tablespoons fat.
Combine:
1 teaspoon dry mustard
2 tablespoons vinegar

½ bottle catsup
1 tablespoon **Worcestershire** sauce
½ cup water
½ teaspoon salt
Few grains pepper

Add onions and simmer for 30 to 35 minutes. Makes ½ cups sauce.

BÉARNAISE SAUCE
(For steak or other meat)

Blend and cook slowly
3 tablespoons dry white wine
3 tablespoons white wine vinegar
8 white pepper kernels, crushed,
2 medium shallots, chopped,

2 sprigs tarragon (preferably fresh)
2 sprigs parsley
1 bay leaf
½ teaspoon meat extract or 1 teaspoon A-1 sauce

Cook wine mixture slowly until reduced to half original amount. Force through a fine sieve. Add 6 slightly beaten egg yolks and, with heat turned off, stir eggs and wine together until well blended. Remove from hot water and add slowly 1 pound melted butter. Beat continually until smooth. If not to be served immediately, hold at moderate temperature. Makes 2 cups sauce.

YELLOW BÉCHAMEL SAUCE

(For croquettes and Surprise Potatoes)

Combine in saucepan:
2 tablespoons butter. Add:
1 tablespoon chopped onion
1 sprig parsley, chopped,
½ teaspoon thyme
1 bay leaf. Cook slowly until onion is golden brown.

Stir in
2 tablespoons flour. Add slowly
¾ cup milk or stock. Cook until thickened. Add a little of mixture to
1 egg yolk

Stir egg mixture into remaining milk or stock. Cook for 1 minute and serve hot with meat. Makes 1 cup sauce.

Variation: Use sauce in preparation of croquettes or Surprise Potatoes, but reserve a little to thin out with hot milk and use as sauce for either dish.

CHEESE SAUCE

(For vegetables or boiled fish)

Heat in top of double boiler
1 cup milk. Blend:
2 tablespoons flour
2 tablespoons melted butter. Stir into hot milk. Season

with salt and pepper. When mixture begins to thicken, add
1 cup grated cheese

Stir until cheese has melted and sauce is smooth. Makes 2 cups sauce.

CUCUMBER DRESSING

(For salmon or other fish)

Combine:
½ cup heavy cream, whipped,
¼ teaspoon salt
Few grains pepper

2 tablespoons vinegar. Add
1 cucumber, pared and chopped fine

Makes 1 cup sauce.

SAUCE DIABLE
(For steak, lamb chops, broiled fish)

Combine:
½ cup melted butter
½ cup light cream
1 teaspoon prepared mustard

2 tablespoons Worcestershire sauce
4 tablespoons A-1 Sauce
1 bottle (6-oz.) Sauce Escoffier Provencale

Makes 2 cups sauce.

EGG SAUCE
(For fish or vegetables)

Prepare 1 cup White Sauce. Let stand, covered, for 15 minutes. Then beat with rotary beater to blend. Season with salt, pepper, a little mustard, and paprika. Add 1 sliced hard-cooked egg. Makes 1½ cups sauce.

HOLLANDAISE SAUCE
(For green vegetables, fish, chicken)

Cream in top of double boiler
½ cup butter. Add
4 egg yolks, one at a time, beating each in thoroughly with rotary beater or wire whisk before adding the next. Add:

¼ teaspoon salt
Few grains cayenne, and very slowly,
½ cup boiling water. Cook until thick. Add
Juice of 1 lemon

During cooking keep top section of boiler well above hot water boiling below. Finally beat mixture well, using a rotary beater. Serve warm over vegetables or cold on salads. Makes 2 cups sauce. (In rare event that this sauce curdles, beat in slowly 1 tablespoon cream which will act as a blending agent.)

HORSERADISH SAUCE
(For beef)

Blend:
4 tablespoons melted fat
2 tablespoons flour. Add:

1 cup milk. Season with Salt. Add
6 tablespoons horseradish

Cook slowly until thickened. Makes 1 cup sauce.

MAÎTRE D'HÔTEL BUTTER
(For potatoes, steak, fish)

Cream
6 tablespoons butter. Add:
Few drops lemon juice
1 teaspoon salt

¼ teaspoon pepper
1 teaspoon finely chopped parsley

Makes ½ cup sauce, enough for 6 medium-sized potatoes.

MINT SAUCE
(For lamb)

Wash, dry, chop fine
1 bunch mint leaves. Mix with

¾ cup currant, plum, or tart apple jelly. Add
Grated rind of ½ orange

Makes about 1 cup sauce.

MUSTARD SAUCE
(For broiled fish, hamburg, steak, tripe)

Sauté until tender
1 tablespoon minced onion in
3 tablespoons butter. Add
2 tablespoons vinegar. Simmer for 5 minutes. Moisten

2 teaspoons dry mustard with
1 tablespoon water. Add to vinegar mixture. Blend in
1 cup brown gravy

Simmer together for about 5 minutes. Makes 1¼ cups sauce. Serves 4.

RAISIN SAUCE
(For baked ham)

Bring to boil:
1 cup water
1 cup sugar. Add:
1 cup seedless raisins
2 tablespoons butter
2 tablespoons vinegar
½ teaspoon salt

¼ teaspoon clove
¼ teaspoon cinnamon
1 glass (6-oz.) grape jelly. Add
1 teaspoon cornstarch, dissolved in a little cold water

Stir over low heat until mixture thickens slightly and raisins are plump. Serve hot. Makes 3 cups sauce. (Sauce for ham should never be of heavy or of thick consistency.)

RAREBIT SAUCE
(For baked fish)

Melt in top of double boiler
2 tablespoons butter. Blend in
1 tablespoon flour
½ teaspoon salt
¼ teaspoon prepared mustard
Add slowly

1 cup milk. Stir until thick.
Add
1 cup grated cheese. Stir until melted. Add
1 egg, slightly beaten

Cook a few minutes more, pour over fish, and sprinkle with paprika. Makes 2 cups sauce.

TARTAR SAUCE
(For fish)

Combine:
4 tablespoons mayonnaise
2 tablespoons chopped gherkins
2 tablespoons chopped olives

2 tablespoons chopped onion
2 tablespoons chopped parsley
½ tablespoon chopped capers

Makes ¾ cup sauce. Serves 4.

WHITE SAUCE OR BASIC CREAM SAUCE
(See Primer for Brides, page 73)

DESSERT SAUCES

BUTTERED RUM SAUCE
(For Baba au Rhum)

Boil for 2 minutes:
2 cups sugar
1 cup cold water. Remove from heat and add

1 tablespoon butter. Cool and add
⅓ cup rum

Makes 3 cups sauce.

BUTTERSCOTCH SAUCE

(For ice cream or over cake)

Combine:

1⅓ cups white sugar	½ cup light corn syrup
2 cups brown sugar	1¼ cups boiling water. Add
	3 tablespoons butter

Boil mixture until the thread stage is reached, 225° F. Cool slightly and serve. Makes 2 cups sauce.

PROFESSIONAL BUTTERSCOTCH SAUCE WITH CREAM

(For ice cream or over cake)

Combine:

1¼ cups sugar	1 tablespoon butter
¾ cup light corn syrup	½ pint light cream
	½ teaspoon salt

Cook mixture until soft ball stage, 234° F. Remove from heat. If too thick, dilute with milk. Serve hot or cold. Makes about 2 cups sauce. (This can be stored in refrigerator. Place over hot water when reheating, and if necessary, add cream or milk to thin. Sauce is the real caramel-type, rich butterscotch sauce and the kind guests at Toll House prefer.)

CHOCOLATE SAUCE

(For ice cream, cream puffs, cake)

Melt in saucepan	¼ cup cocoa
¼ cup butter. Add	¾ cup sugar
¼ cup shaved chocolate. Stir	½ cup light cream
over low heat until smooth.	Pinch salt
Add:	1 teaspoon vanilla

Bring to boiling point. Serve hot or cold. Makes 1½ cups sauce. (This can be stored and reheated over hot water when needed.)

UNCOOKED FUDGE SAUCE

(For ice cream, cream puffs, cake)

Prepare Miracle Fudge Frosting. For a hot sauce increase

amount of milk to ½ cup. For cold sauce increase amount of milk to about ¾ cup. Otherwise consistency is heavy. Makes 1½ cups sauce.

CLARET SAUCE

Boil together for 5 minutes:　1 cup sugar. Add to
½ cup water　　　　　　　　¼ cup claret wine

Serve cold on ice cream or pudding. Makes about 1½ cups sauce.

Variation: Claret Punch or Claret Lemonade. Use sauce diluted with charged water and mixed with ice. Our famous Boston Pop Concerts have featured Claret Punch for many years.

CINNAMON SAUCE

(For waffles or toast)

Cream　　　　　　　　　　　⅓ cup powdered sugar
2 tablespoons butter. Combine:　½ teaspoon cinnamon

Combine butter and sugar mixture and melt slightly over hot water just before serving. Makes ½ cup sauce. Spread on toast which is slipped under broiler to brown for excellent tea-time cinnamon toast.

CUSTARD SAUCE

Heat in top of double boiler　½ cup sugar. Add to
1 cup milk. Mix　　　　　　　2 egg yolks, well beaten
1 tablespoon cornstarch with

Mix well. Pour hot milk slowly into egg mixture. Then return to top of double boiler. Cook 10 minutes. Add 1 teaspoon vanilla. When cold and ready to serve pour over dessert. Makes 1½ cups sauce.

HARD SAUCE

This is a sauce best made with the fingers, I think, because the heat of the hand softens the shortening and the sugar is more readily absorbed. Either confectioners, granulated, or brown sugar may be used and with butter preferably. When butter is expensive, use a vegetable shortening, but add a strong flavor to conceal the taste. With butter, use less flavoring so as not to destroy the good butter taste.

Cream until soft	1 tablespoon cream
⅓ cup butter. Gradually blend in:	1 teaspoon rum, or almond extract or ¼ teaspoon cinnamon or nutmeg
1 cup confectioners sugar	

Beat mixture until fluffy. Pile lightly in serving dish. Chill until cold but not hard. Makes about ¾ cup sauce.

Variations: Substitute for 1 tablespoon cream and 1 teaspoon extract the same amount of brandy, strong coffee, rum, whiskey, orange juice, maraschino cherry juice, preserved ginger with syrup, mashed bananas, strawberries, raspberries, blueberries, or apricot purée.

FLUFFY SAUCE
(For tart fruit puddings)

Combine:	½ cup boiling water. Bring to boil. Add:
1 cup sugar	
2 tablespoons flour. Stir in	1 teaspoon vanilla
	2 egg whites, beaten stiff

Serve hot. Makes 1½ cups sauce.

LEMON SAUCE
(For puddings)

Combine:	to keep mixture smooth. Boil
1 cup sugar	5 minutes. Remove from
3 tablespoons flour	heat. Add:
Few grains salt. Gradually add	Grated rind and juice of 1 lemon
2 cups boiling water, stirring	2 tablespoons butter

Mix well and serve hot. Makes 2 cups sauce.

MOCK MAPLE SAUCE

(For Steamed Chocolate Pudding)

Cream together:

⅓ cup butter

1 cup light brown sugar. Add:

1 egg yolk, beaten,

1 teaspoon vanilla. Mix well. Add

1 egg white, beaten stiff

Makes 1½ cups sauce.

PUDDING SAUCE

(For Fruit Cobbler or Dutch Apple Cake)

Bring to boil:

Juice and grated rind of 1 lemon

⅔ cup sugar

½ cup pineapple or peach juice. Add to

3 egg yolks, beaten well. Cook until thick in top of double boiler. Cool and add

1 cup whipped cream

Makes 2 cups sauce.

ORANGE SAUCE

(For Orange Sponge Pudding or a bread pudding)

Beat

2 egg yolks. Add:

¼ cup powdered sugar

Juice and grated rind ½

orange. Just before serving add

1 cup whipped cream

Serve cold. Makes 1½ cups sauce.

STERLING SAUCE

(For steamed puddings)

Cream together:

½ cup butter

1 cup brown sugar. Add slowly to prevent separation:

4 tablespoons light cream or milk

1 teaspoon vanilla

Makes 1½ cups sauce.

SUNSHINE SAUCE

(For Holiday Plum Pudding or other steamed puddings)

Beat
1 egg yolk. Add slowly while beating
¼ cup sugar. Beat
1 egg white stiff. Add

¼ cup sugar. Fold in egg-yolk mixture. Add
1 teaspoon vanilla. Just before serving fold in
⅔ cup heavy cream, whipped

Chill. Makes 2 cups sauce.

Variation: Flavor with 1 teaspoon rum or brandy instead of vanilla.

TROPICAL SAUCE

(For plain cake or pudding)

In top of double boiler beat
3 egg yolks slightly. Add:
¼ cup sugar
⅓ teaspoon salt. Scald
2 cups milk and add, stir-

ring constantly until mixture coats spoon. Chill. Add:
1 cup whipped cream
3 tablespoons chopped candied fruits

Makes 3 cups sauce.

VANILLA SAUCE

(For steamed puddings or any tart stewed fruit)

Cook for 2 minutes:
2 tablespoons butter, melted,
1 tablespoon cornstarch. Add gradually
½ cup milk. Stir until mixture

boils. Simmer 5 minutes. Beat in bowl
2 eggs until light. Gradually add
1 cup sugar

Place bowl in dish of hot water, and add hot mixture, beating constantly for 5 minutes so that sauce will be hot throughout and quite frothy. Just before serving add ½ teaspoon vanilla. Makes 2 cups sauce.

13. CAKES AND COOK-IES, TOLL HOUSE SPECIALTIES

My grandmother made wonderful cakes and cookies and I have been fortunate to inherit so many of her excellent recipes which were written out in her precise, spidery hand in a ruled copy book. But her recipes weren't set up the modern way and it has been difficult to translate them into standard requirements. Grandmother measured sugar in her "blue cup" and flour in her "yellow bowl" and everything she made was delicious. Two of her triumphs, which you will find here, were Applesauce Cake and Hot Milk Cake. This is our basic cake recipe at Toll House. We use it for Boston Cream Pie, Baba au Rhum, and for layer cakes with various fillings.

At Toll House we also make the new type one-bowl cakes and recommend them also to you, particularly if you have an electric mixer. The Orange Chiffon Cake of this kind is outstandingly good.

I suppose most of you know Toll House Chocolate Crunch Cookies. Their origin and development is really a story by itself. People never seem to tire of them and they carry well too. During the war we shipped thousands of dozens of them to boys and girls in service all over the world. Our Brownies were popular with them too, and that recipe seems to be almost fool-proof. Everyone enthuses over "good luck" with it.

Many questions have been asked me about the problems of cake baking. For the last seven years I have kept these queries in a folder which now bursts with more than a thousand of them. In this latest revision of Toll House Recipes I have answered all these questions, drawing on our Sue's knowledge of baking, and our Jack's of cooking, as well as on my own experience. Here is a whole section on baking. I hope it answers every question you may have. (See also Timetable for Baking, page 20.)

GUIDE TO SUCCESSFUL BAKING

1. Select a reliable recipe and follow it exactly.
2. Use standard ingredients of good quality. Be certain that baking powder, soda, cream of tartar, and other such dry ingredients, as well as perishables like eggs, are fresh.
3. Keep all powdered ingredients *dry* at all times.
4. Use standard level measurements.
5. Follow carefully any special mixing directions of the recipe.
6. In cake-making you may follow the new method, which is to blend vanilla with sugar and shortening at the beginning. Then the fat seals fragrance and flavor and less is lost through evaporation in baking.
7. Fill cake pans no more than two-thirds full.
8. Use cake pans which are level and not warped.
9. Select pans of suitable depth for type of cake you are baking. Too deep a pan for amount of batter will interfere with browning of cake.
10. Bake biscuits and cookies on flat baking sheets or in very shallow pans. The bottom of an inverted cake or pie pan may be used.
11. Remember that dull-finished pans brown cookies and biscuits more than bright, shiny ones.
12. Place pans on oven racks, never on bottom of oven.
13. Avoid crowding oven. Pans too close to sides of oven or too close to each other prevent proper heat conduction, causing hot spots and consequent uneven rising and browning. There must be ample clearance between pan and oven side and between pans on same rack for proper circulation.

14. Length of baking time and temperature vary with size, shape, and type of pan. A lower temperature and longer time is required for larger quantity or thicker food. A loaf cake takes longer than a layer.

15. Time and temperature given in cookbooks are normally for preheated ovens. A preheated oven is one heated to desired temperature before food is placed in it.

16. In preparing pan for cake containing shortening, grease or oil thoroughly and then sprinkle with a tablespoon of flour. Tip pan so that a thin coating of flour covers it. Turn upside down to remove excess. Pour in batter.

CAKE FAILURES AND THEIR CAUSES

Rises Higher on One Side
a. Batter spread unevenly in pan
b. Oven racks or range not level
c. Warped pans
d. Pans placed too close to sides of oven or to other pans on same rack.

Burns on Side and Bottom
a. Oven too full
b. Oven too hot
c. Pans placed too near bottom of oven
d. Glass, granite, or black metal pans intensify condition
e. Pans too close to sides of oven or to other pans on same rack

Humps or Cracks on Top
a. Too hot oven
b. Too much flour or wrong kind—when bread not cake flour used, should decrease each cupful by ⅛

Spongecakes. Also eggs overbeaten, causing loss of moisture

Falls and Is Soggy
a. Insufficient baking
b. Too much shortening
c. Too much leavening
d. Too much sugar
e. Too slow baking

f. Not enough flour or too much liquid

Spongecakes. Also cooled without inverting pan

Dry

a. Too much flour
b. Not enough shortening
c. Not enough sugar
d. Overbeaten mixture
e. Too much leavening
f. Baked too long

Spongecakes. Also overbeaten egg whites

Tough

a. Temperature too high
b. Not enough sugar
c. Not enough shortening
d. Overbeaten

Spongecakes. Also overbeaten egg whites

Soggy Layer at Bottom

a. Insufficient mixing
b. Damp flour used
c. Insufficient baking
d. Insufficient leavening

Yellow spongecakes. Also egg yolks not sufficiently beaten and blended with other ingredients

Coarse-Grained

a. Too much leavening
b. Insufficient mixing
c. Temperature too low

Spongecakes. Also eggs not beaten enough

Cake Runs Over Sides of Pan

a. Too much batter in pan—pan should be only ⅔ full
b. Too much leavening
c. Too slow baking
d. Too much sugar
e. Too much shortening

Pale on Sides and Bottom (Moist Sticky Appearance)

a. Shiny tin or aluminum pan may cause this

b. Oven not hot enough

c. Insufficient baking

d. Left too long in pan, causing steaming—should remove butter cakes after 5 minutes

Sticks to Sides and Bottom of Pan

a. Pan not properly prepared

b. Left too long in pan, causing steaming—Should remove after 5 minutes

c. Insufficient baking

d. Too much sugar

COOKY FAILURES AND THEIR CAUSES

Burn on Bottom

a. Pan set on too low rack in oven

b. Pan too large for oven

c. Black or granite pan used

d. Pan too deep

Too Brown on Top

a. Pan set too high in oven

b. Baking time too long

c. Flue may be obstructed

Burn Around Edges of Pan

a. Oven too hot

b. Pans too large

c. Oven too full for proper air circulation

All measurements for flour are given for flour sifted once before measuring.

CAKES WITH SHORTENING

To be certain of even edges and no breaks, remove all cakes made with shortening most carefully from the pan. Before turning them out, let them cool about 5 minutes, but not much longer. If a baked cake remains too long in the pan, it will "sweat" and the fine, firm outside crust will peel off.

STANDARD LAYER CAKE
(See Primer for Brides, page 77)

ORANGE LAYER CAKE WITH FILLING

Cream
½ cup shortening. Blend in
1¼ cups sugar. Sift
   together:
2½ cups cake flour
¼ teaspoon salt
2½ teaspoons baking powder.

Add alternately to first
   mixture with
¾ cup orange juice and
2 tablespoons lemon juice.
   Beat for 2 minutes. Add
2 eggs

Beat 2 minutes more. Turn into two 8-inch layer pans and bake in moderate oven, 375° F., for 25 to 30 minutes. When cake has cooled, spread the following filling between layers and frost with Orange Icing.

Orange Filling

Mix together:
1 tablespoon cornstarch
3 tablespoons sugar. Add:

1 tablespoon butter
½ cup orange juice
1 tablespoon lemon juice

Cook together until clear. Cool and spread between layers of cake.

VIRGINIA LAYER CAKE

Cream
¾ cup butter. Add gradually
1 cup sugar. Then
1 egg yolk, unbeaten. Beat
   hard. Add
1 egg yolk. Beat hard. Add
1 whole egg. Sift together
   3 times:

2 cups flour
2 teaspoons baking powder
½ teaspoon mace
½ teaspoon salt. Add to first
   mixture alternately with
½ cup milk

Turn into 2 greased 8-inch layer pans and bake in moderate oven, 375° F., for 20 to 25 minutes.

CHOCOLATE CAKE

Cream together:
½ cup butter
¾ cup sugar. Add:
3 egg yolks, beaten light,
½ teaspoon vanilla
2 squares chocolate, melted.
Sift together:

2 cups flour
3 teaspoons baking powder.
Add to first mixture alternately with
¾ cup milk. Fold in
3 egg whites, beaten stiff

Turn into greased loaf pan and bake in moderate oven, 350° F., for 45 minutes, or bake in deep greased 8-inch-square pan at 375° for 30 minutes.

MOTHER'S CHOCOLATE FUDGE CAKE

Cream
½ cup butter. Add
1 cup sugar. Mix well. Add
3 eggs, beating in one at a time. Sift together:
2¼ cups flour
1 teaspoon cream of tartar
½ teaspoon soda
Heat together:

2 squares chocolate
5 tablespoons sugar
3 tablespoons hot water. Add sifted dry ingredients to first mixture, alternately with
1 cup milk. Add chocolate mixture and
1 teaspoon vanilla

Turn into deep greased 8-inch-square pan and bake in moderate oven, 350° F. to 375°, for 30 to 40 minutes.

NEVER-FAIL CHOCOLATE CAKE

Melt
2 tablespoons shortening with
2 squares chocolate. Mix with
1 cup sugar. Add
1 egg, beaten well. Sift together:

1½ cups flour
1 teaspoon baking soda
Speck salt. Add to first mixture alternately with
1 cup sour milk. Add
1 teaspoon vanilla

Beat a few minutes with rotary beater. Turn into deep greased 8-inch-square pan and bake in a moderate oven, 375° F., for 45 minutes. When cool, frost with 7-Minute Frosting. (This is my own favorite recipe for an inexpensive chocolate cake to be used immediately.)

DORIS CUNNINGHAM'S CHOCOLATE CAKE

Melt over hot water:
2 squares chocolate
2 tablespoons milk
2 tablespoons sugar
Egg-sized piece butter or margarine. Stir until smooth. Combine:
1 cup sugar
1 teaspoon cream of tartar

1 heaping cup sifted cake flour
½ teaspoon salt. Add chocolate mixture with:
½ cup milk
1 teaspoon vanilla. Beat until blended. Add
2 eggs

Beat well. Turn into greased 8-inch layer or cupcake pans or loaf pan. Bake in very slow oven, 275° F., for 30 minutes for layer and cupcakes; 40 minutes for loaf cakes. Frost with Doris Cunningham's Beaten Chocolate Frosting.

CROSS-WORD PUZZLE CAKE

Cream together:
½ cup butter
1½ cups sugar. Add:
Grated rind of 1 orange
2 egg yolks, beaten.
Sift together:
2½ cups flour
¼ teaspoon salt
4 teaspoons baking powder.

Add to first mixture alternately with
1 cup milk. Fold in
1 egg white, beaten very light.
Divide batter and add
1½ squares chocolate to one half

Spread batter out in 2 round greased 8-inch layer pans. Start with circle of light batter in center. Surround this with ring of dark, and so on until pan is filled. In second pan start with circle of dark batter in center. Surround this with ring of light batter, and so on until pan is filled. Bake in moderate oven, 375° F., about 20 minutes. Spread Chocolate Frosting between layers and over top and sides.

CRANBERRY CAKE

Cream
½ cup butter. Add gradually
1 cup sugar. Add
3 eggs, one at a time, beating hard after each. Add
1 cup cranberries, stewed with
¾ cup water, and strained.
Sift together:
2 cups flour
3 teaspoons baking powder
⅛ teaspoon clove
⅛ teaspoon cinnamon
¼ teaspoon salt

Add to first mixture. Beat thoroughly. Turn into deep greased 8-inch-square pan or loaf pan and bake in moderate oven, 350° F., for 50 minutes.

GOLD CAKE

Cream
⅓ cup shortening. Add slowly
1 cup sugar. Add
4 egg yolks, unbeaten. Mix well. Sift together twice:
1⅔ cups pastry flour
¼ teaspoon salt
2 teaspoons baking powder. Add alternately to first mixture with
½ cup milk

Beat well and turn into greased loaf pan. Bake in moderate oven, 360° F., for 45 minutes. Frost with 7-Minute Frosting. (You can use whites of eggs for an Angel Cake or a Chocolate Cake.)

GRANDMOTHER'S APPLESAUCE CAKE

Cream
4 tablespoons shortening. Add:
1 cup sugar
1 egg, well beaten. Sift together:
2 cups flour
1 teaspoon cinnamon
1 teaspoon cocoa
½ teaspoon nutmeg
¼ teaspoon clove. Add to first mixture alternately with
1 teaspoon soda, dissolved in
1 cup sour milk, or in 1 cup sour applesauce, and
1 cup chopped raisins

Turn into greased loaf pan and bake in moderate oven, 350° F., for 45 to 60 minutes.

MARY JANE GINGERBREAD

Cream together:
¼ cup butter
½ cup sugar. Add:
1 egg, beaten,
¼ cup dark molasses.
Sift together:
1 cup flour
Pinch salt

1 teaspoon baking soda
¼ teaspoon cinnamon
¼ scant teaspoon clove
¼ scant teaspoon nutmeg. Mix well and add alternately with
½ cup boiling water

Turn into a deep greased 8-inch-square pan and bake in hot oven, 400° F., for 30 to 40 minutes.

Variation: Since this is a very thin mixture, it may be baked in waffle iron. Two waffles with whipped cream between make a delicious dessert. (This was my Grandmother's recipe and she used no ginger!)

SPICECAKE

Cream together:
1½ cups brown sugar
½ cup butter. Beat in
1 egg and
3 egg yolks until light.
Add
1 cup milk.

Sift together:
2½ cups flour
4 teaspoons baking powder
1 teaspoon cinnamon
⅛ teaspoon cloves
½ teaspoon salt

Combine mixtures. Turn into greased 8-inch-square pan and bake in moderate oven, 350° F. to 360°, for 30 to 40 minutes. Cover with Meringue Topping and put back in oven for a few minutes to brown.

Meringue Topping

Beat stiff
2 egg whites.

Gradually add
1½ cups brown sugar.

Beat until very thick and pile on cake.

POUNDCAKE

Cream
1 cup butter. Sift together
and gradually add
1½ cups *sifted* pastry flour
¾ teaspoon baking powder
¼ teaspoon salt
¼ teaspoon mace. Beat
4 egg yolks. Add

1⅓ cups confectioners sugar.
Combine with first mixture. Fold in
4 egg whites, beaten stiff.
Beat all together until
smooth. Add
1 teaspoon vanilla

Bake in greased loaf pan in moderate oven, 350° F., for 45 to 55 minutes. (This recipe was given me by one of my students and is my favorite cake recipe.)

SLOP-OVER CAKE (*Grandma Jones' Neighborhood Favorite*)

Sift together:
1 cup sugar
1¾ cups pastry flour
1 teaspoon cream of
tartar

½ teaspoon soda. Melt
¼ cup butter. Break
1 egg into cup with butter.
Add
Milk to fill cup

Beat mixture well. Turn into two greased 8-inch layer pans and bake in moderately hot oven, 375° F. to 400°, for 25 to 30 minutes.

CAKES WITHOUT SHORTENING

The perfection of cakes made without shortening, such as Spongecake and Angel Cake, depends partly on the way they are removed from the pan. This must not be a hasty process if they are to retain their height and fluffy texture. It is best to invert the baked cake on a cake rack and let it cool for about 1 hour before attempting to remove it from the pan. So inverted, it is gradually cooled by the circulation of air beneath it. If the cake has risen so high that its top would rest on the rack when the pan is inverted, prop it up by resting it on other pans or bowls, placed under the outer edges of the pan. When the cake has somewhat cooled, run a spatula most carefully around the edge and tap the bottom gently to loosen it. Then let the cake slip out on the palm of the left hand and quickly turn the cake right side up onto a plate.

ANGEL CAKE

Beat until frothy:
1 full cup egg whites
¼ teaspoon salt. Add
¾ teaspoon cream of tartar. Continue beating until egg whites will hold form but are moist enough to drop from beater. Gradually add
1¼ cups sugar, beating con-tinually during addition. Avoid overbeating.
Gradually add
1 cup flour, sifted four times, folding into egg whites very carefully. Add
1 teaspoon vanilla and
¼ teaspoon almond extract. Avoid overbeating

Turn into ungreased 9-inch tube cake pan and place in cold oven. Set regulator at 300° F. and bake about 1 hour, increasing temperature to 325° when cake is almost done. Remove cake from oven and invert pan until cake is cold. Frost with Angel Cake Icing.

SPONGECAKE
(See Primer for Brides, page 76)

APRICOT SPONGECAKE OR
APRICOT UPSIDE-DOWN CAKE

Melt in spider:
2 tablespoons butter
1 cup brown sugar. Place flat side down in mixture
1 can (2½ cups) apricot halves, drained.
Beat until light
3 egg yolks. Add:
1 cup sugar
Pinch salt. Beat well. Sift together:
1 cup flour
1 teaspoon baking powder. Add alternately to egg mixture with
½ cup hot water. Beat well. Fold in
3 egg whites, beaten

Pour batter over apricots and bake in moderate oven, 350° F., for 30 to 40 minutes. Turn out on plate so that apricots are on top. Place a maraschino cherry in center of each apricot and serve with whipped cream. Serves 8. (Baked without fruit, this is an excellent spongecake.)

HOT MILK CAKE *(Toll House Basic Recipe)*

Beat stiff
2 egg whites. Beat until light
2 egg yolks. Add to whites and
   beat together. Slowly add
1 cup sugar. Beat with a spoon
   for 5 minutes. Sift together:
1 cup flour

1 teaspoon baking powder
   Pinch salt. Add to egg
   mixture. Beat in
½ cup hot milk in which
1 tablespoon butter has been
   melted

Turn into 7-inch-square pan lined with wax paper. Bake in a moderate oven, 360° F., for 25–30 minutes. (Usually no flavoring is used in spongecake, but we add ½ teaspoon lemon extract and ½ teaspoon vanilla to this recipe.)

DAFFODIL EASTER CAKE

Beat until foamy
1 cup egg whites. Add:
½ teaspoon salt
1 teaspoon cream of tartar.
   Beat until stiff but not
   dry. Fold in carefully
1 cup and 2 tablespoons
   sugar. Divide mixture. Fold
   into one part:

½ cup flour, sifted 5 times
½ teaspoon vanilla. Fold
   into other part:
6 egg yolks, beaten,
⅔ cup flour, sifted
   5 times,
½ teaspoon orange
   extract

Place by spoonfuls into ungreased 9-inch tube cake pan, alternating yellow and white batters as in marble cake. Bake in slow oven, 325° F., for 60 minutes. Invert pan and let stand until cool. (This cake is a Toll House tradition for Easter menus.)

ORANGE CHIFFON CAKE (*A Betty Crocker Masterpiece*)

Sift some cake flour onto a
square of paper. Measure
and sift together:
1½ cups flour
¾ cup sugar
1½ teaspoon baking powder
½ teaspoon salt. Make a well
in center and add:
¼ cup salad oil

2 egg yolks, unbeaten,
1 tablespoon grated orange
rind
Juice of 1 orange plus
water to make ⅜ cup
liquid. Beat smooth. Beat
until very stiff
½ cup (about 4) egg whites
¼ teaspoon cream of tartar

Pour egg-yolk mixture gradually over whites, gently folding them in with rubber scraper until just blended. Do not stir. Pour immediately into ungreased 8- or 9-inch-square pan and bake in moderate oven, 350° F. Or use 9-inch tube pan, 3½ inches deep, and bake at 325° for 50 minutes. Invert pan, resting edges on cooling rack or on two other pans. Let cake hang free of table until cold. Loosen from sides of pan with spatula. Hit edge of pan sharply on table to loosen bottom. Frost or dust with confectioners sugar.

HOLIDAY FRUIT AND NUT CAKES

LIGHT FRUITCAKE

Cream together:
1 cup butter
1 cup sugar. Add:
5 egg yolks, well beaten,
Grated rind and juice of
½ lemon
1¼ cups raisins, cut up,
¾ cup candied cherries

2 cups walnuts, cut up,
¼ pound citron, cut up.
Sift together:
2 cups flour
¼ teaspoon soda. Add to first
mixture alternately with
5 egg whites, beaten stiff

Turn into greased loaf or tube pans lined with wax paper. Bake in slow oven, 275° F., for 2½ to 3 hours. (See Dark Fruitcake for details of baking.) Makes 5 pounds or 3 loaves.

ALMOND CHRISTMAS CAKE

Cream
½ cup butter. Add:
1 cup sugar
½ pound almonds, blanched
   and chopped,
½ pound grated coconut
¼ pound candied cherries
   Blend together with fingers.
   Beat until stiff and dry

5 egg whites. Fold in part of
   egg whites. Sift together
   and add:
1½ cups flour
2 teaspoons baking powder.
   Fold in
½ teaspoon almond extract
   and remaining egg whites

Turn into greased loaf pan and bake in slow oven, 300° F., for about 2 hours. Makes 1 loaf.

DARK FRUITCAKE

Cream together:
1 cup sugar
½ cup butter. Add:
6 egg yolks, well beaten,
½ cup dark molasses. Mix
   well. Sift together and add:
2 cups flour
2 teaspoons allspice
¾ teaspoon mace
½ teaspoon nutmeg
⅛ teaspoon soda
2 teaspoons cinnamon. Flour
   the following well:
1 pound sultana raisins

½ pound currants
1½ pounds raisins
¾ pound citron. Add to
   first mixture. Then add:
¼ cup lemon juice
2 squares chocolate, melted
   with
¼ cup water. Add:
¼ cup fruit juice or
   boiled cider
6 egg whites, beaten stiff
   with
½ teaspoon salt

Fold well into mixture and pour into greased loaf or tube pan lined with wax paper. Bake in slow oven, 275° F., for 3 to 4 hours. Makes 5 pounds or 3 loaves.

The size of the eggs will vary the moisture content. It is wise to use a cake tester. A shallow pan filled with hot water and set in the oven while cakes are baking will improve texture and height, while giving cake a better glaze. This eliminates the old method of steaming and then drying off cake. At Toll House, we decorate with almond halves and candied cherries when cakes are nearly finished baking and tops are still moist. Then we return cakes to oven to complete baking. After baking, let cakes cool. Then remove from pan but retain paper on outside. Brush tops with brandy or rum and store in a cool place until ready to use. The longer ahead fruitcakes are made, the better their flavor. We use this recipe for wedding cake and at Christmas, we include it in hundreds of gift parcels.

SMALL CAKES AND COOKIES

LADY FINGERS

Beat stiff and dry
3 egg whites. Gradually add
⅓ cup powdered sugar. Continue beating. Add:

2 egg yolks, beaten thick,
¼ teaspoon vanilla. Sift together and fold in
⅓ cup flour
⅛ teaspoon salt

Using a pastry tube, shape about 4½ inches long and 1 inch wide on baking sheet covered with unbuttered paper. Sprinkle with powdered sugar. Bake in moderate oven, 350° F., for 8 minutes. Remove from paper with knife. Makes about 1 dozen.

BANDBOX CAKES

Cream
¼ cup butter. Gradually add:
½ cup sugar
5 egg yolks, beaten thick.
Sift together:

⅞ cup flour
1½ teaspoons baking powder.
Add to first mixture alternately with
¼ cup milk

Pour into small greased cupcake pans, filling each about a quarter full. Bake in moderate oven, 375° F., for about 12 minutes. When cool, ice and join in pairs. Place cakes on sides and fasten on a narrow "handle" made of thin strips of angelica.

Garnish in middle with small piece of maraschino cherry. Makes 12 double cakes.

Variation: **DELICIOUS NUT CAKES.** Stir into batter ½ cup broken nut meats and fill pans half full. Makes 16 small cakes.

BROWNIES

Combine:
1 cup sugar
2 eggs, beaten. Sift in
½ cup pastry flour. Add
2 squares chocolate, melted,

⅓ cup butter, melted.
Mix well. Stir in:
1 teaspoon vanilla
1 cup walnuts, broken

Spread about ¾ inch thick in greased 8-inch-square pan. Bake in moderately hot oven, 350° F. to 400°, for 25 to 30 minutes. When cooled a little, cut into squares or strips. Should be more like cake, but chewy. Makes about 16 Brownies.

CAKE-CRUMB MACAROONS

Beat stiff
1 egg white. Measure
½ cup powdered sugar.
Beat 2 tablespoons of the sugar into egg-white mix-

ture. Fold in remainder with:
½ cup fine cake crumbs
½ teaspoon almond flavoring

Shape in rounds on greased baking sheet. Bake in slow oven, 300° F., for 20 minutes. Makes 12 macaroons.

BUTTERSCOTCH PECAN CHEWS

Blend:
⅔ cup better, melted,
2½ cups dark brown sugar. Add
3 eggs. Mix well. Let stand until well cooled. Sift together:

2¾ cups flour
2½ teaspoons baking powder
½ teaspoon salt. Add to first mixture with
1¼ cups pecans, floured

Spread ¾ inch thick in greased 10-inch-square pan. Bake in moderate oven, 350° F., for 25 to 30 minutes. Makes about 25 squares, 2 by 2 inches. Similar to Brownies.

CHOCOLATE NUT CHEWS

Crush graham crackers to make
2 cups crumbs. Combine with:
1 cup sweetened condensed milk

6 oz. (1 c.) semi-sweet chocolate morsels
½ cup broken nut meats

Spread mixture smoothly in greased 8-inch-square pan lined with wax paper. Bake in moderate oven, 350° F., for 30 minutes. Cut while warm. Makes 16 squares.

MERINGUES OR KISSES

Beat until stiff and dry
4 egg whites. Gradually add
⅔ cup sugar. Continue beating until mixture

holds shape. Add
½ teaspoon vanilla. Fold in
⅓ cup sugar

Drop from tablespoon onto greased baking sheet, spacing 1 inch apart, or use pastry bag to shape. Sprinkle with pink and yellow sugar. Bake in slow oven, 275° F., for 20 to 30 minutes or until firm. Makes about 16 meringues.

AFTERNOON TEA CAKES

Cream
5 tablespoons butter. Gradually add
1 cup sugar. Cream well. Add
2 eggs, beaten light. Sift together:

1¾ cups flour
2½ teaspoons baking powder. Add alternately to first mixture with
½ cup milk

Turn into greased cups or muffin pans and bake in moderate oven, 375° F., for about 12 minutes. (If desired, 1 teaspoon lemon juice or vanilla may be added for flavoring.) Makes 16 cakes.

NUT TEA WAFERS
(See Primer for Brides, page 78)

MARSHMALLOW TEAS

Arrange marshmallows on saltines, allowing one to each cracker. Make a deep impression in center of each marshmallow and in each cavity drop a small dot of butter. Arrange on cooky sheet and brown in hot oven, 475° F. or under broiler, placing pan 2 inches below flame. When cold, place a slice of maraschino cherry or a bit of red jelly in center of each. Children love these.

SIMPLE SIMON SNAPS

Cream	1 egg, beaten,
½ cup butter. Gradually add:	¾ cup sifted flour
⅓ cup sugar	½ teaspoon vanilla

Drop small portions from tip of teaspoon onto greased cooky sheet. Place 2 inches apart. Press as thin as possible with a knife dipped in cold water. Bake in hot oven, 400° F., for 8 minutes. Makes 2½ dozen cookies.

GINGER SNAPS

Cream together:	Sift together:
½ cup butter	2⅔ cups flour
½ cup sugar. Add:	1 teaspoon ginger
½ cup dark molasses	1 teaspoon soda. Add to
¼ cup strong coffee.	first mixture

Let stand until flour swells. Roll quite thin and bake in moderate oven, 350° F., for 6 to 8 minutes. Makes about 5 dozen cookies.

SCOTCH SHORTBREAD

Combine:	out on table covered with
1 egg	wax paper. Gradually rub
1 cup sugar. Mix in	in with hands
2 cups washed butter. Turn	4 cups sifted pastry flour

Pat out ¼ inch thick and cut with fancy cutter. Bake in moderate oven, 350° F., about 15 minutes, until brown. Makes 6 dozen cookies.

CORNFLAKE COOKIES

Cream
2 tablespoons butter. Add
1 cup sugar, mixed with
¼ teaspoon salt and
1 teaspoon baking powder.

Add
3 eggs, beaten light.
Add
5 cups cornflakes
1 teaspoon vanilla

Mix well and drop by teaspoonfuls onto shallow greased pan. Bake in hot oven, 400° F., for 6 to 8 minutes. Remove from pan while cookies are still hot. Makes 6 dozen cookies.

CHOCOLATE PINWHEELS

Cream
½ cup butter. Gradually add
½ cup sugar. Drop in
1 egg yolk. Beat mixture well. Add
3 tablespoons milk. Sift together:

1½ cups flour
½ teaspoon baking powder
⅛ teaspoon salt. Add to first mixture. Remove half to floured board. Add
1 square chocolate, melted, to remainder.

Roll white mixture into thin rectangular sheet. Roll chocolate mixture into sheet of same size. Place chocolate dough over white dough and roll both over and over into roll about 2 inches in diameter. Set in refrigerator to stiffen. Cut in thin slices with sharp knife and lay flat side down on greased cooky sheet. Bake in moderate oven, 350° F., about 6 to 8 minutes. Makes about 3 dozen cookies.

DATE-NUT MERINGUES

Beat stiff
2 egg whites. Slowly add:
1 cup confectioners sugar, sifted, beating all the time,

½ teaspoon vanilla
¼ teaspoon salt. Fold in
½ cup blanched almonds, cut fine
¼ pound dates, cut small

Drop from teaspoon onto greased cooky sheet. Bake in slow oven, 325° F., for 20 minutes, or until light straw-colored. Makes 3 dozen small meringues.

SUGAR JUMBLES

Cream together:
1¼ cups butter
1 cup sugar. Add:

2 eggs, beaten,
3 to 3½ cups sifted
flour

Mix well. Sprinkle board with sugar. Take tablespoonful of dough and roll between hands until size of lead pencil. Coil it around in sugar and place on greased cooky sheet. Bake in moderate oven, 375° F., for 6 to 8 minutes. Makes about 6 dozen cookies.

SPICE COOKIES

Cream together:
½ cup butter
1 cup sugar. Add:
1 egg, beaten,
½ cup sour milk in which
½ teaspoon soda has been
    dissolved.

Sift together and add:
2¼ cups flour
1 teaspoon cinnamon
Add:
¾ cup seeded raisins,
    chopped,
¾ cup nut meats, broken

Mix well and drop by teaspoonfuls onto greased cooky sheet. Bake in moderately hot oven, 375° F. to 400°, for 10 to 12 minutes. Makes about 4 dozen cookies.

HONOLULU DATE SQUARES

Place in saucepan:
2 cups dates, cut fine,
½ cup brown sugar
1 cup water
1 tablespoon flour. Cook
    until thick. Add
1 teaspoon vanilla.

Sift together:
1 cup flour
1 teaspoon baking soda. Add:
2 cups rolled oats or wheaties
1 cup brown sugar
¾ cup melted butter

Spread half of flour mixture thinly in greased 8- by 12-inch pan. Cover with date mixture, or filling. Spread other half of flour mixture over this. Bake in moderate oven, 365° F., for about 20 minutes. Cool. Cut in squares. The filling will remain very soft. Makes about 2 dozen squares. (For many years these have been the favorite at the Y.W.C.A. tearoom on the outskirts of Honolulu.)

SOFT GINGER COOKIES

Sift together:
2 cups flour
¼ teaspoon ginger
Few grains salt. Cut in
¼ cup shortening as for baking powder biscuits.

Add:
¾ cup dark molasses
¼ cup sour milk
¾ teaspoon soda, dissolved in small amount hot water

Mix well and drop by teaspoonfuls onto greased cooky sheet. Bake in moderate oven, 375° F., for 10 to 12 minutes. Makes about 3 dozen cookies.

DATE BARS

Combine:
1 egg, beaten light,
1 cup sugar. Beat, and add
1 cup dates, chopped,
1 cup nuts, chopped.
Sift together:

1 cup flour
½ teaspoon baking powder.
Add alternately to first mixture with
½ cup milk

Bake in greased 8- by 12-inch pan in moderate oven, 350° F., about 25 minutes. Let cool a little. Then cut into squares and dust with powdered sugar. Makes about 2 dozen squares.

HERMIT SQUARES .

Cream together:
¾ cup butter
1 cup sugar. Add
2 eggs, beaten light. Sift together:
2½ cups flour
1 teaspoon soda

1 teaspoon cream of tartar
¼ teaspoon cinnamon
¼ teaspoon nutmeg. Add
¾ cup chopped raisins. Add to first mixture alternately with
½ cup milk

Spread mixture ⅓ inch thick in greased 8- by 12-inch pan. Bake in moderate oven, 375° F., about 15 to 20 minutes. Cool.

Cut in squares. Makes about 2 dozen squares. (Brown or white sugar may be used.)

NOVEL LAYER COOKIES

Cream together:	together and add:
½ cup butter	1½ cups pastry flour
1 cup white sugar. Add:	1 teaspoon baking powder
2 eggs, beaten,	½ teaspoon salt.
½ teaspoon vanilla. Sift	

Drop mixture onto greased cooky sheet. With a knife dipped in cold water spread ½ inch thick. Cover with following topping and bake in moderate oven, 350° F., for 6 to 7 minutes. Makes 2 to 3 dozen cookies.

Brown Sugar Topping

Combine:	Smooth over cookies and
1 egg white, beaten well,	sprinkle with
½ teaspoon vanilla	¾ cup chopped walnuts
1 cup light brown sugar.	

This may also be spread on cooled cake and placed under the broiler until browned for a pleasant topping.

TOLL HOUSE CHOCOLATE CRUNCH COOKIES

Cream	2¼ cups flour sifted with
1 cup butter. Add:	1 teaspoon salt. Add:
¾ cup brown sugar	1 cup chopped nuts
¾ cup white sugar	12 oz. (2 c.) semi-sweet choco-
2 eggs, beaten. Dissolve	late morsels,
1 teaspoon soda in	Add
1 teaspoon hot water. Add	1 teaspoon vanilla
alternately with	

Drop by half teaspoonfuls onto greased cooky sheet. Bake in moderate oven, 375° F., for 10 to 12 minutes. Makes 100 cookies.

At Toll House, we chill dough overnight. When mixture is ready for baking, we roll a teaspoon of dough between palms of hands and place balls 2 inches apart on greased baking sheet. Then we press balls with finger tips to form flat rounds. This way cookies do not spread as much in the baking and they keep uniformly round. They should be brown through, and crispy, not white and hard as I have sometimes seen them.

CHOCOLATE COOKIES

Combine:
1 cup sugar
½ cup shortening, melted. Add
1 egg, beaten. Sift together:
1½ cups flour
½ teaspoon soda. Add to

first mixture alternately with
½ cup milk. Add
3 squares chocolate, melted,
½ teaspoon vanilla
¾ cup broken nut meats
¾ cup seedless raisins

Drop from teaspoon onto greased cooky sheet. Bake in hot oven, 400° F., for 8 minutes. Makes about 2 dozen cookies.

COCONUT STRIPS

Cut 2 slices of bread ¾ inch thick. Remove crusts. Cut in strips ¾ inch wide. Pour small amount sweetened condensed milk on a plate. Place ½ cup shredded coconut in another plate. Dip bread strips into milk, drain, and cover with coconut. Toast under broiler flame until brown. Makes about 8 strips.

PEANUT BUTTER COOKIES

Sift together:
3 cups flour
½ teaspoon salt
1 teaspoon soda. Cream together:
1 cup shortening
1 cup white sugar

1 cup brown sugar. Add:
2 eggs
1 cup peanut butter
1 teaspoon vanilla. Beat well. Add dry ingredients. Mix well

Shape dough into balls size of a walnut. Place on greased cooky sheet and press down with a fork so as to leave criss-cross marks on top. Bake in slow oven, 320° F., for 8 minutes. Makes about 3½ dozen cookies.

TOLL HOUSE TING-A-LINGS

Melt in top of double boiler
12 oz. (2 c.) semi-sweet chocolate morsels.
Add:
½ teaspoon salt
4 cups cornflakes
¼ cup chopped walnuts

¼ cup uncooked prunes, stoned and cut small,
¼ cup uncooked dried apricots, cut small,
¼ cup raisins or dates, cut fine,
¼ cup candied ginger, cut fine

Mix well and drop by teaspoonfuls on wax paper. Allow to harden. Serve as cookies with a dessert or as candy. Makes 2 dozen cookies.

MANDELKRÄNZE *(Almond Wreath)*

Cream
½ cup butter. Add
1 cup sugar. Cream well.
Add:
3 egg yolks, slightly beaten,
2 tablespoons cream.
Grind or chop:

1½ ounces bitter almonds
1½ ounces sweet almonds.
Add to first mixture.
Stir in
2½ cups sifted flour (about)

When dough is stiff, form into small cookies. (When possible these cookies are shaped in a Mandelkränze machine.) Bake in moderate oven, 375° F., for 10 to 12 minutes until a very faint brown. Makes 8 to 9 dozen tiny "wreaths." (Almonds may be omitted and 1 teaspoon almond extract used instead.)

MINCEMEAT COOKIES

Cream together:
1 cup butter
2 cups brown sugar. Add
2 eggs. Sift together:
2 cups flour (about)
1 teaspoon salt

1 teaspoon cream of tartar
1 teaspoon soda. Add to first mixture and mix well.
Add:
1 heaping cup mincemeat
1 cup broken nut meats

Add more flour if necessary to make stiff dough. Pack in loaf pans or form into long roll and let stand overnight in cold place. Slice off ¼- to ½-inch slices. Bake in moderate oven, 375° F., for 7 to 12 minutes. Makes 5 dozen cookies. (This dough may be kept for a week and sliced off as needed.)

MORAVIAN CHRISTMAS COOKIES

Combine:
¼ cup butter, melted,
½ cup dark molasses, heated.
Stir in:
¼ cup brown sugar
¼ heaping teaspoon ginger
¼ heaping teaspoon clove

¼ heaping teaspoon cinnamon
⅛ teaspoon nutmeg
⅛ teaspoon allspice
⅛ teaspoon salt
¼ heaping teaspoon soda
1⅞ cups sifted flour

Mix well and let stand in refrigerator several days. Mixture improves with 1 to 2 weeks' ripening. Roll paper thin, keeping dough very cold while rolling and cutting. Use fancy cutter. Bake in moderate oven, 375° F., for 6 minutes. Makes 4 dozen cookies.

---

14. FROSTINGS AND FILLINGS

❦

Frosting has ever been the delight of the small boy and the cake with plenty of icing his favorite. In our family son Don adores cake only for its frosting while my husband prefers cake alone, so they even up. Daughter and I, being on the rotund side, enjoy both. Isn't it always the way!

Toll House guests have been brought up on Richmond Chocolate Frosting which we use on Boston Cream Pie. This frosting is really too heavy for such a feathery cake as Hot Milk Cake but our guests love its soft consistency with the strong chocolate flavor, which is not too sweet.

In New England we consider a layer cake filled with jelly or jam, the top sprinkled with confectioners sugar, as a Washington Pie. It is a dessert most popular at church suppers.

FROSTINGS

7-MINUTE FROSTING

Mix in top of double boiler
1 cup sugar (scant)
1 egg white

3 tablespoons cold water
Few grains salt
Few grains cream of tartar

Melt over plenty of boiling water and beat continuously with rotary beater until mixture is stiff enough to hold its shape when drawn to a peak. Let cool 5 minutes. Then spread on cake. Enough frosting for an 8-inch 2-layer cake. (See also Brown Sugar Seven-Minute Icing)

CHOCOLATE DRIP FROSTING

When Seven-Minute Frosting has set somewhat, melt 2 squares chocolate or ¼ cup Nestle's Semi-Sweet Chocolate Morsels and pour over top of cake. Spread with back of spoon so that some chocolate will run over and drip down sides of cake.

DORIS CUNNINGHAM'S BEATEN CHOCOLATE FROSTING

Cream together:
1 tablespoon butter
1 cup sifted confectioners sugar. Add:
2 squares chocolate, melted,

1 teaspoon vanilla. Beat well.
Add:
1 egg
3½ tablespoons milk

Beat with rotary or electric beater until mixture is fluffy and thick enough to hold shape. Spread on cake.

CHOCOLATE FROSTING

Melt in top of double boiler
2 squares chocolate

1 tablespoon butter. Add
½ cup rich milk

When mixture thickens, remove from heat and let stand until lukewarm. Add confectioners sugar until of consistency to spread. Flavor with ½ teaspoon vanilla. If frosting is too bitter, thin with a little warm milk. Then add more confectioners sugar. Frosting should be very soft and smooth. Enough frosting for 8-inch 2-layer cake.

RICHMOND CHOCOLATE FROSTING AND FILLING

Combine in saucepan:
1 cup sugar
3 tablespoons cornstarch
2 squares chocolate, shaved,
¼ teaspoon salt. Pour over
1 cup boiling water. Boil until

mixture thickens enough to spread. Remove from heat.
Add:
1 tablespoon butter
1 teaspoon vanilla

When cake is cool, spread frosting on cake while chocolate is hot. Then frosting will be glossy. Enough for filling and frosting of 8-inch 2-layer cake.

CHOCOLATE WHIPPED CREAM FROSTING

Combine in bowl:
1 cup heavy cream

1 cup confectioners sugar
4 tablespoons cocoa

Chill in refrigerator for 15 minutes or more. Beat until thick with rotary beater. Spread on cake, leaving rough surface. Enough frosting for 8-inch 2-layer cake.

MIRACLE FUDGE FROSTING
(See Primer for Brides, page 77)

BROWN SUGAR SEVEN-MINUTE FROSTING

Combine in top of double
boiler:
½ cup sugar

½ cup brown sugar
1 egg white
3 tablespoons water

Have enough boiling water in bottom of boiler to come well up along sides of top section. Keep water boiling. Beat for 7 minutes. Set aside for 5 minutes. Then beat until of proper consistency and cool enough to spread. To improve flavor add ½ teaspoon vanilla after cooking. Enough frosting for 8-inch 2-layer cake.

ALMOND CARAMEL FROSTING

Brown in oven
⅓ cup almonds, blanched and
shredded lengthwise. Place
in saucepan:
⅓ cup white sugar
1¾ cups light brown sugar

¾ cup water
⅛ teaspoon cream of tartar.
Let mixture boil until it
reaches 240° F., or spins
thread. Pour slowly over
3 egg whites, beaten stiff

Beat mixture continuously until cool. Place mixture, if not thick enough to spread, over saucepan of hot water. Stir until of proper consistency. Spread roughly over top and sides of cake. Sprinkle with almonds. Enough frosting for 8-inch 2-layer cake.

EASY FLUFFY FROSTING

Beat
1 egg white with
Dash of salt until stiff but
not dry. Pour

½ cup honey, maple syrup,
corn syrup, or melted jelly
in fine stream over egg
white

Beat continuously for about 4 minutes, or until mixture holds
shape. Add ½ teaspoon vanilla if corn syrup is used. Enough
frosting for 8-inch 2-layer cake.

MAPLE ALMOND ICING

Combine in top of double
boiler:
¾ cup maple syrup
Pinch of salt

⅛ teaspoon cream of tartar
2 tablespoons sugar
1 egg white

Keep lower section of boiler two-thirds full of boiling water.
Beat mixture in double boiler until stiff enough to stand in peaks.
Sprinkle top and sides of frosted cake with almonds which have
been sliced and toasted. Enough frosting for 8-inch 2-layer cake.

ORANGE ICING

Place in saucepan
Grated rind of 1 orange
3 tablespoons orange juice

1 tablespoon lemon juice
1 tablespoon butter

Heat just enough to melt butter. Stir in enough confectioners
sugar to make consistency of heavy cream. Let stand 10 minutes
and spread. Excellent for Spongecake or Angel Cake. Enough
frosting for 8-inch 2-layer cake.

ORANGE FROSTING

Mix and let stand 15
minutes:
Grated rind of 1 orange
½ teaspoon lemon juice

1⅓ tablespoons orange juice.
Strain if smooth frosting is
desired. Mix with
1 egg yolk, slightly beaten.

Stir in enough confectioners sugar to make of proper consistency for spreading. Enough frosting for 8-inch 2-layer cake.

ORANGE FROSTING, TOLL HOUSE STYLE

Beat together in top of double
boiler:
1 scant cup sugar
Speck cream of tartar

Pinch of salt
1 egg white
2 tablespoons hot orange juice
1 tablespoon hot lemon juice

Keep lower section of boiler two-thirds full of boiling water. Beat mixture in top of double boiler until stiff enough to stand in peaks. Grate orange rind over top frosting and on lower layer of cake also. Enough frosting for Hot Milk Cake or large layer cake.

PINK PEPPERMINT-STICK ICING

Add ½ cup crushed pink peppermint-stick candy to 1 recipe of 7-Minute Frosting after beating to proper stiffness. This frosting is popular at Toll House on Chocolate Cake.

STRAWBERRY MERINGUE FROSTING

Place in large bowl:
1 cup crushed strawberries
⅔ cup sugar

1 egg white
1 teaspoon lemon juice

Beat with rotary beater until light and stiff. Enough frosting for 8-inch 2-layer cake.

Variation: Use crushed raspberries instead of strawberries.

SUNSHINE FROSTING

Cook together:
1 cup sugar
⅓ cup water until mixture

reaches soft ball stage, 240° F.,
Add very slowly to
2 egg yolks, well beaten

Beat mixture with rotary beater until very stiff. Then beat with spoon until thick enough to spread. Flavor with 1 teaspoon vanilla, lemon, or orange extract. Enough frosting for 8-inch 2-layer cake.

ANGEL CAKE ICING

Blend:
½ teaspoon butter
2 tablespoons hot milk.

Gradually add:
1½ cups confectioners sugar
½ teaspoon vanilla

This should be a thin icing not a frosting. Cover top and sides of Angel Cake.

FILLINGS

APRICOT FILLING

Soak until plump:
½ pound dried apricots in
1½ cups cold water. Cook until soft. Rub through a sieve or use 1½ cups canned apricot purée. Add:
1½ cups sugar
⅓ teaspoon salt
⅓ cup orange marmalade

Spread between layers of cake, reserving small amount for top. Spread over top, cover with whipped cream and garnish with chopped almonds.

CHOCOLATE CREAM FILLING

Place in saucepan:
2 squares chocolate, cut small,
½ cup sugar
¾ cup milk. Bring to boiling point, stirring continuously. Mix with a little cold water
3 tablespoons flour or 1½ tablespoons cornstarch. Add slowly to first mixture, stirring until thick. Remove from heat. Add:
1 tablespoon butter
½ teaspoon vanilla

Cool and spread between layers and on top of cake. Nuts may be broken over top, if desired.

COFFEE CREAM FILLING

Scald
2 cups milk with
2 tablespoons ground coffee. Strain. Mix in top of double boiler:
¾ cup sugar
⅓ cup flour
⅛ teaspoon salt. Add
2 eggs, slightly beaten. Gradually pour over coffee and milk

Cook 15 minutes, stirring continuously until mixture thickens and afterwards occasionally. Cool and add ½ teaspoon vanilla.

Spread between layers of an 8-inch 3-layer cake. This also makes enough filling to fill and cover High Cream Pie.

CREAM FILLING

Combine in top of double boiler:

¾ cup sugar
⅓ cup flour
⅛ teaspoon salt. Add
2 eggs, beaten slightly. Gradually add
2 cups milk, scalded

Cook for 15 minutes, stirring continuously until mixture thickens and afterwards occasionally. Cool and flavor with 1 teaspoon vanilla. Enough to spread an 8-inch 2-layer cake.

SOUR CREAM FILLING

Combine in top of double boiler:

¼ cup sour cream
½ cup sugar
1½ cups nut meats, cut fine,
Small piece of butter. Cook
slowly until thickened. Beat. Add:

½ teaspoon vanilla
¼ cup chopped raisins (optional)

Spread between layers of an 8-inch 2-layer cake. Sift confectioners sugar over top.

PINEAPPLE MALLOW FILLING

Cook together:

1 cup sugar
½ cup water until mixture reaches soft ball stage, 238° F. Add
8 slices canned pineapple,
cubed. Continue cooking until syrup forms but not long enough to darken. When cool, add

1 teaspoon lemon juice

Spread on lower and over top layer of 8-inch, 2-layer cake. Cover top and sides of cake with Seven-Minute Frosting and dot top with small pieces of pineapple.

15. PASTRIES AND PIES

§

§

At Toll House the favorite is Lemon Meringue Pie with its towering meringue. We use once and a half times the recipe with five extra egg whites for the meringue which rises about five inches. Guests vie with each other in guessing its height and rulers are brought out to settle wagers. Children call it sailboat pie!

However, I hardly dare speak of pies after the morning our seven-year-old son asked for five cents to buy a pie at the grocery store to take to school! When I said I would make him one he protested "But, Mother, you don't know how to make this kind." He preferred the baker's little, round, rubbery lemon-filled kind and the teachers were highly amused to see him enjoy his bakery treat. I am happy to report his tastes have improved with age!

Pastry-baking, like cake-baking, has its hazards. Perhaps, indeed, they are greater ones so here again are suggestions to help you improve this certain means to a man's heart.

PIE FAILURES AND THEIR CAUSES

Burns Around Edges
a. Oven too hot
b. Pastry too thin on rim of plate
c. Pans placed too close to oven side or to other pans on same rack

Top Crust Too Light in Color
a. Oven not hot enough
b. Insufficient baking time
c. Oven too full, cutting off proper air circulation
d. Pie set too low in oven

Pastry Tough
a. Not enough fat
b. Handled too much when rolled out
c. Too much flour in dough
d. Too much flour used on rolling board

Not Brown Enough on Bottom, Soggy
a. Set too high in oven
b. Shiny tin or aluminum pans intensify condition
c. Oven not hot enough, especially during first part of baking
d. Pie stood too long before being placed in oven
e. Too much liquid in filling

Double-Crusted Fruit Pies Boil Over
a. Too much fruit used for depth of pan
b. Edges not firmly sealed
c. Crust punctured near edge of pan
d. Oven too hot
e. Baked too long

PASTRIES

PLAIN PASTRY

Sift together:
2 cups flour
¼ teaspoon salt. Measure
⅔ cup shortening

Add half of shortening to flour. Chop fine, using two knives. Add remaining shortening and chop, leaving quite large lumps, which when rolled out make flakes. Add about 4 tablespoons ice water to hold mixture together. Turn out on lightly floured board. Roll thin. Makes one 2-crust 9-inch pie or two pastry shells.

Variation: **SPICE PASTRY.** Add to dry ingredients 1 teaspoon cinnamon and 1 teaspoon nutmeg. This is delicious for apple tarts.

CHEESE PASTRY OR STRAWS

Cut together:

½ cup shortening
½ package processed cheese or
½ cup grated American
cheese. Sift together and add:

1½ cups flour
½ teaspoon salt. Add enough
Ice water to hold mixture
together

Chill and roll ⅛ inch thick. Brush with egg yolk, mixed with 1 tablespoon water. Cut in ½- by 5-inch strips. Place on baking sheet and bake in a hot oven, 450° F., for 12 minutes. Makes 18 straws.

CHEESE PUFF STRAWS

Make a pastry, using

1½ cups sifted flour

½ cup shortening. Cut in well
1 teaspoon salt

Add enough ice water to make mixture hold together. Chill and roll out on a board. Sprinkle with grated cheese. Fold in thirds and roll out again. Sprinkle again with cheese. Roll about ⅓ inch thick and cut in 5- by ½-inch strips. Place on baking sheet and bake in a hot oven, 500° F., until golden brown. Makes 18 strips. Serve with salads.

HOT WATER PIE CRUST

Pour

4 tablespoons hot water over
½ cup shortening. Beat with
fork until liquefied.

Sift together and stir in:
1½ cups flour
⅓ teaspoon baking powder
1 teaspoon salt

Chill and roll out. Makes enough for 1-crust 9-inch pie.

GRAHAM CRACKER CRUST

In an 8-inch pie plate melt
over low heat
3 tablespoons butter. Mix in

½ cup graham cracker crumbs
⅓ cup sugar

Blend well and press mixtures against sides and bottom of pie plate as for a pastry lining. Set in refrigerator to harden. Then pour in filling as in a pastry shell.

PUFF PASTRY

Wash
1 pound butter. Pat until free of water. Reserve 2 tablespoons. Shape remainder into flat, square cake. Place on ice and chill thoroughly.

Sift:
½ teaspoon salt
2 cups flour

Work the 2 tablespoons butter into flour. Add enough cold water slowly, about 3 tablespoons, until dough is of consistency to take up all particles in bowl. Turn dough onto floured board and knead until smooth and elastic. Cover with towel and let stand in refrigerator 15 minutes. Pat and roll ¼ inch thick, keeping dough a little wider than long and corners square. Place remaining butter in center of lower half, fold upper half over this, and press edges together to keep in the air. Fold right side of dough over enclosed butter, and left side under. Turn dough halfway around, cover, and let stand 15 minutes in refrigerator. Pat and roll ¼ inch thick, having dough longer than wide. Lift over to prevent dough from sticking and, if necessary, dredge board lightly with flour. Fold to make 3 even layers with straight edges, and turn halfway around. Cover, and let stand 15 minutes in refrigerator. Do this 8 times in all, turning pastry halfway around each time before rolling. After eighth rolling, fold ends to center and double, making 4 layers. Chill. Roll out, and bake in hot oven, 450° F., for 20 minutes. Use wherever an extra rich pastry is desired as in High Cream Pie. Makes two 9-inch pie shells.

PATTY SHELLS

Roll Puff Pastry ¼ inch thick. Shape with pastry cutter, dipped in flour. With small cutter remove centers from the half rounds. Moisten edges of uncut rounds and place the rings on them. Press lightly. Place on ice for ½ hour or until thoroughly chilled. Bake in hot oven, 450° F., for 20 minutes. Makes 12 shells.

CHIFFON PIES

APRICOT CHIFFON PIE

Bake
1 9-inch shell of Plain Pastry.
Soak for 5 minutes
1 tablespoon gelatin in
¼ cup cold water. Heat
½ cup apricot juice. Add softened gelatin. Add:
½ cup sugar

¼ teaspoon salt
2 tablespoons lemon juice
1 cup canned or cooked apricots, puréed. Cool. When mixture begins to congeal fold in
¾ cup heavy cream, whipped

Fill baked pastry shell with mixture and chill. Before serving spread pie with layer of whipped cream.

CHOCOLATE RUM CHIFFON OR BLACK BOTTOM PIE

Bake
1 9-inch shell of Plain Pastry. Scald
2 cups rich milk. Beat
4 egg yolks, and add to milk. Mix and add:
½ cup sugar
1¼ tablespoons cornstarch. Cook mixture in top of double boiler until custard coats spoon. Remove from heat. Pour out ½ cup of custard and add to it
1½ squares chocolate, melted. Beat until cool.

Add
1 teaspoon vanilla. Pour into baked pastry shell. Chill. Soften
1 tablespoon gelatin in
4 tablespoons cold water. Add to remaining custard while still hot. Combine:
4 egg whites, beaten stiff,
¼ teaspoon cream of tartar
½ cup sugar, gently beaten in. Fold into custard with
3 tablespoons rum

When chocolate layer is firm, cover with the fluffy rum custard. Chill. At serving time, spread with whipped cream sweetened with confectioners sugar. Sprinkle top with shaved chocolate.

COFFEE CHIFFON PIE

Bake
1 9-inch shell of Plain Pastry.
Soak for 5 minutes
1 tablespoon gelatin in
¼ cup strong cold coffee. Combine in top of double boiler:
4 egg yolks, slightly beaten,
½ cup sugar
½ teaspoon salt
½ cup strong hot coffee. Cook until of custard consistency.
Add gelatin, mixing thoroughly. Add
1 tablespoon lemon juice.
Cool. When mixture begins to congeal fold in
4 egg whites, beaten stiff, with
½ cup sugar, gradually beaten in

Turn into baked pastry shell. Chill. At serving time, spread with whipped cream.

LEMON CHIFFON PIE

Bake
1 9-inch pastry shell of Plain Pastry. Soak for 5 minutes
1 tablespoon gelatin in
¼ cup cold water. Combine in top of double boiler:
½ cup sugar
½ cup lemon juice
½ teaspoon salt
4 egg yolks, beaten. Cook until of custard consistency. Add:
1 teaspoon grated lemon rind and softened gelatin. Cool.
When mixture begins to congeal fold in
4 egg whites, beaten stiff, with
½ cup sugar, gradually beaten in

Turn into baked pastry shell. Chill. At serving time, spread with whipped cream.

MOCHA CHIFFON PIE

Bake
1 9-inch shell of Plain Pastry.
Soften
1 tablespoon gelatin in
¼ cup cold water. Combine in top of double boiler:
⅓ cup cocoa
½ cup sugar
½ teaspoon salt
4 egg yolks, beaten,
1 cup strong coffee. Cook until of custard consistency.
Add gelatin. Cool. When mixture begins to congeal fold in
4 egg whites, beaten stiff, with
½ cup sugar, gradually beaten in

Turn into baked pastry shell. Chill. At serving time, spread with whipped cream.

ORANGE CHIFFON PIE. See Lemon Chiffon Pie. Substitute 1 teaspoon lemon juice, 1 tablespoon grated orange rind, and ½ cup orange juice for lemon juice and rind.

PINEAPPLE CHIFFON PIE

Bake
1 9-inch shell of Plain Pastry.
Soften
1 tablespoon gelatin in
¼ cup cold water. Combine in top of double boiler:
4 egg yolks, beaten,
¼ cup sugar
1 tablespoon lemon juice
1¼ cups canned, crushed pineapple

¼ teaspoon salt. Cook until of custard consistency. Add gelatin. Cool. When mixture begins to congeal fold in
4 egg whites, beaten stiff, with
¼ cup sugar, gradually beaten in

Turn into baked pastry shell. Chill. At serving time, spread with whipped cream.

PUMPKIN CHIFFON PIE

Bake
1 9-inch shell of Plain Pastry.
Place in top of double boiler
1 cup steamed, strained fresh or canned pumpkin. Cook 10 minutes, stirring occasionally. Combine:
3 egg yolks, beaten,
½ cup sugar
1 cup milk. Stir into pumpkin. Add:
½ teaspoon salt
½ teaspoon ginger
¼ teaspoon nutmeg

1 teaspoon cinnamon
2 tablespoons melted butter. Cook until of custard consistency. Remove from heat. Add
1 tablespoon gelatin softened in
¼ cup cold water. Stir until dissolved. Chill. When mixture begins to congeal fold in
4 egg whites, beaten stiff, with
½ cup sugar, gradually beaten in

Turn into baked pastry shell. Chill. At serving time, spread with whipped cream. Sprinkle with candied ginger. Or spread with cream cheese delicately flavored with Roquefort cheese.

STRAWBERRY CHIFFON PIE

Bake
1 9-inch shell of Plain Pastry. Combine in top of double boiler:
4 egg yolks, beaten slightly,
½ cup sugar
1 tablespoon lemon juice
½ teaspoon salt. Cook until of custard consistency. Add
1 tablespoon gelatin softened in

¼ cup cold water. Add
1 cup strawberry pulp and juice. Add a little red coloring to give pleasing color. Cool. When mixture begins to congeal fold in
4 egg whites, beaten stiff, with
¼ cup sugar, gradually beaten in

Turn into baked pastry shell. Chill. Before serving spread with thin layer of whipped cream. Garnish with strawberries.

FRUIT AND CUSTARD PIES

APPLE PIE
(See Primer for Brides, page 78)

APPLE CHEESE PIE

Prepare
1 recipe Plain Pastry. Line a 9-inch pie plate. Fill with
6 to 8 medium-sized apples, peeled, cored, sliced. Cover with:
⅔ cup sugar
1 tablespoon butter, cut in

pieces. Roll out upper crust. Sprinkle
3 tablespoons grated cheese over dough. Fold. Roll out again. Sprinkle with
3 tablespoons grated cheese. Fold. Roll out second time.

Moisten edges of lower crust with cold water. Arrange top cheese crust and press edges together. Bake in hot oven, 425° F., for 15 minutes. Reduce heat to 350° for 20 to 35 minutes to finish baking.

APRICOT PIE

Bake
1 9-inch shell of Plain Pastry.
Beat stiff
3 egg whites. Fold in:

1 cup cooked apricot pulp
¼ cup sugar
1 tablespoon lemon juice

Turn mixture into baked pastry shell and bake in moderate oven, 350° F., for about 25 minutes.

BANANA CREAM PIE

Bake
1 9-inch shell of Plain Pastry or prepare Graham Cracker Pastry Shell. Combine in top of double boiler:
½ cup sugar
6 tablespoons flour
¼ teaspoon salt. Slowly add
2 cups milk. Mix well and cook until thick. Allow to cook 10 minutes more, stirring occasionally. Beat
2 egg yolks and stir into them small amount hot mixture. Pour back into remaining

hot mixture, beating continuously. Cook 1 minute. Remove from heat. Beat in:
1 tablespoon butter
½ teaspoon vanilla. Cool. Pour half of custard into pastry shell. Slice into custard
2½ bananas. Pour on remaining custard. Whip
½ cup heavy cream. Fold in:
1 tablespoon sugar
½ teaspoon vanilla

Spoon whipped cream over top of pie. Garnish with remaining ½ banana, sliced.

DOWN-MAINE BLUEBERRY PIE

Bake
1 9-inch shell of Plain Pastry. Pick over and wash
1 quart blueberries. Reserve 3 cups and cook remaining blueberries until soft with:
1 cup sugar

¾ cup water. Make a paste of:
2 tablespoons flour
¼ teaspoon salt
¼ cup water. Add to blueberries and cook slowly until thickened. Add hot mixture to uncooked blueberries

Turn all into baked pastry shell. Chill for 3 hours. Serve topped with whipped cream or ice cream.

BUTTERSCOTCH PIE

Bake
1 9-inch shell of Plain Pastry. Heat in top of double boiler
1½ cups milk. Mix:
  4 tablespoons cornstarch
  2 tablespoons flour
½ cup cold milk. Stir into hot milk and cook, stirring until thickened. Melt

2 tablespoons butter. Add
1¼ cups brown sugar. Cook until sugar is melted and bubbly. Stir into first mixture. When dissolved, add
1 egg, beaten. When thickened, add:
¼ teaspoon salt
½ teaspoon vanilla

Cool. Turn mixture into baked pastry shell. Chill. Cover with whipped cream before serving.

COCONUT CUSTARD PIE

Prepare
½ recipe Plain Pastry. Line a 9-inch pie plate. Combine:
3 eggs, beaten,
¼ cup sugar

⅛ teaspoon salt
2 cups milk
½ cup grated or shredded coconut
½ teaspoon vanilla

Turn mixture into lined pie plate. Bake in hot oven, 450° F., for 10 minutes. Reduce heat to 325° and bake 30 to 40 minutes more, or until knife inserted in custard comes out clean.

CRANBERRY PIE

Prepare
1 recipe Plain Pastry. Line a 9-inch pie plate. Chop:
1 cup cranberries
1 cup raisins. Add:

1 cup sugar
2 tablespoons flour
½ cup water
1 teaspoon vanilla

Mix well. Turn into lined pie plate. Arrange lattice top. Bake in hot oven, 450° F., for 15 minutes. Reduce heat to 350° and bake 15 minutes more.

COCONUT CREAM PIE

Bake
1 9-inch pastry shell of Plain Pastry or prepare Graham Cracker Pastry Shell. Combine in top of double boiler:
½ cup sugar
6 tablespoons flour
¼ teaspoon salt. Slowly add
2 cups milk. Mix well. Add
1 cup grated coconut. Cook until thick. Allow to cook 10 minutes more, stirring occasionally. Beat slightly
2 egg yolks. Stir in small amount of hot mixture. Pour back into remaining hot mixture, beating continuously. Cook 1 minute. Remove from heat. Beat in:
1 tablespoon butter
½ teaspoon vanilla.

Cool. Pour into baked pastry shell. Spread with whipped cream sweetened with confectioners sugar. Sprinkle with additional coconut.

HIGH CREAM PIE

Prepare 1 recipe Plain Pastry. Roll out and cut circle of dough large enough to cover top of pie plate. Place dough on baking sheet and prick. Cover outside of pie plate with remaining pastry. Bake both in hot oven, 450° F., until golden brown. Fill baked pastry shell with Coffee Cream Filling, cover with baked circle of pastry and spread with remaining filling to make a "layer" pie. Garnish with whipped cream and pecan nuts.

KEY LIME PIE

Bake
1 9-inch shell of Plain Pastry or prepare Graham Cracker Pastry Shell. Beat with rotary beater until thick:
1 can sweetened condensed milk
½ cup lime juice
1 teaspoon grated lime rind
3 egg yolks

Turn mixture into pastry shell. Prepare meringue:

Beat until frothy
3 egg whites. Add slowly
6 tablespoons sugar. Beat until meringue stands in peaks

278

Spread over filling. Brown in preheated oven, 350° F. **Cool.**
Allow to stand in refrigerator for 1 hour or more before serving.
(To retain lime flavor, never heat juice.)

LEMON PIE

Prepare
1 recipe Plain Pastry and line
9-inch pie plate. Combine:
1 cup sugar
1 egg, beaten,

⅛ teaspoon salt
Grated rind and juice of 1
lemon. Add:
2 large apples put through
coarse knife of food chopper

Turn mixture into lined pie plate. Arrange top crust and
prick. Bake in hot oven, 425° F., for 15 minutes. Reduce heat to
350° and bake 20 to 25 minutes more.

LEMON FLUFF PIE

Bake
1 9-inch shell of Plain Pastry.
Beat in top of double boiler
3 egg yolks. Gradually add
½ cup sugar. Mix thoroughly.
Add:
Grated rind and juice of

1 lemon
3 tablespoons hot water. Cook
until consistency of thin
custard. Beat
3 egg whites. Add gradually
½ cup sugar. Beat until stiff

Fold egg whites into custard mixture and turn into baked
pastry shell. Place in moderate oven, 350° F. for about 12 to 15
minutes, or until brown.

TOLL HOUSE LEMON MERINGUE PIE

Bake
1 9-inch shell of Plain Pastry.
Melt in top of double boiler:
1 tablespoon butter in
1 cup hot water. Mix in a bowl:
1 cup sugar

2 tablespoons flour. Add:
2 egg yolks, beaten
Grated rind and juice of 1
lemon. Add this mixture to
butter.

Cook until thick, stirring constantly. Cool thoroughly. Turn
into baked pastry shell and top with meringue. Place in moderate
oven, 350° F., for 12 to 15 minutes, to brown.

Meringue Topping

Probably the most talked-of food at Toll House is the tall meringue on our pies. But we have no secrets. It is all accomplished by using plenty of egg whites. For the filling of our Lemon Meringue Pie we use one and one-half times the recipe for our 10-inch pie plate. We allow 5 egg yolks for the filling and 5 egg whites for the meringue with 10 tablespoons granulated sugar.

When you make meringue for pie, beat the egg whites with a pinch of salt until they hold a firm peak. Then add the granulated sugar, 1 tablespoon at a time, allowing 2 tablespoons for each egg white. Beat thoroughly to dissolve the sugar. Keep adding sugar until all 10 tablespoons are absorbed by the egg whites and a marshmallowlike, shiny, silky consistency results. Some cooks add ¼ teaspoon cream of tartar or baking powder at the very end of the beating to insure stiffness.

Our meringue is so stiff we have to "pack" it down on the pie fillings. We spread the top smoothly as a too rough top results in uneven browning. The meringue should remain in the oven (preheated) at 350° F., for 12 to 15 minutes. Then it will be thoroughly cooked and will stay high and fluffy. Do not expect a good meringue to result from quick-broiler browning.

Much also depends upon the eggs. They should be over 1 day old, but preferably not more than 1 week old. Old eggs may have "watery" whites which are not likely to give good results.

The size of eggs varies. If eggs are small or of pullet size, measure ½ cup of egg whites for a high meringue on a 10-inch pie and allow the same 10 tablespoons sugar.

If meringue is cooked too long, the top is apt to be leathery and it "weeps." After cooking and spreading a meringue topping, place pie in refrigerator or other cold place.

LEMON SPONGE PIE

Bake
1 9-inch shell of Plain Pastry.
Combine in saucepan:
3 egg yolks, beaten,
Juice of 1 lemon
¼ cup sugar

¼ cup hot water. Simmer over low heat until mixture thickens. Remove from heat.
Fold in
3 egg whites, beaten stiff

Turn into baked pastry shell. Bake in a moderate oven, 350° F., for about 25 minutes.

LEMON CHEESE PIE

Prepare
1 Graham Cracker Pastry Shell. Mix:
½ pound cottage cheese
3 tablespoons sugar. Add
3 egg yolks, one at a time, and beat thoroughly. Stir in until combined:
3 tablespoons flour

¼ teaspoon salt
3 tablespoons lemon juice
2 teaspoons grated lemond rind. Add
1 cup light cream or rich milk. Beat until stiff
3 egg whites. Gradually add
½ cup sugar

Fold egg whites into cheese mixture. Turn into lined pie plate. Sprinkle with additional graham cracker crumbs, and bake in slow oven, 325° F., for 55 minutes. Serves 6. (Many recipes for cheesecake require a special spring-form pan which the average kitchen lacks. This recipe is an adaption of the favorite cheesecake and has a light, delicate flavor. The pie will shrink somewhat after baking, which is to be expected with this type of mixture. Any shallow pan may be used instead of a pie plate.)

PECAN PIE

Prepare
½ recipe Plain Pastry and line 9-inch pie plate. Combine:
2 eggs, beaten light,
1 cup sugar

1 cup sour cream
1 teaspoon flour
¼ teaspoon lemon extract
¼ teaspoon cinnamon and cloves, mixed

Turn into lined pie plate. Cover with pecan halves. Bake in slow oven, 350° F., for 40 minutes, or until firm. Cool and cover with sweetened whipped cream.

RICH PECAN PIE

Prepare
½ recipe Plain Pastry and line
9-inch pie plate. Combine:
4 eggs, beaten,
1 cup sugar
1 cup dark corn syrup

1 tablespoon flour
½ teaspoon salt
3 tablespoons melted butter
1 cup pecan meats
2 teaspoons vanilla

Turn into lined pie plate. Bake in moderate oven, 350° F., for 40 minutes. Chill and before serving spread with whipped cream.

PINEAPPLE PIE

Bake
1 9-inch pastry shell of Plain
Pastry. Heat in top of
double boiler
1 cup pineapple juice. Mix:
3 tablespoons cornstarch
½ cup sugar
⅛ teaspoon salt. Combine with
hot pineapple juice. Cook
30 minutes, stirring until
mixture thickens.

Pour over
2 egg yolks, slightly beaten.
Return to heat and cook 3
minutes. Add
1 cup crushed pineapple,
drained. Cool slightly. Turn
into baked pastry shell. Top
with meringue made from
2 egg whites, beaten stiff, with
4 tablespoons sugar gradually
beaten in

Brown in moderate oven, 350° F., for 12 to 15 minutes.

PINEAPPLE PIE (*Chinese Style*)

Prepare
1 recipe Plain Pastry and line
9-inch pie plate. Put through
coarse knife in food chopper
2 small apples, cored and pared.
Add:

½ can (1¼ cups) crushed
pineapple
1½ cups sugar
2 tablespoons melted butter
⅛ teaspoon salt. Mix thoroughly

Turn into lined pie plate. Arrange top crust and prick. Bake in hot oven, 425° F., for 15 minutes. Reduce heat to 350° and finish baking. (If this mixture is not enough to fill your pie plate, add another apple, chopped.)

PINEAPPLE AND RAISIN PIE

Prepare
1 recipe Plain Pastry and line
9-inch pie plate. Chop
1 slice pineapple. Add:
1 cup raisins
½ cup water. Mix:
⅜ cup sugar

2 tablespoons cornstarch. Stir
into fruit mixture. Cook 10
minutes. Add:
Juice of ½ lemon
½ cup pineapple juice
Pinch of salt

Cool. Turn into lined pie plate. Arrange top crust and prick. Bake in hot oven, 450° F., for 25 minutes.

PRUNE AND APRICOT PIE

Soak prunes and apricots separately overnight, using ⅔ prunes and ⅓ apricots. Allow about 2 cups pitted prunes and 1 cup apricots. Cook each a short time. Add sugar to taste.

Combine:
1 egg, beaten,
Pinch of salt

¼ teaspoon cornstarch
2 tablespoons lemon juice.
Add to fruit mixture

Prepare 1 recipe Plain Pastry and line 9-inch pie plate. Turn mixture into lined pie plate. Arrange top crust or lattice strips. Bake in hot oven, 425° F., about 30 minutes.

Variation: Substitute pineapple and peaches for prunes and apricots.

RHUBARB PIE

Prepare
1 recipe Plain Pastry and line
9-inch pie plate. Cut into
small pieces
1½ cups rhubarb. Turn into
strainer and pour over it

Boiling water. Drain. Add:
1 cup sugar
2 tablespoons flour or 1 tablespoon cornstarch
1 egg
½ teaspoon salt. Mix well

Turn into lined pie plate. Dot rhubarb with a little butter. Arrange lattice top. Bake in hot oven, 450° F., for 20 minutes. Reduce heat to 350° and bake 15 minutes more, or until done.

RAISIN PIE

Prepare
1 recipe Plain Pastry and line 9-inch pie plate. Cook for 10 minutes:
2 cups seeded raisins
1½ cups cold water. Mix and add:

1 cup sugar
4 tablespoons cornstarch. **Cook** until thickened. Stir in
Juice of 2 lemons
Grated rind of 1 lemon
1 tablespoon butter
1 egg, beaten

Cool. Turn into lined pie plate. Arrange top crust and prick. Bake in hot oven, 450° F., for 25 minutes.

SQUASH PIE

Prepare
½ recipe Plain Pastry and line 9-inch pie plate. Combine.
2½ cups cooked squash
2 cups milk
1 teaspoon salt
1 teaspoon cinnamon
1 teaspoon ginger

1 tablespoon dark molasses
1 tablespoon butter. Beat slightly
2 egg yolks and
1 egg white. Add to squash mixture. Beat stiff
1 egg white. Beat into mixture, using rotary beater to prevent skin forming on top

Turn into lined pie plate. Bake in hot oven, 450° F., for 10 minutes. Reduce heat to 325° and bake for 30 minutes more.

TARTS, TURNOVERS, AND PUFFS

CREAM CHEESE TARTLETS

Cream together:
1 package cream cheese

¼ pound butter. Cut into
1 cup sifted flour. Mix well

Chill. Roll out thin and cut with cooky cutter. Place on baking sheet. Bake in hot oven, 450° F., for about 15 minutes. While still warm, dent with back of spoon and fill with jam. Makes about 8 tartlets.

ICE CREAM TARTS OR PIE

Prepare ½ recipe Plain Pastry. Cover an inverted pie plate with pastry, bringing it well over sides and trimming off at edge of plate. Prick pastry several times on bottom and sides and bake in hot oven, 500° F., for 20 minutes, or until brown. Cool. Prepare a meringue:

Beat stiff	½ cup sugar, beating constantly. Add
3 egg whites. Add slowly	
	1 teaspoon vanilla

Fill baked pastry shell with 1 pint ice cream (chocolate or coffee is delicious). Cover with meringue and brown quickly under broiler until meringue is set and golden brown. This is a safe procedure only for meringues which are to be eaten immediately.

Variation: Individual shells may be made by covering inverted muffin pans with pastry. One pint of ice cream is enough for 6 tart shells.

SOUTHERN APPLE TURNOVERS

Prepare 1 recipe Spice Pastry. Roll out and cut into rounds or squares. Pare, core, and slice 4 or 5 apples. On half of pastry rounds place sliced apples. Add sugar according to tartness of apples. Dot with butter. Cover with remaining pieces of pastry and slit to allow steam to escape. Moisten edges with water and press together well. Bake in hot oven, 450° F., for 10 minutes. Reduce heat to 350° and bake until cooked through, about 10 minutes. Makes 6 turnovers.

CREAM PUFFS

Bring to boil in saucepan:	1 cup flour. Mix vigorously. Remove from heat. Add
½ cup butter	
1 cup boiling water. Add all at once	4 unbeaten eggs, one at a time

Beat well between additions. Drop by tablespoonfuls onto buttered sheet. Space one and a half inches apart. Shape with handle of spoon into rounds, piling mixture slightly in center. Bake in hot oven, 400° F., for 30 to 35 minutes. Take care not to remove from oven before puffs are baked or they will fall. Slit and fill with whipped cream, Cream Filling, or ice cream. Serve with hot Chocolate Sauce or Butterscotch Sauce. Makes 18 large puffs or 50 tiny tea-sized ones.

Variation: Fill puffs with creamed chicken and serve at luncheon.

16 CANDIES TO MAKE AT HOME

ॐ

At holiday time it's a lot of fun to try your hand at making candy. A box of homemade confections is always a welcome gift and there are many kinds which children can prepare alone. Even when they were little, our children made the Gypsy Brown Burrs most successfully to the delight of their grandmothers and friends who received boxes of these first masterpieces. For those who are willing to undertake a more ambitious recipe I have given basic directions for chocolate dipping and the making of bonbons. With a little imagination you can develop many new fillings. I remember when I was in college we even chocolate-dipped sweet gherkin pickles and loved them! In the summer, ripe strawberries are delicious dipped in chocolate, leaving the tops and stems exposed.

CRUNCHY CREAM MINTS

Mix in deep saucepan:

3 cups sugar	1 teaspoon vinegar
¾ cup boiling water	¼ teaspoon cream of tartar

Stir with fork wrapped in wet cloth while mixture slowly dissolves. Wipe sugar away from sides of pan. When mixture boils, put on cover for 2 minutes and let cook to soft crack stage 270° F. Pour into buttered pan or onto marble slab. While cooling, fold in edges and when cool enough to handle, pull like taffy. Divide into 3 equal parts. Add oil of cinnamon and green coloring to the first part, oil of lemon and yellow coloring to the second part, and oil of clove and red coloring to the third. When pliable, pull out into strips 6 to 8 inches long. Roll each strip in powdered sugar, cut with shears into 1-inch pieces turning the piece halfway around each time to make an attractive shape. Let stand on tray overnight until dry and sugary. Store in a covered tin can. Makes about 3 dozen pieces.

PRALINES

Shell out
2 cups pecans. Melt in saucepan
2 tablespoons butter. Add:
2 cups sugar
1 cup maple syrup and
⅔ cup milk. Stir until sugar is dissolved. Bring to boiling point, and, without stirring, boil to soft ball stage, 238° F. Remove from heat. Let stand until cool. Add:
¼ teaspoon salt
½ teaspoon mapleine or vanilla

Beat with wooden spoon or pour onto marble slab and work with spatula until candy begins to harden. Then place in saucepan and stir over hot water until softened. Add nuts. Drop from spoon in 3-inch rounds onto buttered slab or baking sheet. Makes about 20 pralines.

PRALINE POWDER

Chop ¾ cup walnuts and add to ¾ cup sugar. Place in heavy spider over low flame. Stir until sugar is melted to golden brown. Turn onto oiled platter. When mixture is cold, grind in food chopper. Store powder in covered jar for use over puddings or ice cream.

GYPSY BROWN BURRS

Toast
1 cup grated or shredded coconut. Set aside. Wash and seed
1 cup dates. Mix with
¼ cup figs. Put through medium knife of food chopper

Rinse hands in cold water, knead mixture well, and form it into rolls ½ inch thick and 1 inch long. Roll in toasted coconut. Makes 1 dozen pieces.

GINGER CREAM CANDY

Combine in saucepan:
2 cups white sugar
1 cup light brown sugar
¾ cup milk and
2 tablespoons light corn syrup.
Boil to soft ball stage, 238°
F. Remove from heat. Add:

2 tablespoons butter
2 tablespoons crystallized ginger, cut fine. Do not stir. When cooled to lukewarm, add
1 teaspoon vanilla

Beat until creamy. Pour into two 8-inch-square buttered pans. When cool cut in squares. Makes 3 dozen pieces.

SCOTCH KISSES

Brush sugar and starch from
½ pound marshmallows. Boil together in heavy spider:
2 cups sugar

¾ cup water
¼ cup butter and
Few grains salt until slightly caramelized

Place pan over hot water to keep hot. Dip marshmallows quickly into syrup. Remove to wax paper to cool. Makes enough syrup for about ½ pound marshmallows.

TURKISH DELIGHT

Prepare and set aside
grated rind and juice of
1 lemon and
1 orange. Soak

3 tablespoons gelatin in
½ cup cold water. Put
2 cups sugar and
½ cup hot water in saucepan

When mixture reaches boiling point, add gelatin and simmer 20 minutes. Add fruit juice and color red or green. Strain into a bread pan which has been rinsed in cold water. When cold and firm turn out on board, cut into 1-inch cubes and roll in confectioners' sugar. Makes 2 dozen pieces.

FUDGE

Mix in saucepan   2 squares chocolate or 3
2 cups sugar   tablespoons cocoa
1 cup milk   ½ teaspoon salt

Stir over low heat until mixture comes to a boil. Simmer to soft ball stage, 238° F. Set saucepan in pan of cold water and leave until mixture cools. Add 1 tablespoon butter and 1 teaspoon vanilla. Beat mixture until thick and creamy. Pour into 8-inch-square buttered pan. When set, cut into squares. Makes 2 dozen pieces.

FRUIT FUDGE

Combine in saucepan: ball stage, 238° F. Add:
2 cups sugar   1 teaspoon vanilla
1 cup milk   ½ cup candied fruits, cut in
¼ cup butter. Cook to soft   small pieces

Finish as for plain Fudge. Makes 2 dozen pieces.

FUDGE DROPS

Melt 2 packages Nestle's Semi-Sweet Chocolate Morsels and stir in 1 cup condensed milk. When well blended drop by teaspoonfuls onto wax paper. Press half a walnut or pecan into each drop. Or you may add 1 cup chopped nuts to mixture and pour into 8-inch-square pan. When cool, cut into squares as for fudge. Makes 2 dozen pieces without nuts, 3 dozen pieces with nuts.

BROWN SUGAR PANOCHA

Melt in deep saucepan   1 cup white sugar
2 tablespoons butter. Add: 1 cup thin cream
2 cups brown sugar   Few grains soda

Stir over low heat until sugar is dissolved. Bring to boiling point and cook to soft ball stage, 238° F. Remove from heat.

Add:
1 heaping tablespoon marsh-
    mallow cream. Pour onto mar-
    ble slab or platter, sprinkled
    with cold water.
    When cool, add:

¼ teaspoon salt
1 teaspoon vanilla. Work
    with spatula until creamy.
    When firm, knead in
1 cup chopped nuts

Turn into buttered pan. When cold, cut in squares. Makes about 3 dozen pieces.

CHOCOLATE PEANUT-RAISIN CLUSTERS

Empty 1 package Nestle's Semi-Sweet Chocolate Morsels into top of double boiler with warm not hot water in lower section. Stir occasionally while melting. As soon as chocolate is melted, remove from heat and cool a little, beating frequently. Shell 1 pint freshly roasted peanuts and remove skins. Measure after shelling, and add equal amount of seedless raisins. Stir peanuts and raisins into melted chocolate. Drop blended mixture by teaspoons onto piece of oilcloth or marble slab. Do not let a drop of water get into chocolate. Work in room where temperature averages 60° F. to 65°. Makes 3 dozen pieces.

BRAN BRITTLE

Place in saucepan:
2 cups white sugar
1 cup brown sugar
½ cup light corn syrup
1 cup water. Cook, stirring
    until sugar is dissolved.
    Continue cooking without
    stirring, until temperature

of 300° F. is reached (a
    little above hard crack
    stage). Remove from heat.
Add:
⅛ teaspoon salt
¼ cup butter. Stir only
    enough to blend. Add
1½ cups bran flakes

Turn at once onto greased slab or greased baking sheet. Smooth out with spatula. After half a minute take hold of edges of candy and lifting it slightly from slab, pull it as thin as possible. Break into irregular pieces. Makes 2 to 3 dozen pieces.

HAYSTACKS

Combine:
1½ cups white sugar
½ cup light corn syrup
½ cup rich milk
¼ cup dark molasses

⅛ teaspoon salt. Cook to soft ball stage, 238° F. Add:
1¼ pounds shredded coconut
3 teaspoons butter

Pour onto buttered platter. When cool enough to handle, form into cone-shaped "haystacks." Wrap in wax paper or place on buttered platter. Makes about 2 dozen pieces.

HAZELNUT CRISP

Melt in heavy spider
1 cup sugar, stirring constantly. Add

1 cup hazelnuts, chopped and lightly toasted in oven

Mix thoroughly. Invert an 8-inch-square cake pan and butter base. Turn mixture onto this. Then cool and shape, with 2 buttered knives, into squares or strips. Makes about 2 dozen pieces.

PEANUT CANDY

Place in heavy spider
1 cup sugar. Stir over slow heat. (It will lump, then

gradually melt.) When melted, add
1 cup peanuts, finely chopped

Mix thoroughly and proceed as for Hazelnut Crisp. Makes about 1½ to 2 dozen pieces.

CANDIED GRAPEFRUIT OR ORANGE PEEL

Soak fruit peel in cold, salted water for 24 hours (using 1 teaspoon salt to 1 quart water). Drain, cover with cold water, and boil until tender. Change water three or four times. Drain and cut in squares or strips. Measure peel and add equal amount sugar, ½ cup water, and few drops coloring. Heat slowly and cook until fruit is transparent and sugar is dissolved. Remove from heat, cool, and roll in powdered sugar.

HONIED ORANGE PEEL

Cook quartered orange peel until tender, about 30 minutes. Drain for 5 minutes, by placing in sieve and running cold water over it. Then place on board and slice very thin. If skin is very thick, remove some of white part of rind. Make a syrup by combining ⅓ cup honey with 1 cup hot water. Drop slices into this and cook very slowly until thick. Avoid overcooking. Cool, place in covered jar in refrigerator, and before using, dip in sugar.

CHOCOLATES

The centers of chocolate-coated candies may be made of Peanut Candy, Fudge, Fondant, Candied Grapefruit, or Orange Peel.

CHOCOLATE COATING

Place 6 oz. (1 c.) semi-sweet chocolate morsels in top of double boiler over warm, not hot water. Do not cover and *do not add water* to chocolate. Stir constantly while it melts. When half melted, remove from heat and stir until lumps are dissolved. (A thermometer test should indicate 110° F.) Beat vigorously with a spoon to cool the chocolate and bring up the oil globules. Chocolate should now register 85° F. and be ready for coating nuts or prepared centers. Dip by hand or with two-tined fork and work quickly. Place the freshly coated candies on board covered with square of table oilcloth or wax paper.

It takes a little experience to turn out perfect chocolates. If the coating is shiny, chocolate has not been thoroughly beaten. If base forms under each candy, chocolate was not sufficiently cooled before dipping, or you may have placed candies on oilcloth before you smoothed off the excess chocolate.

"Bursters" sometimes occur, a term for candies with bubbly coatings or thin places through which centers show. To avoid this, particularly with cream or crystallized fruit centers, use heavy coating.

Gray and streaked chocolates result from melting over too

great heat, too slow cooling, moisture in palm of hand when hand-dipping, or allowing chocolate to run between fingers into palm. If candy is subjected to extreme heat, in the sun, or extreme cold, in the refrigerator, color will also be affected.

BONBONS

There are two processes involved in making bonbons: preparation of fondant or outside coating and preparation of centers. Bonbons can be made in infinite variety. Try rose or wintergreen flavoring with pink coloring; pistachio flavor with green coloring; violet flavor with violet color. Almond paste is good for centers or a mixture of chopped nuts and white fondant with coating of maple.

FONDANT

Combine in a deep saucepan:	¾ cup hot water
2 cups sugar	⅛ teaspoon cream of tartar (scant)

Stir over low heat until sugar is dissolved and begins to boil. Cover for 2 to 3 minutes to steam any grains of sugar down into syrup. Avoid jarring or stirring after syrup begins to boil. If any grains of sugar remain on sides of saucepan, wash them down with cloth dipped in cold water and wrapped around fork. When well steamed, remove cover and carefully insert thermometer. Cook to a soft ball stage, 238° F.

To test for soft ball, dip fork into syrup and let syrup drop from fork back into pan. If a long hairlike thread remains after all drops have run off, sugar has boiled enough.

Dampen pan, platter, or marble slab with the hand dipped in cold water. Then pour hot syrup quickly and carefully into pan. Do not let last of syrup drip out and never scrape the kettle. The drippings and scraping may cause whole mass to granulate. Let remain in pan, without jarring, until just warm, testing with back of hand. In passing hand over it, mixture will feel firm and smooth.

With scraper, begin at edge of platter and work toward center, scraping clean from edge each time and working until mass is creamy. Then quickly gather mass into hands and knead. Place in bowl with damp cloth to sweat. Wrap in wax paper to exclude air. It is ready for use in 24 hours but may be kept several days or much longer.

CENTERS

Combine in small equal amounts finely chopped candied cherries, citron, and nuts, or ⅓ nuts alone with ⅔ fondant. Knead and add few drops of flavoring. Shape into small balls. Drop onto wax paper to harden. Then coat with fondant.

COATING

Place prepared Fondant in top of double boiler or in a bowl set in pan of hot water over very slow heat. Add few drops of hot water and stir until fondant is melted. Add few drops of desired coloring and appropriate flavoring—as pink with strawberry.

Place one center at a time on a two-tined fork. (Avoid piercing center.) Dip each center into fondant. (Stir fondant after each dipping.) Lay bonbons on wax paper and bring dipping fork over top, thus leaving a little swirl of fondant as a finish.

17. TEA TIME AND SANDWICHES

ॐ

Tea time should be an hour of relaxation in an atmosphere of friendliness and intimacy. Too often it is time of hectic rushing and dashing from kitchen to dining or living room if you are maidless and have planned too elaborate and difficult a tea menu. Of course every detail of the tea service should be perfection. The silver, linen, and china should be of the loveliest and the tea itself an ambrosia of deliciousness.

Do be sure to have everything ready before guests arrive so that when you pour your tea there will be no nervous restlessness but rather an atmosphere of companionability and cheerfulness. To attain this, nothing is more satisfactory than the dainty sandwich, either the usual closed, wafer-thin one, or the open-faced more colorful sandwich of canapé type. But by all means plan kinds which you need not worry over—"will the bread become soaked" or "will the filling remain hot while I am pouring tea." Such thoughts will not add to your peace of mind and it is impossible to be a perfect hostess and worry: your guests will sense it.

So plan a variety of sandwiches, supplemented by dainty cakes and pastries, which will be of different shapes, fillings, and coloring, but will be at their best when it is convenient for you to serve them.

Your first requisite is good bread of several kinds—white, whole wheat, rye, and good old Boston brown bread. A sharp knife is your best friend in this hour of preparation and its companion is soft butter. Let butter stand outside the refrigerator for half an hour ahead of time. Then cream it a bit before spreading.

Have your sandwich fillings ready before preparing the bread and after making and cutting, place the sandwiches on a tray or platter. Wrap them tightly in wax paper and then cover with a damp towel. Place them in the refrigerator and your worries are over! When sandwiches have to stand around in the dining room, cover them with lettuce leaves whose moisture will keep the bread from drying out quickly.

SANDWICH FORMS

PLAIN SANDWICHES

Trim entire sandwich loaf of crust. Cut lengthwise into thin slices which have been spread evenly with creamed butter before slicing. Cover one slice with prepared filling, spreading *clear out* to edges and corners. Cover spread slice with a buttered slice. Cut with knife into desired shapes—squares, oblongs, or diamonds—or use a cooky cutter to make shapes. By all means keep sandwiches small, both for daintiness and economy in the cutting.

RIBBON SANDWICHES

Cut two thin slices of white bread and then one of whole wheat. Spread with butter and then cover one white slice with one kind of filling and the whole wheat with another, each filling being of a different color. Put the three slices together with the dark bread in the middle. Wrap in a damp cloth. Place under a weight in the refrigerator until butter hardens and slices are firmly pressed together. Then cut this three-layer sandwich into ¼ inch slices.

CHECKERBOARD SANDWICHES

Both white and dark bread are needed for these sandwiches. Cut the two loaves of bread lengthwise into ½ inch slices and then into long strips, ½ inch wide. Spread strips with the sandwich spread. Alternate dark with white strips, pressing together so as to make two loaves of checkerboards. Wrap in a damp cloth, place under a weight in refrigerator until thoroughly chilled. Cut into slices from 1/4 to 1/2 inch thick.

PINWHEEL SANDWICHES

Remove crusts from loaf of sandwich bread. Cut lengthwise into thin slices, spreading loaf with softened butter before cutting off each slice. Spread liberally with a moist, finely cut sandwich spread and beginning at the long side, roll like a jelly roll, giving a little pressure at each turn so as to keep roll in shape. Spread softened butter over outer edges of each roll and wrap tightly in a damp cloth. Place in refrigerator until butter hardens so that rolls will hold their shape. Cut roll into slices from 1/4 to 1/2 inch thick.

HUB SANDWICHES

Cut white and dark bread into circles 2 1/2 inches in diameter. With small cutter cut out centers of some white and some dark pieces of bread. Spread the whole circles with filling. On white circles put ring of dark bread and place smaller circle of white bread in the open center of the ring. Place ring of white bread on dark circles or cut half the centers in fourths and alternate brown and white segments on the whole pieces of bread.

ROLYPOLY SANDWICHES

Cut and make like Pinwheel Sandwiches but use a bulky filling such as a stalk of asparagus, or a piece of stuffed celery and roll the bread around it. Seal with softened butter. Sometimes it helps to fasten with a toothpick until butter has hardened.

CORNUCOPIAS

Cut bread into slices 1/4 inch thick and remove crusts. Spread with filling. Bring opposite corners of bread together to form a cornucopia, spreading the overlapping edges with butter so as to hold shape. Wrap in a damp cloth and place in refrigerator until butter hardens and sandwiches will hold shape. Serve with a sprig of watercress or parsley stuck in the top of each cornucopia.

OPEN SANDWICHES

Cut buttered slices of bread in fancy shapes. Cover with filling and garnish as for a canapé with slices of stuffed olive, hard-cooked egg, pimento, ripe olive, anchovy, pickle, or watercress.

SANDWICH FILLINGS

FRAMINGHAM SANDWICH LOAF

Cut sandwich bread lengthwise in ¾ inch slices. Remove crusts. Spread bread with softened butter. Combine 1 cup cubed chicken, ½ cup diced celery, 2 pimentos, sliced, and 6 olives, sliced. Make a 3-tiered sandwich. Place lettuce on slice of bread, add some chicken mixture to cover, spread with mayonnaise, and place next slice of bread on top. Repeat procedure with lettuce, chicken mixture, and mayonnaise. Cover with third slice of bread. Make a bed of lettuce on platter. Place sandwich on lettuce and garnish with olives. To serve, cut into inch slices and serve on lettuce. This sandwich may be made 2 or 3 hours ahead and wrapped in wax paper and then in a damp towel until ready to serve.

Variation: Instead of chicken use crab meat or tuna fish. Or in place of lettuce and the mixture, use cream cheese and seasonings. Frost with Mayonnaise Dressing.

HOLLYWOOD REDUCING TEA SANDWICHES

Equal parts of figs and prunes mashed together and moistened with orange and lemon juice make excellent tea-time dainties. Spread on Ry-Krisp or health bread and garnish with a bit of orange peel.

Another Hollywood favorite, although not for weight watchers, is a sandwich with a filling of equal parts of alligator pear and salmon mashed together and moistened with highly seasoned Russian Dressing.

MUSHROOM

Slice unpeeled mushrooms. Melt a good-sized piece of butter in a frying pan, add mushrooms, and cook slowly until nicely browned but not crisp. While hot, chop fine or put through food chopper. Season well with salt and pepper, to make a smooth filling. Spread between thin slices of bread and garnish with an olive. These sandwiches lead the parade.

TONGUE AND HORSERADISH

Chop tongue fine and season well with horseradish and perhaps a bit of chopped pickle. Spread on rye bread. This is preferable to a sliced meat filling which is not easily eaten except at the luncheon table or on a picnic.

MIAMI DELIGHTS

Peel 1 orange, remove membrane and mash pulp. Work in 1 package cream cheese and 1 tablespoon chopped chives. Season well with salt and paprika. Also use sliced canned brown bread and fill with mashed dates moistened with orange juice, a little French Dressing and cream cheese, if you wish.

CREAM CHEESE AND PINEAPPLE

Chop slices of canned pineapple and mix with cream cheese. Add pineapple juice if cheese needs softening. Spread between buttered slices of bread and cut in shapes desired.

SPRING

Mix 1 cup cream cheese with 2 or 3 chopped green peppers, 1 can pimentos, 1 small mild onion, chopped, and 1 teaspoon salt. Spread on thin slices of dark bread and cut into fancy shapes.

CHERRY TEA

Mix together 2 cups marshmallow cream, 1⅓ cups chopped walnuts, 1⅓ cups chopped raisins, ⅓ cup chopped maraschino cherries and a little juice. Spread on small circles of bread, cover with other circle and with a thimble make an indentation in the center. Press a cherry into the depression.

FRENCH TOASTED HAM

Cut 1 pound cooked ham in small pieces. Mix 1 cup mayonnaise with a little prepared mustard and moisten ham well. Cut bread in ¼-inch slices. Butter one side of sandwich and spread the other with ham mixture. Put slices together, and dip one sandwich at a time in a batter made of ½ cup milk and 1 slightly beaten egg. Melt butter in frying pan and sauté sandwiches until brown. Serve very hot. These are excellent for Sunday night supper or for luncheon.

EGG AND CHEESE

Mash 3 hard-cooked eggs with a fork and blend in ½ cup finely grated American cheese. Add drop of Worcestershire sauce, salt and pepper, and enough mayonnaise to moisten for spreading.

DRIED BEEF AND CHEESE

Chip fine ½ cup dried beef and work in 1 package cream cheese. Moisten with horseradish, a bit of Worcestershire sauce, enough cream for spreading consistency.

ORIENTAL SANDWICH

Fry ¼ pound bacon until crisp and brown. Crumble it fine and mix with ½ cup pimento cheese and ½ cup chopped candied ginger. Moisten with syrup from candied ginger.

APRICOT CHEESE

Moisten cream cheese with cream and mash with canned or fresh apricots. Add a few drops of lemon juice to pep up flavor.

ROQUEFORT SPREAD

Mash together with a fork equal parts Roquefort and cream cheese. Moisten with cream and add chopped pecan meats before spreading. This is best used on dark breads.

CHEESE AND CHIVES

Add 2 tablespoons chopped chives to 1 package cream cheese or 1 pound cottage cheese. Season highly with salt, pepper, tabasco sauce, and paprika. Allow to stand a short time before spreading to let cheese ripen and absorb flavor of seasoning.

PIMENTO AND OLIVE

Use either pimento cream cheese or chopped pimentos with plain cheese. Add chopped olives, moisten with cream, and season with drop of tabasco, salt and pepper.

BAR LE DUC AND CHEESE

Mash together Bar le Duc jelly and cream or cottage cheese until of a consistency to spread. Serve on bread as an open sandwich or on toasted crackers.

DATE, CHEESE, AND NUT
Moisten cream cheese with orange juice and add ¼ cup chopped dates and ¼ cup chopped nuts.

CHICKEN LIVER
Cook chicken livers in chicken stock. Then chop or grind fine and moisten with chicken gravy. Season well and add an equal amount of sautéed mushrooms which have also been chopped fine.

SHAD ROE
For lovers of shad roe a sandwich well prepared is a real delicacy. Blend melted butter and lemon juice with cooked roe and add crisp bacon which has been chopped fine. Do not use too much bacon or the flavor of the fish roe will be lost.

CALF'S LIVER AND BACON
Grind leftover liver, which has been fried, broiled, or baked. Mix with it crisp bacon, crumbled, and enough melted butter or mayonnaise to make a spread.

SARDINE
The sardine may be used whole but a better blend results if sardines are drained of oil and mashed. Moisten with plenty of lemon juice and season with salt and cayenne. Use equal amount of hard-cooked eggs if a strong sardine flavor is not desired.

RED PEPPER JAM
Drain 1 small can of pimentos and force through food chopper. Place in saucepan with ¾ cup sugar and ½ cup mild vinegar. Stir until sugar is dissolved. Simmer until mixture is consistency of jam. Spread on white or dark bread for a different sandwich. This mixture is excellent as filling for one layer of a ribbon sandwich with cream cheese and green pepper for the alternating layers.

PEANUT BUTTER AND BACON
Combine ½ cup peanut butter with 8 slices crisp crumbled bacon. Mix well and spread on bread or better still serve on crisp crackers.

PEANUT BUTTER AND BANANA

Mash 1 small banana into ½ cup peanut butter. Add a little lemon juice if desired for tartness.

TOMATO AND BACON

Skin and slice tomatoes. Cut rounds of bread the same size as the tomato slices. On top of bread place a small firm slice of lettuce cut crosswise. Spread with mayonnaise and place slice of tomato on top. Dot with mayonnaise and garnish with a 1-inch square of crisp bacon, cooked to be as crinkly as possible. A bit of watercress set into the mayonnaise at each side of the bacon adds color.

LOBSTER AND CUCUMBER

Cut lobster meat fine enough to spread well. Moisten with melted butter. Add cucumber, chopped fine, and mix all together with mayonnaise or Boiled Dressing, salt, pepper, and paprika. Cucumber is a pleasant variation from celery.

CALIFORNIA "CHICKEN" SPREAD

Mash 1 can tuna fish with 1 cup chopped mustard pickle until well blended. Spread on dark bread.

SWISS CHEESE AND HAM

No more popular sandwich, barring chicken, can be served guests than rye bread, well buttered, and covered with thin slices of Swiss cheese. Spread with English mustard and top with a slice of tender baked ham.

TURKEY

Combine small pieces of turkey with stuffing. Or use turkey alone (but by all means include stuffing when you have it).

CHINESE CHICKEN

Combine ½ cup chopped chicken and ½ cup crushed pineapple, drained. Season with salt, pepper, and paprika and moisten with mayonnaise. Spread and sprinkle with toasted almonds, sliced or chopped. Serve either as an open or a closed sandwich.

SALMON AND CUCUMBER

Mash 1 cup salmon with a fork. Add ½ cup chopped cucumber or celery and moisten with mayonnaise and a little horse-radish but have flavor of horseradish dominate mayonnaise.

LETTUCE

No more delicate sandwich can be served at teatime than one of crisp Boston lettuce broken or cut up and placed on white or dark bread and spread with Mayonnaise, Russian, Roquefort, or Boiled Dressing. Serve while lettuce is still crisp.

WATERCRESS

Place tender stalks of watercress on soft, fresh rye or whole wheat bread. Spread with peppy Russian Dressing, and serve before dressing soaks bread.

DEVILED EGGS

Slice hard-cooked eggs. Separate yolks from rings of white. Mash yolks with deviled ham, chopped onion, and mayonnaise. Season to taste and blend well. Place the white rings on the buttered bread. Fill with the mashed yolks. Garnish with radish rings, anchovy curls, caviar, or pimento.

18. RELISHES AND ODDMENTS

Is there any aroma more wonderful floating out of a kitchen than that of cooking relishes? In New England these relishes served as "side dishes" at luncheon and dinner are concocted in summer from the bounty of our farms. The Piccalilli which always appears at Toll House along with Saturday night Baked Beans is made from one of my own most cherished family recipes. When we first opened Toll House, Mother made Piccalilli by the gallon at home so that we could bring to our new business one of the best of our traditional family recipes.

When I put up relishes at home, I make a point of filling all the odd mayonnaise and other jars I have saved since the last preserving. I suppose this is my Yankee thrift. Anyway it is these odd-sized containers which I tuck into the gift packages I send to shut-in friends or give for going-away, birthday, and Christmas gifts. Try giving a present of a gaily wrapped jar of such Toll House favorites as Pickled Watermelon Rind or Spiced Orange Peel. You will find that your friends will appreciate either of these tremendously. One of our most distinguished guests, Cole Porter, always carries home a few jars of the Spiced Orange Peel, which he has enjoyed here for years. If you make Catsup for a Maine friend use very little sugar. Down Maine they like their relishes sour.

BEET RELISH

Mix together:
1 pint chopped, cooked beets
1 quart chopped cabbage
1 cup sugar
½ cup prepared horseradish
1 teaspoon salt
1 teaspoon pepper

Cover with vinegar and cook 20 to 30 minutes, or until vinegar is absorbed. Turn into jars and seal hot. Makes about 4 pints.

CABBAGE AND CELERY RELISH

Mix and salt in layers:
4 large cabbages, shredded,
8 onions, chopped,
3 red peppers, cut fine,
3 bunches celery, chopped (about 24 stalks)

Let stand for 24 hours. Drain, wash off salt, cover with mild vinegar. Let stand 24 hours. Then squeeze out moisture.

Add:
¼ pound dry mustard
4 pounds brown sugar
1 cup white mustard seed
Cover with cold vinegar

Seal in jars. This will be ready for use in 2 to 3 days. Makes about 10 pints.

CATSUP

Combine:
8 quarts strained tomatoes
6 tablespoons salt
4 teaspoons dry mustard
½ teaspoons black pepper
1 teaspoon ground clove
1 teaspoon ginger
1 quart vinegar
1 to 3 cups brown sugar (according to taste)

Simmer until quantity is reduced by half. Turn into hot clean bottles. Makes about 3 pints.

CHILI SAUCE

Combine:
12 large, ripe tomatoes, skinned,
4 onions, chopped,
2 red peppers, chopped,
4 cups vinegar
2 tablespoons sugar
1 tablespoon salt

Boil hard 1 hour and turn into clean bottles. Makes about 2 pints.

CHILI SAUCE WITH SPICES

Mix:
24 ripe tomatoes, peeled, blanched, cut fine,
3 green peppers, chopped,
3 onions, chopped,
½ cup sugar
1 quart vinegar

2 tablespoons salt
1 tablespoon ground cloves
1 tablespoon ground nutmeg
1 tablespoon ground ginger
1 tablespoon ground allspice

Simmer until thick, about 2 hours. When cool pack in sterile jars. Makes 4 pints

CLOVELLY CHUTNEY

Mix and simmer until very thick:
4 pounds apples, pared and sliced,
2 ounces salt
1 ounce mustard seed

Few grains cayenne
2 pounds brown sugar
2 pounds raisins
1 ounce ground ginger
3 pints vinegar

Bottle and seal. Makes about 3 quarts.

CUCUMBER RELISH

Mix together:
1 quart small whole cucumbers
1 onion, sliced,
1 red pepper, chopped and seeded. Cover with
⅛ cup salt. Let stand over-

night. In morning drain, wash off salt, and add:
½ cup brown sugar
Pinch tumeric
1 teaspoon white mustard seed
1 teaspoon horseradish

Cover with vinegar and heat to boiling point. Turn into clean jars. Makes 2 pints.

PEPPER RELISH

Pour boiling water over:
12 red peppers, chopped
12 green peppers, chopped,
3 onions, chopped. Let stand

10 minutes. Drain and add:
2 cups sugar
1 tablespoon salt. Cover with
Vinegar

Simmer for 20 minutes. Turn into clean jars. Makes 2 pints.

GREEN PEPPER RELISH

Remove seeds and put
through. food chopper
twice, using fine blade:
8 green peppers
2 red peppers. Pack solidly
into 2 cups using juice to
overflow cups. Add
1½ cups vinegar and bring to

a hard boil. Set aside in
warm place for 15 minutes,
uncovered. Stir occasionally.
Bring again to rolling boil
and boil 2 minutes. Remove
from heat and stir in
1 bottle pectin

Skim and stir continuously for 8 minutes. Turn into clean glasses and seal. Makes six 6-ounce glasses of relish.

PICCALILLI

Mix:
1 peck green tomatoes, sliced,
1 cup salt. Let stand overnight. In morning drain,
wash off salt, and add:

1 package (1½-oz.) mixed
spices, tied in a bag,
½ dozen onions, sliced,
1 pound brown sugar
2 quarts mild vinegar

Cook until tender, about 1 hour. Turn into clean jars and seal. Makes about 12 pints.

ORIENTAL RELISH

Cook together for
5 minutes:
10 cups canned tomatoes
10 cups chopped apple
5 lemons, ground in food

chopper,
1¼ cups preserved ginger,
chopped fine. Then add
15 cups sugar.
Simmer until thick.

Turn into hot sterilized jars. Seal. Makes 4 quarts.

STRING BEAN RELISH

Cook together in small amount salted water until not quite done and still crispy:
4 pounds string beans, cut in 2-inch pieces,
6 onions, sliced,
1 bunch celery, cut in large pieces. Drain. (Reserve

water for soup.) Bring to a boil
1 quart vinegar with
1½ pounds brown sugar. Combine
½ cup flour
1 tablespoon tumeric
1 tablespoon celery seed

Add a little hot vinegar to flour to make a smooth paste. Then add remaining liquid and pour over hot vegetables. Simmer about 45 minutes. Pack hot in sterilized jars. Makes 5 to 6 quarts.

REED FAMILY TOMATO RELISH

Bring to a boil:
3½ pounds sugar
1 pint vinegar. Put in
7 pounds tomatoes. As soon as skins break, take out tomatoes and drain 3 days. Return to syrup and boil several hours. Add:

1 tablespoon cloves (whole and ground)
1 tablespoon cinnamon (whole and ground)
1 tablespoon whole allspice
1 stick cinnamon
3 to 4 red peppers

Simmer until mixture is thick and dark red color. Turn into clean jars. Makes 6 to 7 pints.

Variation: Add pieces of ginger to make this taste like chutney.

CRANBERRY RELISH

Put through food chopper:
1 quart cranberries
2 oranges. Add:

½ cup crushed pineapple
2 cups sugar

Mix well and store, covered, in refrigerator. Do not cook. Serve with turkey or chicken. Serves 10 to 12.

SPICED CRANBERRY JELLY

Combine:
1 cup water
4 cups cranberries. Cook until soft. Rub through a sieve. Cook
½ cup raisins in water to cover until tender. (There should be ¾ cup raisins and liquid.) Soften
1½ tablespoons gelatin in ¼ cup cold water. Add to hot cranberry pulp and dissolve.
Add raisins and:
1¾ cups sugar
¼ teaspoon powdered clove
½ teaspoon cinnamon
Juice of 1 lemon

Pour into molds. Chill. Serve with poultry. Serves 4.

CRANBERRY JELLY

Pick over and wash
4 cups cranberries. Put in saucepan with
2 cups boiling water. Boil 20 minutes. Rub through a sieve and cook 3 minutes more. Add
2 cups sugar. Cook 2 minutes more

Turn into mold and chill. Serves 4.

DELICIOUS PICKLES

Dissolve in a bowl
3 pounds brown sugar in
1 quart apple vinegar. Cut
12 large vinegar pickles into ⅓ inch thick rounds. Place pickles in bowl.
Sprinkle each layer with a few tablespoons of mixed spices, using
½ box (¾-oz.) mixed spices in all

Let stand several hours in bowl, stirring occasionally. Then turn into jars or crocks. Makes 4 pints.

PICKLED BEETS

Boil and skin
½ peck small beets. Mix together:
1 cup sugar
2 cups vinegar
3 cups water

Add beets and cook mixture until beets are heated through. Turn into pint jars. Makes 6 pints.

RIPE CUCUMBER PICKLE

Sprinkle with salt
1 quart sliced ripe cucumbers. Let stand 3 hours. Drain, wash off salt, and add:
¾ cup sugar

2 green peppers, chopped,
1 red pepper, chopped,
2 onions, chopped
1 tablespoon horseradish. Cover with Vinegar

Bring to boil and simmer until cucumbers are transparent. Seal in jars. Makes about 3 pints.

SPICED ORANGE PEEL

Peel orange carefully so that no fruit clings to rind. Cut rind into 2-inch lengths and measure until there are 12 quarts. Soak overnight in cold water. Drain.

Cover with water and bring to boil. Discard water. Do this three times to remove bitter flavor. Cook rind until tender during third cooking. Drain. Make a syrup by simmering together for about 5 minutes:

5 quarts white sugar
2 pints vinegar
1 package (1½-oz.) whole cloves

1 package (1½-oz.) stick cinnamon

Add orange peel to syrup. Mixture will be very thick but after cooking peel about 5 minutes, you will find mixture is of proper consistency. Bottle while hot, leaving cinnamon and clove in syrup. Makes 3 gallons.

Variation: **SPICED GRAPEFRUIT PEEL.** This same syrup may be used with grapefruit peel. Or try fresh pineapple or tiny carrots, cooking them in a little water. Then add them to the syrup.

SWEET PICKLED PRUNES

Wash and soak overnight 2 pounds prunes. In morning boil together for 5 minutes:

1 pound brown sugar
1 cup vinegar
2 large sticks cinnamon, broken

Insert 1 whole clove into each prune. Place prunes in syrup. Simmer for at least 2 hours. Turn into sterilized jars and seal. Makes 3 pints. This is delicious served with chicken.

PICKLED WATERMELON RIND

Cover with water 7 pounds cubed watermelon rind. Cook until you can pierce rind easily with fork. Make a syrup of:
1 pint water

1 pint vinegar
3½ pounds sugar
½ teaspoon oil of cinnamon
½ teaspoon oil of cloves

Pour syrup over rind and let stand overnight. Next morning pour off syrup and bring it to a boil. Pour over rind. Repeat procedure two more times. Turn into jars. Makes 8 pints.

Variation: To make a crisp pickle, soak rind first for 2½ hours in 3 quarts water mixed with 3 tablespoons slaked lime. Drain off lime water before adding water to cook.

ODDMENTS

APPLE CIRCLETS

Core large red apples and cut in slices ¾ inch thick. Dip in melted butter and then in a mixture and cinnamon. Place in pan and cook under broiler until one is puffed and brown. Turn and brown other side. Serve as garnish with pork or ham.

CARROT AND PINEAPPLE HONEY

Combine:
4 cups grated raw carrots
6 cups granulated sugar

1½ tablespoons grated lemon rind
½ cup lemon juice
2 cups crushed pineapple

Stir over low heat until sugar dissolves. Then bring to boil and cook vigorously for 2 minutes. Remove from heat and add ½ cup pectin. Stir well. Skim and fill hot sterilized jars. Makes 2 quarts.

JIFFY GRAPE JUICE

Place in a quart jar   1½ cups Concord grapes
½ cup sugar

Fill jar with boiling water. Seal and let stand for 6 months, if possible, before using. Strain, chill, and serve. Makes 1 quart.

TOMATO SOY

Blanch, skin, core, and cut   1 pint vinegar
up   1½ cups sugar
20 tomatoes. Mix with: ½ cup salt (scant)
10 onions, sliced,   1 teaspoon celery seed
 8 green peppers, chopped,

Simmer until thick. Turn into clean bottles and seal. Makes about 4 pints.

CUCUMBERS IN SOUR CREAM

Mix together: 2 heaping teaspoons horse-
1½ cups sour cream   radish
1½ teaspoons salt   ¾ teaspoon dry mustard
 1 teaspoon black pepper   2 tablespoons grated Parme-
 ¼ cup lemon juice   san cheese
                                   1 large onion, sliced

Pour this dressing over 3 cucumbers, sliced. Let stand so that flavor is absorbed.

Variation: This dressing may also be used with slices or wedges of tomatoes.

꿗   # 19. JELLIES, JAMS, CONSERVES   꿗

꿗

Who can resist making Strawberry Jam or Grape Jelly when fruit is in season, and what tastes better on a cold winter morning than breakfast toast with a homemade spread? Children enjoy the drama of preserving and ours like particularly to pour the paraffin and label all the small, pretty, odd-shaped containers that come our way for the gift Christmas food baskets. There is nothing more attractive and acceptable than a jar of homemade jam or jelly attractively wrapped and beribboned.

GUIDE TO PRESERVING

Acid, pectin, and sugar are necessary for the jellying of fruit. Because the quantity of acid decreases as fruit matures and reaches the peak of flavor, it is best to use a mixture of slightly under-ripe fruit for pectin and acid, and of ripe fruit for flavor and color.

Combinations of fruits rich in pectin with others rich in acid result in interesting blends of flavor and colors; for example, crabapple with grape, currant with raspberry, tart apple with quince, or quince with cranberry.

If fruit lacking pectin is available, the commercial pectins may be used; if acid is needed, lemon juice or citric acid will supply it.

JELLIES

Prepare the selected fruit in small quantities. Six quarts of berries, 8 quarts of apples or grapes can be handled quickly enough for them to jell successfully.

Two pounds of prepared fruit yield 1 pint of juice. One pint of fruit juice, plus an equal quantity of sugar yields 1½ pints or 4 regular-sized, 6-ounce jelly glasses.

Place washed fruit in a broad, flat-bottomed kettle. Allow about 1 cup water to 1 pound crushed fruit. In cooking, count time after fruit begins to boil. Berries, currants, and grapes require 5 to 10 minutes; apples and quinces 20 to 25 minutes, to cook soft.

Pour hot cooked fruit into jelly bag at once. Let juice drip into a bowl. When dripping is almost over, press jelly bag to obtain remaining juice. Clarify by re-straining through a fresh jelly bag which has been wrung out in hot water.

Wash jelly glasses and cover with hot water. Boil them from 15 to 20 minutes. Keep them hot until jelly is ready.

For best results, prepare at one time no more than 8 cups juice, using ¾ to 1 cup sugar to each cupful.

Heat the fruit juice and sugar quickly to the boiling point. The flat-bottomed pan permits rapid evaporation. Stir mixture only until the sugar is dissolved. Boil rapidly until jelly stage is reached and the amount of juice is reduced to about half.

JELLY TEST

Dip out a large spoonful of boiling syrup. Then pour it slowly back into the kettle. When the last of the syrup separates into two distinct lines of drops which "sheet" together off the edge of the spoon, the jelly has cooked enough. Fruit juice and sugar usually require 3 to 5 minutes of boiling before they jell.

Allow hot syrup to stand in kettle while jelly glasses are lifted from boiling water, drained, and placed on a tray. Before pouring remove any scum from top of hot syrup.

Fill hot jelly glasses to within ¼ inch of top. Cover glasses with a large sheet of wax paper and allow to cool.

When cold, add a layer of paraffin no thicker than a coin. Tip and rotate glass before the paraffin hardens so that it will run up to the rim and form a good seal. Be sure no drops of juice remain on the inside of the glass in the area of the paraffin or you will not achieve a tight seal.

JAMS AND PRESERVES

When, without heat, sugar is added to fruit, the fruit loses juice, shrinks somewhat, and becomes more firm. Little if any sugar is absorbed by raw fruit under these conditions, but cooking changes the cell walls of the fruit so that sugar penetrates more rapidly. The passage of sugar syrup into fruit is a slow process, so after fruit has been heated in syrup, it is sometimes desirable to let it stand for a time to "plump" before the final cooking.

When without preliminary softening, fruit is cooked in a very concentrated syrup, it tends to shrink too rapidly, becomes tough, and fails to regain its shape on standing. For example, unless firm fruits, such as cherries are started in syrup thin enough to allow the cellulose to soften before cooking concentrates the syrup, the fruit will be tough and hard. Rather soft fruits, such as berries and peaches, need firming to preserve their shape, so they are cooked at once in a heavy syrup, or allowed to stand overnight in sugar.

Jams are made from crushed fruits cooked with sugar until mixture is thick. Well-ripened but sound berries and soft-fleshed fruits like apricots, peaches, and plums make good jams. The same proportions of 1 pound fruit to ¾ to 1 pound of sugar applies. Sterilized jars, well paraffined, are best for jams too.

Preserves are made with 1 pound fruit to ¾ to 1 pound sugar. In most cases, the fruit and sugar can be combined in alternate layers and let stand overnight or 8 to 10 hours before cooking. If you prefer, add sugar and ¼ cup water for each pound of fruit and cook at once. Stir until boiling point is reached. Boil rapidly until syrup is somewhat thick, taking care to prevent scorching. Pour at once into hot sterilized jars and seal.

GRAPE JELLY

Select somewhat under-ripe grapes. Stem, wash, and place in an agate or enamel-lined saucepan over low heat. Simmer very gently, until fruit is softened throughout. A peculiarity of grape jelly is its tendency to crystallize on standing. One cup of diced tart apples added to 1 quart of grapes during the cooking prevents crystallization (or half as much apple juice may be combined with the grape juice). The flavor of apple will not be apparent. Pour grapes into bag and let juice drain off. Do not squeeze the bag of juice but let juice drain slowly, overnight if necessary. For each cup of juice allow 1 cup sugar. Heat sugar by spreading it on shallow pans in the oven. After draining, heat juice to boiling point and let boil rapidly for 10 minutes, skimming as needed. Add sugar and let boil until a little will jell on a cool saucer or until thermometer reads 220° F. Skim, and pour into sterilized glasses. Cool and seal. Expect from each quart of juice 8 glasses (6-ounce) of jelly.

WILD GRAPE JELLY FOR VENISON

Wash and stem
4 quarts grapes, preferably wild grapes. Add:

1 quart vinegar
¼ cup whole cloves
¼ cup stick cinnamon

Heat slowly and simmer until soft. Strain through jelly bag. Do not squeeze. Pour juice into large kettle and boil 20 minutes. Add 6 pounds brown sugar and cook until mixture jells. Pour into hot, sterile glasses. Cool and seal. Makes sixteen 6-ounce glasses jelly.

PIMENTO JAM

Drain
1 can (7-oz.) pimentos. Put through food chopper and

place in saucepan. Add.
¾ cup sugar
½ cup vinegar

Stir over low heat until sugar is dissolved. Simmer until mixture is consistency of jam. Pour into small glasses, cool, and seal. Makes two 3-ounce glasses of jam. (Spread on white or dark breads to make a delicious and different sandwich.)

STRAWBERRY JAM

Wash, hull, and mash 2 quarts ripe strawberries, to make 4 cups. Turn into a large kettle, and stir in 7 cups sugar. Bring to a rolling boil, stirring continuously and boil hard for 1 minute. Remove from heat and stir in ½ bottle liquid pectin. Stir and skim off white froth at 5-minute intervals until top is clear of foam, and jam has cooled slightly and fruit no longer floats to top. Ladle jam into drained, scalded glasses, filling to within ½ inch of top. Seal at once, cool, label, and store in a cool, dry place. (I prefer strawberry jam made with pectin. A brighter color, fresher fruit flavor, and firmer berries result than when the longer cooking method is followed.)

AMBER MARMALADE

Wash, dry, cut in paper-thin slices   1 orange
                                         1 lemon
1 grapefruit

Add half as much water by measure as fruit and let stand overnight. Then place fruit over heat and bring to a boil. At once place mixture, covered, in moderate oven, 350° F., and cook for 10 minutes. Reduce heat to 300° and continue cooking for 50 minutes more. Remove from oven. Again let mixture stand overnight. Measure cooked fruit and add equal amounts of sugar. Place sweetened mixture over heat until it reaches boiling point. At once place mixture, uncovered, in a moderate oven, 350° F., and cook for 10 minutes. Then reduce heat to 300° and continue cooking for 50 minutes or until mixture "sheets" off edge of metal spoon. This is the Jelly Test. Turn into sterile jars, cool, and seal with a thin layer of paraffin. Put on covers and store in dark place. Makes four 6-ounce glasses of marmalade.

RHUBARB AND ORANGE MARMALADE

Quarter, seed, slice thin 3 oranges. To 1 cup fruit add
2 cups water. Let stand 48 hours. Bring to boil. Add

2 pounds rhubarb, cut into ½ inch pieces. Boil 30 minutes. Add
1¼ pounds sugar

Simmer until mixture jells. Turn into hot sterilized jars. Cool and seal. Makes six 6-ounce glasses.

GINGER MARMALADE

With a sharp knife remove thin skin from

3 large oranges and
1 lemon. Shred peel very fine and place in saucepan with:

1½ cups water
¼ teaspoon soda. Cook 10 minutes, stirring continuously. Remove white membrane from skinned fruit. Add to cooked peel and water. Cover and simmer 20 minutes. Chop

2 cups crystallized ginger. Measure fruit and water, adding more water to make 3 solidly packed cups. Add ginger and

5½ cups sugar. Simmer 2 minutes. Remove from heat. Stir in

½ cup pectin

Let stand 5 minutes with occasional stirring. Then turn into jelly glasses and seal. Makes twelve 6-ounce glasses of jelly.

CARROT PRESERVE

Put through food chopper with a little water:

4 pounds carrots
4 lemons. Cook until soft. Add

6 cups sugar. Cook mixture until thick enough to heap on spoon. Add

¾ pound soft almonds, blanched and cut fine

Remove from heat. Turn into jelly glasses. Cool and seal. Makes eleven 6-ounce glasses of preserve.

RHUBARB AND STRAWBERRY PRESERVE

Wash and hull

8 cups strawberries. Add:
8 cups rhubarb, cut into ½ inch pieces.

4 cups sugar
¼ cup water

Boil about 10 minutes or until juice has been extracted. Pour into hot, sterilized jars. Adjust top clamp. Place in a slow oven, 275° F., for 30 minutes to insure sterilization. Remove and adjust lower clamp at once. Makes 8 pints of preserve.

CRANBERRY CONSERVE

Simmer for 10 minutes
1 orange, washed and put
  through food chopper, in
1 pint water. Cook until
  very soft
1 quart cranberries with
1 cup water. Rub through

sieve and add to orange.
  Add:
¼ cup raisins, put through
  food chopper,
2½ cups sugar
1 pint water

Cook until mixture heaps on spoon. Remove from heat and stir in 1½ ounces broken walnut meats. Turn into sterile glasses, cool, and seal. Makes about eight 6-ounce glasses of conserve.

PEAR CONSERVE

Peel, core, and quarter
8 pounds pears. Put through
  food chopper, using medium
  blade. Add:

8 pounds sugar
½ pound preserved ginger
4 lemons, put through food
  chopper, using small knife

Cover and let stand overnight. In the morning bring to a boil, over heat. Then place in moderate oven, 350° F., and cook for 10 minutes. Reduce heat to 300° and cook until thick and amber-colored, about 1½ hours. Turn into hot, sterile jars. Cool and seal. Makes about 5 quarts of conserve.

RHUBARB AND PINEAPPLE CONSERVE

Bring to a boil
1 cup fresh pineapple, finely
  cut. Add:
1 quart rhubarb, cut in 1-inch
  pieces,
Juice and grated rind of

1 orange.
1 quart sugar. Simmer until
  thick, stirring occasionally
  to prevent burning. Add
¼ cup chopped nut meats

Fill sterilized jars. Cool and seal. Makes six 6-ounce glasses.

MINCEMEAT

Put through food chopper, using large blade;

2 pounds cooked lean meat
1 pound suet
3 quarts sour apples. Add:
3 pounds raisins, chopped,
2 pounds currants, chopped,
1 tablespoon citron, chopped,
3 oranges, and
3 lemons, washed, grated and juice removed,

2½ pounds sugar
1 cup dark molasses
2 tablespoons salt
2 tablespoons cinnamon
2 teaspoons nutmeg
2 teaspoons mace
2 teaspoons powdered clove
1 teaspoon allspice
1 quart beef broth
3 cups boiled cider
2 cups sour jelly or sweet pickle syrup

Simmer for 2 hours. Turn into sterile jars and seal while hot. Makes 8 to 9 pints.

GREEN TOMATO MINCEMEAT

Chop fine, drain, and rinse in cold water

1 peck green tomatoes. Add:
1 cup vinegar
4 cups water. Simmer for 2 hours. Add:
2 pounds raisins, chopped,

3 pounds white sugar
1 pound brown sugar
2 tablespoons cinnamon
2 tablespoons allspice
2 tablespoons salt
2 tablespoons nutmeg
1 teaspoon clove

Simmer for 2 hours more. Turn into sterilized jars and seal while hot. Makes 8 to 9 pints.

321

20. CANNING FRUITS AND VEGETABLES

⅋

Too often homemakers use the first tender products of the garden directly for the table. Then when the garden is on the wane and fruits and vegetables are not so tender and choice, they start canning. But only choice products are worth preserving. To avoid waste of time and materials and to obtain the finest products, the early crops not the end ones should be canned. No more than two hours from garden to can is a good rule to follow. (The suggestions in this chapter are based on new information developed by United States Department of Agriculture.)

FOR BEST RESULTS

1. If you do not raise your own produce, buy locally, choosing only fresh, firm, ripe, tender fruits or vegetables.
2. Prepare at one time only one canner load.
3. Sort for size and ripeness to insure more even cooking.
4. Wash very clean, handling gently.
5. Dip apples, peaches and pears in a solution of 2 tablespoons salt, 2 tablespoons vinegar and 1 gallon water to prevent fruit from turning dark.
6. Have ready jars, caps, and rubber rings in a pan of warm water with rack or cloth placed on bottom so jars will not touch, bringing to boil just before time to fill them.
7. Pack food while hot and cover with boiling liquid. Pack well

but do not cram in too much solid food. Work out air bubbles by gliding knife blade down sides of jar. Wipe sealing edge and rubber ring clean as a seed or sticky place may prevent a perfect seal.

8. Before processing, completely seal a jar closure that is made of rubber on a metal disk. Partly seal other screw types before processing. Screw the cap tight. Then turn it back about a quarter inch. Snap the top wire clamp of a lightning-type jar into place and leave the side clamp up.

9. For the boiling water bath you can use as a canner a wash boiler or any deep kettle or other clean vessel. It must have a good fitting lid and be large enough to hold a convenient number of jars and deep enough to allow covering tops of jars with at least 1 to 2 inches of water. Fit a wire or wooden rack in canner to support jars above the bottom so that water may freely circulate around and under them. Have water boiling in canner and put in each jar of food as it is filled. After all jars are in the canner, add more boiling water if it is needed to cover jars. Put lid on and start counting time as soon as water boils briskly. Keep it boiling steadily for as long as timetable indicates for type food you are processing. Add boiling water as needed to keep jars adequately covered.

10. If you are using a steam pressure canner keep about 1 inch of boiling water in canner. Place jars on rack. Do not let them touch as steam must circulate around each jar. Fasten cover securely so that no steam escapes except at open petcock. After steam has poured steadily from petcock for 7 minutes, close petcock, and let pressure rise to desired point on gauge. Count time from moment required pressure is reached. Regulate your stove or heat to keep pressure even. Never try to lower pressure by opening petcock. Keep drafts from blowing on canner. After processing time is completed, let canner cool gradually before opening. When gauge falls to zero, slowly open petcock. Then unfasten cover. Tilt the cover away from you so that steam will escape on opposite side.

11. If you have no jar lifter or tongs, dip some water out of

canner before removing jars when using the boiling water bath method. Lift out jars and tighten at once any clamps or caps which are only partly sealed. *Do not open a jar* to replace lost liquid. Seal as is. Place jars right side up to cool. Keep them out of draft but do not cover with a cloth. When cool, carefully tilt jar to see if it leaks. If jar leaks, open it, heat contents, and process again in another jar with a new closure.

12. Wipe jars shining clean, label contents, and mark date. Watch jars for a few days then store in a dark, cool, dry place.

13. It has been determined that the discoloration noticeable in peaches, pears, applesauce, sweet corn, carrots, and some berries after canning is due to low Vitamin C (ascorbic acid) content. It has been suggested that 2 one-grain ascorbic acid tablets be added per pint or quart jar of food to correct this loss in flavor and color.

14. Proportions for Canning Syrup:
    Thin: 1 cup sugar and 3 cups water or juice.
    Moderately thin: 1 cup sugar and 2 cups water or juice.
    Medium (for sour fruit): 1 cup sugar and 1 cup water or juice.

15. The boiling water bath method of processing is not recommended for the following foods: meats, fish, poultry, sweet corn, asparagus, squash, beans of all types, peas, beets, or any other foods which are non-acid.

GUIDE FOR PURCHASING FRUITS AND VEGETABLES

(Legal weight of a bushel of fruit varies in different states.)

Food	Fresh	Quarts after Canning
Apples	1 bu. (48 lbs.)	16–20
	2½–3 lbs.	1
Berries, except straw-	24-qt. crate	12–18
berries	5–8 cups	1
Cherries, as picked	1 bu. (56 lbs.)	22–32
	6–8 cups	1

Food	Fresh	Quarts after Canning
Peaches	1 bu. (48 lbs.)	18–24
	2–2½ lbs.	1
Pears	1 bu. (50 lbs.)	20–25
	2–2½ lbs.	1
Plums	1 bu. (56 lbs.)	24–30
	2–2½ lbs.	1
Strawberries	24-qt. crate	12–16
	6–8 cups	1
Tomatoes	1 bu. (53 lbs.)	15–20
	2½–3 lbs.	1
Asparagus	1 bu. (45 lbs.)	11
	4 lbs.	1
Beans, Lima (in pods)	1 bu. (32 lbs.)	6–8
	4–5 lbs.	1
Beans, Snap	1 bu. (30 lbs.)	15–20
	1½–2 lbs.	1
Beets (without tops)	1 bu. (52 lbs.)	17–20
	2½–3 lbs.	1
Carrots (without tops)	1 bu. (50 lbs.)	16–20
	2½–3 lbs.	1
Corn (in husks)	1 bu. (35 lbs.)	8–9
	6–16 ears	1
Okra	1 bu. (26 lbs.)	17
	1½ lbs.	1
Peas, Green (in pods)	1 bu. (30 lbs.)	6–7
	2–2½ lbs.	½
Pumpkin	50 lbs.	15
	3 lbs.	1
Spinach	1 bu. (18 lbs.)	6–9
	2–3 lbs.	1
Squash, Summer	1 bu. (40 lbs.)	16–20
	2–2½ lbs.	1
Sweet Potatoes	1 bu. (55 lbs.)	18–22
	2½–3 lbs.	1

TIMETABLES FOR CANNING

FOR FRUITS AND TOMATOES, PICKLED BEETS, SAUERKRAUT

Solid food in the jar should be covered by liquid and a half-inch head-space left in each jar.

Processing times are given for sea level. If canning is done at higher altitude, add 1 minute per 1,000 feet when processing time is 20 minutes or less. Add 2 minutes per 1,000 feet when processing time is longer.

In the following chart the time is indicated for processing in a boiling water bath at 212° F.

Food	Preparation	Minutes per Pint	Minutes per Quart
Apples	Pare, core, cut in pieces. Steam or boil in thin syrup or water 5 minutes. Pack hot, cover with hot liquid.	20	25
	Or make applesauce, sweetened or unsweetened. Pack hot	10	10
Apricots	Same as Peaches.		
Beets, Pickled	Cook beets until tender in water to cover. Remove skins, slice or dice. Pack hot, add ½ teaspoon salt per pint. Cover with boiling vinegar sweetened to taste.	30	30
Berries (except strawberries)	If berries are firm, precook, adding just enough medium syrup or juice to prevent sticking to pan. Pack hot, cover with hot liquid.	15	20

Food	Preparation	Minutes per Pint	Minutes per Quart
Cherries	Can cherries with or without pits. Follow directions for berries. For sour cherries, use medium syrup. For sweet cherries, use thin syrup.	15	20
Peaches	Remove skins and pits. Precook juicy fruit slowly until tender, adding ¼ cup sugar to 1 pound fruit to draw out juice. Precook less juicy fruit in thin to medium syrup. Pack hot, cover with boiling juice or syrup.	25	30
Pears	Peel, cut in halves, core. Proceed as for peaches.	25	30
Pimentos (ripe)	Place in hot oven for 6 to 8 minutes. Dip into cold water. Remove skins, stems, and seed cores. Pack and add ½ teaspoon salt per pint. Do not add liquid.	40	—
Plums, Prunes	Can plums whole or in halves. Prick skin of each whole plum. Precook 3 to 5 minutes in juice, or thin to medium syrup to sweeten. Pack hot, cover with boiling juice or syrup.	25	30
Rhubarb	Cut into ½-inch lengths. Add ½ cup sugar per quart rhubarb. Let stand to draw out juice. Boil until tender. Pack hot, cover with hot juice.	15	20

Food	Preparation	Minutes per Pint	Minutes per Quart
Sauerkraut	Heat well-fermented sauerkraut to simmering point, do not boil. Pack into jars, cover with hot sauerkraut juice. Leave ¼-inch head-space.	25	30
Strawberries	Stem berries. Add ½ cup sugar per quart fruit. Bring slowly to boil. Remove from stove. Let stand overnight. Bring quickly to boil. Pack hot, cover with hot juice.	15	20
Tomatoes	Scald and peel. Remove stem end and any bad spots. Quarter or leave whole. Heat to boil. Pack hot. Add 1 teaspoon salt per quart.	10	10
Tomato Juice	Remove stems and any green or bad spots. Cut into pieces. Simmer until softened. Put through a fine sieve. Add 1 teaspoon salt per quart. Reheat at once just to boil. Pour into hot jars immediately. Leave ¼-inch head-space.	15	15
Fruit Juices	Use berries, red cherries, currants, grapes, plums, or blends of these. Remove any pits. Crush fruit. Heat gently to 170° F. (below simmering) until soft. Strain through a cloth bag. Add sugar if desired, about ½ to 1 cup sugar to 1	15	15

Food	Preparation	Minutes per Pint	Minutes per Quart
	gallon juice. Heat again to 170°. Pour into hot jars or bottles. Leave ⅛-inch head-space.		
Fruit Purées	Use any soft fruit. Cook until softened. Put cooked fruit through a fine sieve. Proceed as for fruit juices.	20	20

FOR VEGETABLES
(Processed in Pressure Cooker)

Add 1 teaspoon salt per quart when packed. Leave ½-inch head-space for non-starchy vegetables. Leave 1-inch for starchy vegetables such as corn, peas, Lima beans. Be sure solid food is covered by liquid.

Time and pressure are given for sea level. If canning is done at a higher altitude follow time indicated but increase pressure ½ pound per 1,000 feet. Time is indicated to process in pressure cooker at 10 pounds (240° F.).

The boiling water bath method of processing is not recommended for meats, fish, poultry, sweet corn, asparagus, squash, beans (all types), peas, beets, or any other food which is non-acid, because it is not possible to obtain a high enough temperature inside the jar to kill all the spores which cause disease in human beings.

Food	Preparation	Minutes per Pint	Minutes per Quart
Asparagus	Cut into 1-inch lengths. Cover with boiling water. Boil 2 or 3 minutes. Pack hot. Cover with hot cooking liquid.	25	40

Food	Preparation	Minutes per Pint	Minutes per Quart
Beans			
Lima	Can only young tender beans. Cover with boiling water. Bring to boil. Pack hot. Cover with hot cooking liquid.	35	55
Snap	Cut into 1-inch pieces. Cover with boiling water. Boil 5 minutes. Pack hot. Cover with hot cooking liquid.	20	25
Green Soy	Cover shelled beans with boiling water. Boil 3 or 4 minutes. Pack hot. Cover with fresh boiling water.	60	70
Beets	Before washing, trim off tops leaving taproot and 1-inch of stem. Boil until skins slip easily. Allow 15 minutes for baby beets, older beets take longer.	25	45
Carrots	Slice and boil 5 minutes in water to cover. Pack hot, cover with hot cooking liquid.	20	25
Corn	Whole-grain. Cut corn from cob so as to get the kernel but not the husk. Add 1 teaspoon salt per quart and half as much boiling water as corn. Heat to boil. Pack hot. Add no more salt and no extra water.	55	75

Food	Preparation	Minutes per Pint	Minutes per Quart
Greens	Discard imperfect leaves and tough stems. Carefully wash out all dirt. Boil in small amount of water until wilted. Pack hot and not too solid. Cover with hot cooking liquid.	40	70
Okra	Can only tender pods. Cover with boiling water. Bring back to boil. Pack hot. Cover with hot cooking liquid.	35	40
With Tomatoes	Heat sliced okra and tomato sections to boil. Pack hot. (Tomatoes will provide enough liquid.)	25	35
With Corn and Tomatoes	Heat sliced okra, whole-grain corn, and tomato sections to boil. Pack hot. The processing time indicated is for a mixture of 3 parts tomato pulp to 1 part each of okra and corn.	75	95
Peas, Green	Cover with boiling water. Boil about 5 minutes. Pack hot. Cover with hot cooking liquid.	40	40
Black-Eyed	Proceed as for Lima beans.		
Pimentos	See Table for Fruits and Tomatoes.		
Pumpkin	Peel and cut into 1-inch	55	90

Food	Preparation	Minutes per Pint	Minutes per Quart
	cubes. Add a little water and bring to boil. Pack hot. Cover with hot cooking liquid.		
Sauerkraut	See Table for Fruits and Tomatoes.		
Squash, Summer	Do not peel. Proceed as for pumpkin	30	40
Winter	Proceed as for pumpkin.	55	90
Sweet Potatoes	Boil or steam until skin slips easily. Skin. Cut into pieces. Pack hot. Cover with boiling water	100	110
Vegetable Soup Mixtures	Use 2 or more of these: tomato pulp, corn, Lima beans, peas, okra, carrots, celery, onion. Cut vegetables into small pieces or cubes. Add a little water if necessary. Heat mixture to boil. Pack hot. Cover with hot cooking liquid. Season to taste.	60	70

21 PRESSURE COOK-ERY, A SPECIAL TECHNIQUE

𝕰

Today, no cookbook completely fulfills its mission if it does not take into account the new technique of pressure cookery. This is as it should be since food prepared the pressure way is full of flavor and nutrition and the method is both quick and economical.

The following material is to be considered supplementary to the specific directions that came with your cooker. The cooking periods indicated here must necessarily be adjusted according to the type and grade of meat and the amount of fat on it, as well as your family's preference for it, rare or well done. With vegetables, size and freshness are factors to be considered. Mature beets pulled yesterday, for instance, take longer than the little fellows of the first crop which you brought in half an hour ago from the garden.

POINTS TO REMEMBER

1. Prepare food in usual manner. Do not fill pan over ⅔ full. Soups, stews, cereals are placed on bottom of pan. Use trivet for meats and vegetables.
2. Pour required hot water and seasonings into cooker.
3. Secure cover, following directions for your type of cooker.

4. Place pan over high heat (or full flame). Then watch for steam to issue from vent. Dead air is first exhausted and then steam flows freely.

5. When a steady flow of steam has emerged for 1 minute, close steam vent with its indicator weight, by flipping dial gauge forward or by turning the valve. It depends on the type of cooker used. Bring pressure quickly up to notch or the required pressure, and start counting cooking time immediately.

6. Reduce heat for pressure can be maintained with very little flame or heat. When cooking time is up, remove pan at once from heat. Allow pointer to drop to zero. Run cold water over top of cooker for certain starred (*) foods, since heat retained by pan can prolong cooking time.

7. Open gauge or remove weight when pointer has reached zero, *never before.* Use caution to prevent burns when opening cover of cooker.

8. Season food further, using if desired small amount of liquid left in cooker for sauces or gravies. Serve as usual.

TIMETABLE FOR PRESSURE COOKERY

For all foods marked with star (*) set cooker in cold water to reduce heat quickly or pour cold water over top of cooker.

Vegetable	Preparation	Cups of Hot Water	Minutes to Cook	Pounds of Pressure
*Artichoke	Wash, trim, pare, if desired.	½	10	15
French	Stand heads upright.			
Jerusalem	Peel, prepare like potatoes.	¼	10	15
*Asparagus	Wash, cut off tough ends. Place on trivet.	½	1–2	15
*Beans	Wash, string, snap into desired	⅓	2–2½	15
Green or Wax	lengths.			
Lima	Shell and wash.	⅓	1½–2	15
* Beets, cut	Wash, peel, cut.	¼	4	15
whole	Wash, trim tops leaving 2 inches of stem and root. Cook, slip skins.	½	15	15

Vegetable	Preparation	Cups of Hot Water	Minutes to Cook	Pounds of Pressure
*Broccoli	Wash, cut off tough lower portion. Split stalks, if very large. Place no trivet.	½	1½	15
* Brussels Sprouts	Remove outside wilted leaves.	½	2	15
*Cabbage	Wash, slice.	¼	1	15
* Carrots, sliced	Wash, scrape, slice.	½	2	15
whole	Wash, scrape	⅓	3	15
*Cauliflower,	Remove leaves, wash, place on			
whole	trivet.	¼	4	15
flowerets	Break into flowerets.	¼	2	15
*Celery	Wash, remove strings from outer stalks, retain top leaves for flavor, dice.	⅓	1–2	15
*Corn on Cob	Remove husks and silk, place on trivet.	½	3–5	15
*Eggplant	Pare, slice or cube, cover with salt water to prevent discoloration.	¼	¼	15
*Greens	Wash well, remove tough por-			
Beet	tions of stems. Soak a few min-	¼	3	15
Chard, Swiss	utes in salt water to kill any	¼	1½	15
Dandelion	worms or insects. Drain well,	¼	2½	15
Kale	cut through whole amount a	¼	4	15
Mustard	few times to reduce bulk.	½	5	15
Spinach		¼	1	15
Turnip		½	5	15
*Kohlrabi	Wash, peel, slice, or dice.	½	3	15
*Okra	Wash, cut off ends, cut into ½-inch pieces.	½	3	15
*Onions, cut	Wash, peel, cut.	½	3	15
whole	When cooked whole, shape is retained perfectly.	½	1–10	15
*Parsnips, sliced	Wash, peel, slice.	½	3	15
halved	May be halved lengthwise.	½	10	15
*Peas	Shell and wash.	¼	1	15
With carrots		¼	1½	15
*Potatoes, Irish	Wash, cook with skins on or off.			
whole	Gauge time according to size	1	9–12	15
quartered	of potato.	1	5–8	15
*Potatoes, Sweet	Wash, cook unpared.			
whole	Skins slip off easily after cook-	1	10–15	15
cut	ing.	1	8	15

Vegetable	Preparation	Cups of Hot Water	Minutes to Cook	Pounds of Pressure
•Pumpkin	Wash, pare, cut into small pieces.	½	3	15
•Rutabagas	Pare, cut into 1-inch cubes.	½	6	15
•Squash Acorn	May be steamed whole.	½	10	15
Hubbard	Cut into small pieces, pare before or scrape after cooking.	½	10–12	15
Summer	Wash, cut in 1-inch lengths.	½	2–3	15
Zucchini	Wash, cut in 1-inch slices.	¼	¼	15
•Tomatoes	Remove stem end, peel.	¼	1	15
Stewed	Quarter, no water needed.	—	½	15
•Turnips	Peel, slice.	¼	4	15

FROZEN VEGETABLES

Defrost 1 Hour Before Cooking

Vegetable	Preparation	Cups of Hot Water	Minutes to Cook	Pounds of Pressure
›Asparagus, cut or tips	Break up block and separate as much as possible.	¼	1	15
•Beans, Green or Wax	Break up block and separate.	¼	4	15
Lima	Gauge time according to size.	¼	1–4	15
•Broccoli	Separate stalks.	¼	1–1½	15
• Brussels Sprouts	Break up block.	¼	1½	15
•Carrots	Break up block.	¼	½	15
•Carrots and Peas	Break up block.	¼	½	15
•Cauliflower	Break up block.	¼	½	15
•Corn, cut	Break up block.	¼	1	15
on cob	Be sure to defrost first	¼	1½	15
•Greens, Chard	Separate defrosted block well	¼	1½	15
Spinach	to insure center cooking.	¼	1	15
Mixed Vegetables	Break up block.	¼	2	15
•Peas	Break up block. Remove from heat as soon as brought to pressure.	¼	—	15
Succotash	Break up block.	¼	1½	15
Squash	Break up block.	½	2	15

DRIED VEGETABLES

Vegetable	Preparation	Cups of Vegetables	Cups of Water	Minutes to Cook	Pounds of Pressure
Beans					
Baked	Soak in water 1 hour.	2	4	80	15
Kidney	Soak in water 1 hour.	1	2½	50	15
Lima	Soak in water 1 hour.	1	2½	45	15
Soy	Soak in water 1 hour.	1	3	40	15
Navy	Soak in water overnight.	2	4	80	15
Lentils	Wash and soak.	1	3	40	15
Peas					
Green or Yellow	Wash, do not soak.	1	2½	20	15
Split		1	2½	15	15
Rice					
White	Wash, add to salted boiling	1	2	6	15
Wild	water, reduce heat, seal pan and cook. Serve directly from cooker.	1	3	13	15

DRIED FRUITS

Fruit	Preparation	Cups of Fruit	Cups of Water	Minutes to Cook	Pounds of Pressure
*Apples	Do not soak. Add sugar as soon as cover is removed from cooker.	2	2½	8	15
*Apricots		2	2½	¼	15
*Figs		1	2	25	15
*Peaches		2½	3	8	15
*Pears		2	1	6	15
*Prunes	Wash first, cook with slices of lemon, if desired.	2½	3	3	15

MEATS AND POULTRY

Beef	Preparation	Cups of Hot Water	Minutes to Cook per Pound	Pounds of Pressure
Corned Beef	Freshen by soaking in cold water, if brine seems excessively salty. Reserve some liquid after cooking to use in cooking potatoes, cabbage, onions, turnips, parsnips, beets, which can be cooked together in pressure pan. Plan 4 minutes cooking time for vegetables uniformly cut.	Water to cover	25	15
Flank Steak	Stuff, if desired, roll and tie. Brown first in hot fat, place on rack, season with salt and pepper. Cook a few onions with meat for flavor. Add to water 2 tablespoons vinegar to tenderize meat.	½	45	15
Pot Roast	Dredge with flour and sear well. Place on trivet. Season. If enough room remains in cooker, potatoes, onions, carrots may be added during last 5 minutes of cooking.	½	15	15
Rump Roast	Sear well. Season and place on trivet. Wine may be used in place of water.	½	15	15
Rolled Rib Roast	Sear well. Season and place on trivet.	½	10, rare 12, medium 15, well done	15
Braised Short Ribs	Sear well and season. Barbecue Sauce may be poured over meat instead of water.	¾	25	15
Meat Loaf	Follow favorite recipe.	1	15	15

Beef	Preparation	Cups of Hot Water	Minutes to Cook per Pound	Pounds of Pressure
Meat Balls	Brown before cooking. Use tomato soup or juice for liquid.	1	10	15
Swiss Steak	Brown well, season, place on trivet. Tomato soup or juice may be used as liquid.	½	30–40	15
Liver	Dredge with flour and sear well before cooking.	only 1 tablespoon	2½	15
Stew	Dredge beef cubes with flour and brown well in hot fat. Cook a few onions with beef for flavor. Add vegetables after cooking time for meat given per pound and cook 5 minutes more.	1½	10	15
Chicken				
Fried	Flour, brown in fat, season before cooking.			
2 pounds		¼	15	10
2½–3 pounds		¼	18	10
Fricassee	Flour, brown well, season.	½	30	10
Roast	Stuff, season well, cook. Brown in oven using pan juices to make gravy while chicken is browning.	½	25	10
Stewed	Disjoint, cook with celery tops and onion for flavor. ¼ cup rice may be sprinkled over top of chicken before cooking.	1½	45	10
Lamb				
Chops	Brown first, place on rack.	½	10	15
Leg (4–5 pounds)	Remove skin, sear well.	½	18	15
Shanks or Neck	Brown well, rice and vegetables may be added at the start.	1	20	15

Lamb	Preparation	Cups of Hot Water	Minutes to Cook per Pound	Pounds of Pressure
Stew	Trim off fat and cube meat. Add 3 lemon slices to cut strong flavor. Cook rice and vegetables at same time if desired.	1½	10–15	15
Stuffed Breast	Stuff, fold over and tie. Brown well, place on rack and season.	½	12	15
Pork				
Chops	Cook to tenderize. Remove from cooker, place on broiler rack with apple slices dipped in sugar and cinnamon. Brown on both sides.	¼	10	15
Roast Loin	Brown fat side, set on trivet.	¼	14	15
Spareribs	Sear ribs. Sauerkraut may be cooked with ribs.	¼	20	15
Ham				
Butt or Shank	Cook, remove from pan, skin, score and brown under broiler. A mixture of brown sugar, mustard, and cloves spread over fat side adds flavor before browning.	1	20	15
Slice	Place in pan, rub well with brown sugar, sprinkle with cloves and use cider or pineapple juice for liquid.	½	25	15
Veal				
Roast	Sear well. Place on trivet.	½	15	15
Veal Birds or Steak	Stuff birds and bread steak, if desired, season, brown in fat.	¼	10–15	15

CEREALS

Place required amount of water in cooker, add salt, bring to rapid boil. Add cereal slowly to avoid lowering heat below boiling point. Stir until smooth. Adjust cover and proceed by usual directions for pressure. Do not fill cooker over two-thirds full.

Type	Cups of Cereal	Teaspoons of Salt	Cups of Hot Water	Minutes to Cook	Pounds of Pressure
Pearl Barley	½	½	2½	25	15
Corn Meal (Hominy)	½	¾	2	10	15
Cracked Wheat	⅔	½	2	20	15
Cream of Wheat	½	¾	2	3	15
Farina	½	¾	2	2	15
Grapenut Wheat Meal	½	½	2½	10	15
Macaroni	1	1	3	5	15
Oatmeal (Quick)	1	¾	2½	2½	15
Ralston	½	¾	2	10	15
Rice	½	½	2	6	15
Wheatena	½	¾	2	4	15
Wheatsworth	1	½	3	15	15
Whole Wheat	1	½	4	25	15

22. COOKING FOR ONE HUNDRED

§

Although these recipes from Toll House are planned for family cooking, it is not hard to increase them so they can be used for church suppers, club meetings, grange dinners, and service club meetings. The greatest problem in large-quantity cooking is of course the purchasing. If there is too little it is embarrassing; if too much, there is no profit. To assist with the marketing of the major ingredients I have prepared the following chart which includes the most popular foods for luncheon, supper, and dinner dishes. The seasonings I leave to you.

Dish	*Principal Ingredients*
Fruit Cocktail	10–12 cans (No. 5)
	Add fresh fruit, if desired
Tomato Bisque (24 qts.)	12 quarts tomatoes
	12 quarts milk
Vegetable Soup (28 qts.)	20 quarts beef or chicken stock
	2 cups each diced carrots, peas, string beans, potato, cabbage, onions, celery, etc.
	2 quarts tomatoes
Clam Chowder	10 quarts shucked clams
	20 pounds (10 qts.) diced potato
	1 pound salt pork
	3 pounds onions
	14 quarts milk

Dish	**Principal Ingredients**
Corn Chowder	20 pounds (10 qts.) diced potato
	1 pound salt pork
	3 pounds onions
	14 quarts milk
	10 cans (No. 2) corn
Fish Chowder	Same as Clam Chowder. Omit clams and add 30 pounds cod or haddock
Scrambled Eggs	8 dozen eggs
	4 quarts milk
Cheese Fondue	4 quarts soft stale bread crumbs
	4 quarts milk
	2 pounds American cheese
	2 dozen eggs
Macaroni and Cheese	4 pounds (4 qts.) macaroni
	3 pounds American cheese
	8 quarts milk
Baked Beans	8 quarts pea beans, measured before baking
	3 pounds salt pork
Piccalilli	5 quarts
Cole Slaw	12 pounds cabbage
	4–6 cups cooked dressing
Chicken Salad (For 10 platters)	10–12 quarts diced chicken
	10–12 quarts diced celery
	2 cups French dressing (for marinating)
	1 gallon mayonnaise (more or less)
	10 heads lettuce
Golden Glow Salad	12 tablespoons gelatin
	6 cups pineapple juice
	6 cups crushed pineapple
	6 cups grated raw carrots
Lobster Salad	100 pounds lobster in shell (about 25 lbs. cut up)
	3 quarts diced celery

343

Dish	*Principal Ingredients*
	10 heads lettuce
	1 gallon mayonnaise
Potato Salad	36 pounds (18 qts.) cooked potato cubes
	6 onions, finely minced (more, if desired)
	2 cups French dressing (for marinating)
	1 gallon mayonnaise (more, if needed)
Vegetable Salad (For 10 platters)	3 quarts peas
	4 quarts diced beets or carrots
	3 quarts diced celery
	1 quart French dressing
	10 heads lettuce
Corned Beef (For Boiled Dinners)	40 pounds
	(See separate vegetables)
Pot Roast of Beef	30 pounds bottom round
	5 pounds carrots
	7 pounds onions
	30 pounds potatoes
Roast Beef	30–50 pounds, depending on cut
Roasted Hamburg Steak (Meat Loaf)	20 pounds top round
	10 pounds lean pork
	2 loaves bread, crumbled
	20 onions, cut fine
	7 quarts milk
	1 dozen eggs
Hamburgers	20 pounds chopped beef
	12½ dozen rolls
Lamb Stew	32 pounds forequarter
Roast Lamb	6 8-pound legs
Roast Chicken or Turkey	60 pounds, dressed
Boiled Ham	50 pounds
Roast Fresh Ham	3 16-pound hams

Dish		*Principal Ingredients*
Roast Pork	40	pounds, loin or rib
Pork Chops	30	pounds
Baked Fish	12	5-pound cod, haddock, bluefish, mackerel, etc.
Fried Fish Fillets	35	pounds flounder
Stuffing for Roast Turkey or Chicken	8	quarts crumbs
	2	tablespoons poultry seasoning
	2	quarts oysters, if desired
Stuffing for Chops or Fish	14	cups cracker or bread crumbs
Shrimp Wiggle	4	quarts White Sauce
	16	cans (7-oz.) wet shrimp
	6	quarts peas
Cooked Beets	25	bunches
Cooked Cabbage	25	pounds
Cooked Carrots	20	bunches
Cooked Peas	5	cans (No. 10) cans or 5 large packages, frosted
Mashed Potato	1	bushel
Escalloped Potato	32	pounds potatoes
	7	quarts milk
	3	pounds onions (more or less)
Mashed Squash	50	pounds
Mashed Turnip	20	pounds
Tartar Sauce (with fish)	3	quarts
Iced Celery	12	bunches
Gherkin Pickles	3	pounds
Iced Radishes	2½	dozen bunches
Rolls or Biscuits	17	dozen
Table Butter	3	pounds (cut 48 pieces to pound)
Coffee	3	pounds (6 gals.)
Coffee Cream	1½	pints heavy cream mixed with
	6	quarts milk
Loaf Cake (served with ice cream)	9	cakes (cut 12 servings each)

Dish	*Principal Ingredients*
Layer Cakes (served alone)	20 cakes (cut 6 servings each)
Cream Filling (for layer cakes)	2 quarts
Gelatin Desserts	1½ cups gelatin
	9 quarts fruit juice or water
	6 cups cold water
	6 cups sugar
	5 quarts cut fruit, as desired
Ice Cream	2¾ gallons brick ice cream (cut 9 servings to qt.)
Indian Pudding	9 quarts milk
	3 cups corn meal
	4 cups dark molasses
	6 cups sugar
	1 dozen eggs
	1 pound butter
Pie	20 pies (cut each in 6 servings)
Pastry	9 quarts flour
	12 cups lard
Strawberry Shortcake	100 shortcake biscuits
	8 boxes strawberries, fresh, or 5 boxes, frosted
	1 quart heavy cream
Cheese	4 pounds American loaf cheese (cut 25 servings to lb.)
Tapioca Cream Pudding	4 cups minute tapioca
	8 quarts milk
	1 dozen eggs
	6 cups sugar

23. SOLVING KITCHEN PROBLEMS

It is ticklish business to attempt to remove stains except from white materials. When spots occur on colored fabrics or materials not washable, you can injure a garment just by rubbing too hard. Dry cleaning firms beg you to leave the stain alone and to pin a note to your garment telling the nature of the stain—coffee, coffee with cream, butter, or ink. Be as specific as you can for the cleaner uses different methods for coffee-with-cream-and-sugar spots from what he does on clear-coffee spots. My cleaner tells me that on most spots he first uses cold water, so if you wish to attempt to remove stains from unwashable fabrics, try cold water first. I prefer to play safe and send colored garments immediately to my cleaner before the spot is "set." He has so many safe removers I can always be sure the stain has not ruined the garment forever. Here are safe methods for removing stains from white or washable fabrics.

STAIN REMOVAL

Blood

Hot water will set protein in blood stains and should never be applied until after treatment with cold water. Use any of following agents:

1. Cold water. If material is washable, soak stains and rub gently in cold water until they turn light brown; then proceed with usual laundering methods.

347

2. Ammonia. If the material is white and washable, soak in a solution of about 2 tablespoons household ammonia to 1 gallon water until stains are loosened; then wash in usual manner. For old stains ammonia is somewhat more satisfactory than soap.

3. Hydrogen Peroxide. First apply cold water. Then sponge a white material with a little hydrogen peroxide. This will often remove last traces of blood stains after the main part has been removed by cold water.

Butter

Stains from butter are essentially grease spots, although they also contain salt, casein, and sometimes coloring. Launder in the usual way but with soap containing naphtha and kerosene. Take care to rub spots thoroughly.

Candle Wax and Paraffin

Since paraffin does not spread but hardens on cloth, scrape away wax with dull knife, place blotting paper under cloth, and press with warm iron. Then if wax is colored, dissolve dye on fabric by sponging with wood alcohol or cleaning fluid.

Chewing Gum

1. If material is washable, soften gum stain with egg white; then launder as usual.
2. Sponge unwashable material with cleaning fluid.

Chocolate and Cocoa

1. Use soap and hot water on washable materials.
2. Apply grease solvents to unwashable materials scraping what you can from fabric; then apply cleaning fluid.

Coffee

1. If possible remove at once with ordinary laundering and dry in sun.
2. Pour boiling water on stain from height of 2 to 3 feet. This is effective on fresh stains. Pressure helps greatly.

Egg

1. Ordinary laundering often suffices.
2. Sponge spots with cold water and allow to dry. Then apply cleaning fluid.

Fruits

1. Stretch spotted area over bowl and pour boiling water on it from height of 3 to 4 feet. Pressure helps greatly. Alternate pouring with rubbing, if necessary.
2. Treat more stubborn stains by moistening them with lemon juice and then exposing to sun. This is only possible with white fabrics.

Glue

1. Soak washable material in warm water and, if necessary, boil.
2. Sponge spots on other materials with acetic acid or white vinegar.

Grass Stain

1. On washable material use hot water and soap, rubbing stain vigorously. If any stain remains, bleach out with commercial bleaching water.
2. On unwashable fabrics use ether or alcohol to dissolve stains.

Ink

1. For some types of ink stain ordinary washing is satisfactory.
2. When this is unsuccessful, soak stains for a few seconds in a solution of 3 tablespoons oxalic acid to 1 gallon water; then rinse in clear water and, finally, in water to which few drops of ammonia have been added.
3. If material is colored or not washable, send to dry cleaner.

Iodine

Sponge material with alcohol.

Iron Rust

1. With white material stretch stained area over vessel of actively boiling water and squeeze lemon juice over stain. After few minutes, rinse fabric and, if necessary, squeeze lemon juice on again. Another method is to sprinkle stain with salt, moisten with lemon juice, place material in the sun, and squeeze on more lemon, if necessary.
2. Your cleaner has "rusticator" to use on colored or unwashable fabrics.

Medicines

1. Pour on boiling water the same way as for fruit stains.
2. Sponge with alcohol.

Mildew

1. Wash very fresh stains with soap and water and then dry in sun.
2. Soak in sour milk and then place in sun without rinsing.
3. Moisten stains with lemon juice and salt and allow material to remain in sun.

Oil Paints and Varnishes

Sponge stains with turpentine and then wash as usual.

Road Oil, Axle Grease, etc.

1. Sponge stains with carbon tetrachloride or a cleaning fluid; then launder as usual.
2. Rub cooking fat thoroughly into stain; then wash in hot soapy water. Repeat if necessary.

Tea

1. Soak in borax solution—1 teaspoon borax to 1 cup water—then rinse in boiling water.
2. Boil stained material in solution of ½-inch cube soap to 1 cup water.

First Aid Treatment for Burns or Scalds

by

Walter E. Deacon, M.D.

Any burn or scald destroys the outer layer of skin and paves the way for infection. Therefore it should be treated like a cut or an abrasion. Soak the area in Zonite (1 tablespoon to 2 cups of boiled water) for 15 minutes. Dress with boric acid ointment and apply a sterile bandage (Steripad).

If severe, soak in Zonite as outlined above. Dress with boric acid ointment and apply a pressure dressing, i.e. wrap the burned area in a snug bandage.

If after treatment, blisters form consult your doctor as the dead tissue will probably have to be removed under aseptic technique.

INDEX

373

A CATALOGUE OF SELECTED DOVER BOOKS
IN ALL FIELDS OF INTEREST

A CATALOGUE OF SELECTED DOVER
BOOKS IN ALL FIELDS OF INTEREST

RACKHAM'S COLOR ILLUSTRATIONS FOR WAGNER'S RING. Rackham's finest mature work—all 64 full-color watercolors in a faithful and lush interpretation of the *Ring*. Full-sized plates on coated stock of the paintings used by opera companies for authentic staging of Wagner. Captions aid in following complete Ring cycle. Introduction. 64 illustrations plus vignettes. 72pp. 8⅝ x 11¼. 23779-6 Pa. $6.00

CONTEMPORARY POLISH POSTERS IN FULL COLOR, edited by Joseph Czestochowski. 46 full-color examples of brilliant school of Polish graphic design, selected from world's first museum (near Warsaw) dedicated to poster art. Posters on circuses, films, plays, concerts all show cosmopolitan influences, free imagination. Introduction. 48pp. 9⅜ x 12¼. 23780-X Pa. $6.00

GRAPHIC WORKS OF EDVARD MUNCH, Edvard Munch. 90 haunting, evocative prints by first major Expressionist artist and one of the greatest graphic artists of his time: *The Scream, Anxiety, Death Chamber, The Kiss, Madonna*, etc. Introduction by Alfred Werner. 90pp. 9 x 12. 23765-6 Pa. $5.00

THE GOLDEN AGE OF THE POSTER, Hayward and Blanche Cirker. 70 extraordinary posters in full colors, from Maitres de l'Affiche, Mucha, Lautrec, Bradley, Cheret, Beardsley, many others. Total of 78pp. 9⅜ x 12¼. 22753-7 Pa. $5.95

THE NOTEBOOKS OF LEONARDO DA VINCI, edited by J. P. Richter. Extracts from manuscripts reveal great genius; on painting, sculpture, anatomy, sciences, geography, etc. Both Italian and English. 186 ms. pages reproduced, plus 500 additional drawings, including studies for *Last Supper*, Sforza monument, etc. 860pp. 7⅞ x 10¾. (Available in U.S. only) 22572-0, 22573-9 Pa., Two-vol. set $15.90

THE CODEX NUTTALL, as first edited by Zelia Nuttall. Only inexpensive edition, in full color, of a pre-Columbian Mexican (Mixtec) book. 88 color plates show kings, gods, heroes, temples, sacrifices. New explanatory, historical introduction by Arthur G. Miller. 96pp. 11⅜ x 8½. (Available in U.S. only) 23168-2 Pa. $7.95

UNE SEMAINE DE BONTÉ, A SURREALISTIC NOVEL IN COLLAGE, Max Ernst. Masterpiece created out of 19th-century periodical illustrations, explores worlds of terror and surprise. Some consider this Ernst's greatest work. 208pp. 8⅛ x 11. 23252-2 Pa. $6.00

ART FORMS IN NATURE, Ernst Haeckel. Multitude of strangely beautiful natural forms: Radiolaria, Foraminifera, jellyfishes, fungi, turtles, bats, etc. All 100 plates of the 19th-century evolutionist's *Kunstformen der Natur* (1904). 100pp. 9⅜ x 12¼.   22987-4 Pa. $5.00

CHILDREN: A PICTORIAL ARCHIVE FROM NINETEENTH-CENTURY SOURCES, edited by Carol Belanger Grafton. 242 rare, copyright-free wood engravings for artists and designers. Widest such selection available. All illustrations in line. 119pp. 8⅜ x 11¼.
23694-3 Pa. $4.00

WOMEN: A PICTORIAL ARCHIVE FROM NINETEENTH-CENTURY SOURCES, edited by Jim Harter. 391 copyright-free wood engravings for artists and designers selected from rare periodicals. Most extensive such collection available. All illustrations in line. 128pp. 9 x 12.
23703-6 Pa. $4.50

ARABIC ART IN COLOR, Prisse d'Avennes. From the greatest ornamentalists of all time—50 plates in color, rarely seen outside the Near East, rich in suggestion and stimulus. Includes 4 plates on covers. 46pp. 9⅜ x 12¼.   23658-7 Pa. $6.00

AUTHENTIC ALGERIAN CARPET DESIGNS AND MOTIFS, edited by June Beveridge. Algerian carpets are world famous. Dozens of geometrical motifs are charted on grids, color-coded, for weavers, needleworkers, craftsmen, designers. 53 illustrations plus 4 in color. 48pp. 8¼ x 11. (Available in U.S. only)   23650-1 Pa. $1.75

DICTIONARY OF AMERICAN PORTRAITS, edited by Hayward and Blanche Cirker. 4000 important Americans, earliest times to 1905, mostly in clear line. Politicians, writers, soldiers, scientists, inventors, industrialists, Indians, Blacks, women, outlaws, etc. Identificatory information. 756pp. 9¼ x 12¾.   21823-6 Clothbd. $40.00

HOW THE OTHER HALF LIVES, Jacob A. Riis. Journalistic record of filth, degradation, upward drive in New York immigrant slums, shops, around 1900. New edition includes 100 original Riis photos, monuments of early photography. 233pp. 10 x 7⅞.   22012-5 Pa. $7.00

NEW YORK IN THE THIRTIES, Berenice Abbott. Noted photographer's fascinating study of city shows new buildings that have become famous and old sights that have disappeared forever. Insightful commentary. 97 photographs. 97pp. 11⅜ x 10.   22967-X Pa. $5.00

MEN AT WORK, Lewis W. Hine. Famous photographic studies of construction workers, railroad men, factory workers and coal miners. New supplement of 18 photos on Empire State building construction. New introduction by Jonathan L. Doherty. Total of 69 photos. 63pp. 8 x 10¾.
23475-4 Pa. $3.00

THE DEPRESSION YEARS AS PHOTOGRAPHED BY ARTHUR ROTH-STEIN, Arthur Rothstein. First collection devoted entirely to the work of outstanding 1930s photographer: famous dust storm photo, ragged children, unemployed, etc. 120 photographs. Captions. 119pp. 9¼ x 10¾.
23590-4 Pa. $5.00

CAMERA WORK: A PICTORIAL GUIDE, Alfred Stieglitz. All 559 illustrations and plates from the most important periodical in the history of art photography, Camera Work (1903-17). Presented four to a page, reduced in size but still clear, in strict chronological order, with complete captions. Three indexes. Glossary. Bibliography. 176pp. 8⅜ x 11¼.
23591-2 Pa. $6.95

ALVIN LANGDON COBURN, PHOTOGRAPHER, Alvin L. Coburn. Revealing autobiography by one of greatest photographers of 20th century gives insider's version of Photo-Secession, plus comments on his own work. 77 photographs by Coburn. Edited by Helmut and Alison Gernsheim. 160pp. 8⅛ x 11.
23685-4 Pa. $6.00

NEW YORK IN THE FORTIES, Andreas Feininger. 162 brilliant photographs by the well-known photographer, formerly with Life magazine, show commuters, shoppers, Times Square at night, Harlem nightclub, Lower East Side, etc. Introduction and full captions by John von Hartz. 181pp. 9¼ x 10¾.
23585-8 Pa. $6.95

GREAT NEWS PHOTOS AND THE STORIES BEHIND THEM, John Faber. Dramatic volume of 140 great news photos, 1855 through 1976, and revealing stories behind them, with both historical and technical information. Hindenburg disaster, shooting of Oswald, nomination of Jimmy Carter, etc. 160pp. 8¼ x 11.
23667-6 Pa. $5.00

THE ART OF THE CINEMATOGRAPHER, Leonard Maltin. Survey of American cinematography history and anecdotal interviews with 5 masters—Arthur Miller, Hal Mohr, Hal Rosson, Lucien Ballard, and Conrad Hall. Very large selection of behind-the-scenes production photos. 105 photographs. Filmographies. Index. Originally Behind the Camera. 144pp. 8¼ x 11.
23686-2 Pa. $5.00

DESIGNS FOR THE THREE-CORNERED HAT (LE TRICORNE), Pablo Picasso. 32 fabulously rare drawings—including 31 color illustrations of costumes and accessories—for 1919 production of famous ballet. Edited by Parmenia Migel, who has written new introduction. 48pp. 9⅜ x 12¼. (Available in U.S. only)
23709-5 Pa. $5.00

NOTES OF A FILM DIRECTOR, Sergei Eisenstein. Greatest Russian filmmaker explains montage, making of Alexander Nevsky, aesthetics; comments on self, associates, great rivals (Chaplin), similar material. 78 illustrations. 240pp. 5⅜ x 8½.
22392-2 Pa. $4.50

AMERICAN ANTIQUE FURNITURE, Edgar G. Miller, Jr. The basic coverage of all American furniture before 1840: chapters per item chronologically cover all types of furniture, with more than 2100 photos. Total of 1106pp. 7⅞ x 10¾. 21599-7, 21600-4 Pa., Two-vol. set $17.90

ILLUSTRATED GUIDE TO SHAKER FURNITURE, Robert Meader. Director, Shaker Museum, Old Chatham, presents up-to-date coverage of all furniture and appurtenances, with much on local styles not available elsewhere. 235 photos. 146pp. 9 x 12. 22819-3 Pa. $6.00

ORIENTAL RUGS, ANTIQUE AND MODERN, Walter A. Hawley. Persia, Turkey, Caucasus, Central Asia, China, other traditions. Best general survey of all aspects: styles and periods, manufacture, uses, symbols and their interpretation, and identification. 96 illustrations, 11 in color. 320pp. 6⅛ x 9¼. 22366-3 Pa. $6.95

CHINESE POTTERY AND PORCELAIN, R. L. Hobson. Detailed descriptions and analyses by former Keeper of the Department of Oriental Antiquities and Ethnography at the British Museum. Covers hundreds of pieces from primitive times to 1915. Still the standard text for most periods. 136 plates, 40 in full color. Total of 750pp. 5⅝ x 8½. 23253-0 Pa. $10.00

THE WARES OF THE MING DYNASTY, R. L. Hobson. Foremost scholar examines and illustrates many varieties of Ming (1368-1644). Famous blue and white, polychrome, lesser-known styles and shapes. 117 illustrations, 9 full color, of outstanding pieces. Total of 263pp. 6⅛ x 9¼. (Available in U.S. only) 23652-8 Pa. $6.00

Prices subject to change without notice.

Available at your book dealer or write for free catalogue to Dept. GI, Dover Publications, Inc., 180 Varick St., N.Y., N.Y. 10014. Dover publishes more than 175 books each year on science, elementary and advanced mathematics, biology, music, art, literary history, social sciences and other areas.